Fairway to Justice

Her Fearless Fight Against Power And Intimidation

Written by

Cordell Parvin

Printed in the United States of America

About The Author

Cordell Parvin is a retired Texas lawyer whose storytelling explores themes of justice, resilience, and the human spirit. Drawing on decades of legal experience, Parvin brings a sharp eye for conflict and character to the page.

"Fairway to Justice" is Parvin's latest novel - a gripping courtroom drama about ambition, betrayal, and the pursuit of fairness in an increasingly complex world.

Chapter 1

Lauren

I jerk back at the newspaper headline shoved into my face. "That's not what I said!"

Robert Benton's glare was as cold as his office décor. "Biological men competing against girls and women would destroy golf." He slams the paper down on his desk and rubs his forehead. "My phone has been ringing off the hook. Call the reporter and retract this."

"No. My views have nothing to do with you or my design of the Lake Tierra Golf Course." Benton removed his suit jacket and leaned back in his gray chair.

Benton straightened the newspaper and set it neatly to the side. "Then, your contract is terminated."

"Go to—"

"And, delete the statement on your website that you are designing the Lake Tierra Golf Course. The contract you signed with me gives me the right to the design when I terminate your contract. You should read the contract you signed."

I can feel the color draining from my face. Benton's daring me to challenge him. I had witnessed him do it over and over again to contractors.

"I'm not retracting what I've said about girls' and women's sports. I am offended by reports of biological boys and men exposing themselves in the locker rooms designated for girls and women. I'd be open not to speaking out on the subject any further if you pay me my one-million-dollar bonus you already owe me."

Benton leans forward. His gray chair squeaks, "Did you consider where most of my land and home purchasers and golf members come from? You offended my best clients when you called the transgender athletes biological boys and men."

"So tell me who they—"

"No. You're not entitled to any bonus even if you agree to retract what you've said about transgender athletes. I'm terminating your contract for cause. I don't owe you another cent. If you sue me, claiming that you have any right in the design of the Lake Tierra Golf Course, you will pay a steep price. My attorney, Harvey Morgan, can run up your expenses, delay your case, and use what we've found on your computer, including your photos, to make your life miserable. You should move on."

"What photos?" I rub at the sweat collecting at the collar of my silk blouse.

"Let's put it this way," he says. "I will post photos of you that will destroy your squeaky-clean image."

It's not until I get into my car that I'm able to shout, "Fuck you."

***

Benton follows up our conversation by giving an interview in the newspaper. It's clear he wants to inflict as much pain as possible and turn the public against me. Benton has never had any trouble lying and repeating the lie so frequently that at least some in the media think he's telling the truth.

After reading his public relations piece, I call Seth Ashford, my corporate lawyer at McKenzie Simmons in Dallas. My voice shakes with frustration as I relay the story. I've poured everything into building the most successful women's golf course design business in the country, and now, instead of giving me what I deserve, Benton wants to tear it all down.

I started a golf course design business, West Design Company, with nothing. I spent months waiting for the first opportunity to design a golf course. After more than a year, Dallas County asked me to design a public golf course in South Dallas with the stipulation that it had to be user-friendly for children taking up the game for the first time. The Oakwood Golf Course I designed gained national recognition, which propelled me to design at least a dozen more golf courses in urban low-income areas.

I'm among McKenzie Simmons' few female business clients. Seth has told me that the young male lawyers in his firm say I am aggressive and describe me as the "badass." They're intimidated by me. Seth has also told me his law firm's young female lawyers say, I'm confident and self-assured, I have "gravitas," and they want to be like me.

I like those depictions. I hope I have gravitas, and I have no problem being a badass since that's what it takes for me to make it in a male-dominated sport and industry. I'm not a badass when it comes to conflict. Just the opposite. I don't like conflict because it takes time, energy, and money away from my work designing the next golf course.

A national business magazine did a cover story on me, titled: "Lauren West: Breaking Barriers on the Green." I'm sitting in a golf cart on the cover. The writer describes me as a brilliant woman who played on the LPGA tour, retired, and created a top golf course design company, West Design, focused on designing top-rated golf courses in luxury golf communities. The article also covers my Lauren West Foundation to help students impacted by the COVID shutdown. My foundation buys computers and provides tutoring to compensate for what the students lost while being away from school.

But, none of my work to help others matters now. Ashford warns me not to underestimate the damage Benton can do to my career and life. I agree. He says, I have a good case, but fighting Benton in court will take time and money away from my design business. I can't afford to lose either, but I have no choice. Benton wrongfully terminated my contract to avoid paying my bonus, and he took ownership of my Lake Tierra Golf Course design.

"I can't let Benton get away with it," I tell Seth. I designed the Lake Tierra Golf Course. It's already in the Top 50 of Golf Digest and Golf Magazine, and it's only been open less than a year," I say.

"Don't make any decisions while you are angry," Seth recommends.

"Easier said than done." I slump back in my chair.

Seth has a copy of the newspaper article Benton planted to discredit me. He tells me Benton must have connections in the media. He begins reading. "Robert Benton, the well-known Silicon Valley philanthropist, says he was stunned when she learned that Lauren West had railed against the idea of transgender athletes competing in sports."

"Benton donates money to charities to gain recognition," I say.

Seth continues. "Miss West is a loser. She was supposed to be the superstar golfer on the LPGA tour and she flopped. No one would hire her to design golf courses, so she begged me to give her a chance. I've had to make changes to each of her designs. Now, after I told her to keep her politics private, she has severely damaged my real estate development sales and golf course membership by making transphobic public statements. They say her comments are putting transgender individuals at risk of violent attacks. When she graduated from the University of Texas, West was supposed to be the next big thing in the LPGA. Instead, she was an overrated golfer who never lived up to the hype. The same is true about her golf designs. They haven't been anything special. I've had to fix each one of them."

"Bullshit," I say. "Benton claims credit for everything and uses insults and lies to get his way. We started developing the Lake

Tierra Hill Country Development at the beginning of COVID-19 when many of Benton's clients began working remotely. If anything, they chose to build second homes in the Lake Tierra development because they liked my golf course design."

Seth continues. "I repeat: Miss West did not design the Lake Tierra Golf Course. I fixed her flawed design, and that's why the Lake Tierra Golf Course won awards.

"Before he terminated my contract, I played the Lake Tierra Golf Course with many of his clients who built homes. They'll tell you they built multi-million-dollar homes and paid a hefty initiation fee so they and their families could be among the first members of the country club. Benton is mad that I've become the brand of his developments. Most purchasers don't even recognize his face and name. He says that when he terminated my contract for cause, I gave up the right to claim that I designed the Lake Tierra Golf Course. I don't care what the contract says. I designed the golf course, and I'm entitled to claim credit. He lists himself as the designer on all his current advertising and on scorecards."

Seth continues, "After I terminated Miss West's contract for cause, she demanded I pay her ten percent of the net profits on the sale of land and the country club initiation fees on all the golf courses she designed. Since I terminated her contract for cause, she's not entitled to claim she designed the golf course, and she's not entitled to any bonus."

"I've done nothing that permits Benton to terminate my contract for cause. When asked by a reporter what I thought about transgender athletes competing against girls and women, I gave my opinion. How can expressing my opinion be considered a breach of a contract to design a golf course? I want to file a lawsuit to collect my bonus and win recognition for designing the Lake Tierra Golf Course."

"Benton doesn't care whether he wins the lawsuit. Instead, he wants to make you wish you had never filed it," Seth says. "He'll do everything possible to destroy you in the media and financially ruin you. Are you sure you want to take that substantial time and money away from your design business?"

"Yes. Benton's counting on me being more interested in not going broke, paying lawyers and saving my wholesome image than I am saving my time and money. He believes he can run over me by drowning me in legal costs and negative publicity while he delays the trial as long as possible. I won't let him get away with it. Benton is taking credit for my design of the number one golf course in Texas and one of the top golf courses in the world. In addition, Benton wrongfully terminated my design contract so he could take credit for the design and not pay the bonus I earned. I'm not the only one. The golf course builder and the contractor who built the clubhouse told me Benton failed to pay their contract price."

Seth looks at me over the top of his reading glasses. "Benton makes one other allegation in the newspaper."

"What's that?" I ask.

"I terminated Miss West's design contract for cause. As a result, I don't owe her any additional money. Instead, she owes Benton Land Company for our loss of sales due to her misconduct."

"The cause he fabricated is bullshit," I reply. "There's no way Benton Land Company lost sales because of me."

"True. And when Benton bought the land, and he promised to pay you for your work, which included finding the land, doing a feasibility study, a market analysis, and preparing a detailed golf course design. He also promised to pay you a ten percent bonus on net profits. We have to show that Benton wrongfully terminated your contract, took credit for your design, and what are the net profits from the sale of real estate and golf initiation fees."

I pick up my phone. Another reporter is texting me asking for a comment. "Who in the law firm can represent me?"

"We can't represent you," Seth says. "Since we helped you negotiate the contracts and gave you advice on both receipts of payments and benefits from Benton, we might receive a subpoena to testify and turn over documents. Also, you don't want a Dallas lawyer to try your case to a Corona County jury."

"So, who do you recommend I hire to represent me and my companies?"

Ashley Shine can tell you who the best Texas Hill Country trial lawyer is. He summons Ashley to his office.

After introductions, Shine tells me that she and Seth went to law school with Luke Hartley, who grew up in Corona. Luke's an outstanding trial lawyer, and he has tried dozens of cases in Corona County.

I shake my head and raise my voice. "No way, I'm hiring Luke Hartley to represent me," I tell them.

"Why?" Shine asks.

"He represented landowners who fought the rezoning for the Lake Tierra Golf Course. I don't believe we can work well together, and he may feel the same way."

Shine shoots me a quizzical look. "I've called Luke to ensure that Benton doesn't hire him first. He told me he fought you on the rezoning. He says he'd never represent Benton."

I hadn't thought of that angle. Benton's attack dog lawyer, Harvey Morgan, will likely represent him. But, they'd need a local counsel. Shine's point made me more inclined to at least meet with Luke. That way, he couldn't be Benton's local counsel.

"Luke's not just the best trial lawyer in the Texas Hill Country. He also has connections with the judges, and as you probably discovered in the Zoning hearing, most Corona County residents know and like him. Luke's the lawyer you should hire. He'll want to represent you against Benton."

"I know from my experience against him in the Corona County rezoning hearings that Luke is the best lawyer. I wasn't pleased with the lawyer we hired for the rezoning. I'm just not sure Luke and I will get along with each other."

"Before you make a final decision, will you at least meet with Luke?"

"I need to do some research and think about it. I'll let you know."

When I get home, I go to Luke's law firm webpage for the first time. On his home page, I find a photo of Luke and his two daughters, Abby and Megan. I read in his bio that Abby is autistic and that Luke is active in the Organization for Autism Research. There are photos of Abby riding horses and photos of Megan playing soccer. I don't find a photo of Luke's wife, which causes me to wonder if he is divorced.

I think about it. Before I do anything, I call my LPGA best friend, Courtney Barr and ask what she thinks.

"Damn, Lauren, you don't have a choice," Courtney says. "If Luke Hartley is the best lawyer to get your bonus, you've got to hire him."

I hate that I don't have a choice, but Courtney is right. Luke is the best lawyer to represent me. Thirty minutes later, I call Shine. "Call Luke. I want to meet with him right away. I'm not saying I will hire him, and I'm not sure he'll be willing to represent me in a lawsuit against Benton, but we might as well find out right away."

I must file the lawsuit against Benton to recover my bonus money and be credited with designing the Lake Tierra Golf

Course, but I know he'll do everything he can to make me wish I hadn't.

Chapter 2

Luke

What suit should I wear to my meeting in Dallas? I look in my closet for my navy blue Brioni pinstripe suit. It cost me a ton of money, but when I want to make a good impression, I pick off the rack in my closet.

I've spent my entire career representing small and medium-sized Hill Country businesses and tried dozens of cases in Corona County. My clients have been great friends, but none get up in the morning and say, "Oh boy, I get to go visit Luke Hartley, my lawyer today."

I receive frequent calls from recruiters and law firms urging me to join their firms and relocate to Dallas, Houston, Austin, or San Antonio. I reject every offer to earn far more money because I want my girls, especially Abby, to grow up in Corona.

Lauren and I crossed paths during our time at the University of Texas. She was two years behind me and played on the golf team while I played on the baseball team. At one point in my senior year, my teammate tried to play matchmaker for us. According to my teammate, Lauren's father insisted she focus on her academics and golf. I took that to heart and never called her.

Before my trip to Dallas, I search for more information about Lauren West. In one article, the writer describes Lauren as the most driven athlete at UT. She had the dream, the discipline, and the grit to qualify for the LPGA tour. I find several articles discussing her distinctive golf course design concept. She's known for her strong will and unwavering confidence, and she is never shy about expressing her opinions to anyone. I expect that will make Lauren a difficult client to represent, and I'm not sure, given my health, that I can handle that now.

According to reports, Lauren experienced anxiety and depression following Ben's departure and subsequent death from cancer.

Lauren left the tour after injuring her back and failing to win again on the LPGA tour. She pursued a master's degree in landscape architecture and began designing golf courses.

I've never had the opportunity to represent someone famous before. I'd love to represent Lauren, but I've not recovered from what is now called Long COVID. Very few people outside of my family know I'm still recovering from my two-week stay in the ICU. Being on a ventilator for several days saved me, but it changed my life in profound ways. I decide to at least meet with Lauren and then decide if I would be the best trial lawyer to represent her.

As I listen to my law school classmate tell me that Lauren West wants to meet me, I am torn whether I should tell Seth, I am still having memory and concentration issues.

Before the Lake Tierra development, I hadn't followed Lauren's golf course design career other than reading about it in magazine articles. I ask Seth to tell me more.

"When she was on the tour, she was all business. When she was at the top of the leaderboard and scheduled to play in the final group on Sunday, she'd practice after her round on Saturday until she was the only one on the practice tee, and it was too dark to see golf balls. Many admired her work ethic, but she had only a few friends; she had her father, Ben, caddying for her, and he made a big difference.

"Disclosing no lawyer-client confidences, what can you tell me about representing Miss West?" I'm trying to judge if I will be mentally able to focus and represent her.

"Don't worry; Lauren has given me permission to tell you about our work for her. She is highly motivated, self-reliant, brutally straightforward, and fiercely competitive. She takes immense pride in her achievements on the tour and her current work in golf course design."

Most elite athletes think and act the same way.

Seth continues. "Even if you asked her to play pickleball for the first time, she'd still be determined to beat you and would make every attempt to do so. The guys at our law firm feel stressed and intimidated by Lauren's impatience and perfectionism.

"When a man is a perfectionist, many people say he is brilliant. When a woman is a perfectionist, many people say she is bitchy."

"How so?" I ask.

"She sets high standards for herself and our lawyers, making her expectations clear. When one of our lawyers does a project for her, she asks if that's the best they can do. She's also impatient. I tell our lawyers to use a statement I heard long ago—when Lauren asks a question, she doesn't want the answer to tell her the history of Swiss watchmaking. She just wants to know what the time is."

I burst out in laughter while Seth continues.

"Lauren asks why the task they are doing for her is not yet complete. Some think she's high maintenance and would rather care for her business without our help. She's paying top dollar and has every right to expect and demand the best and most efficiently done legal work we offer. They never complain when she pays our bills."

"I'm not surprised. I know from my research that Ben West was obsessed with making her the number one woman golfer in the world. Has Lauren had any support system since her father's death from cancer a few years ago?"

"No," Seth replies. "Lauren's a loner. Her mother lives with her. Lauren claims she's too busy, and that could be true."

"What makes Lauren a challenge to represent?" I ask, once again sensing that I know the answer.

"She'll ask for updates and challenge you every step along the way."

I laugh.

We discuss Robert Benton and his motive for terminating Lauren's design contract.

"He's motivated to terminate her contract so he can save over one million dollars and claim credit for the design of an award-winning golf course," Seth says.

Benton insisted on having a clause in Lauren's design contract giving him the ownership of her design and denying her the right to take credit for the design and deny any further payment if he terminated her contract for cause. To make it difficult to terminate her contract for cause, Seth added a clause which only gave Benton the right to terminate Lauren's design contract for cause limited to a material breach of the agreement by Lauren and which she fails to remedy to Benton Land Company's reasonable satisfaction.

I burst out laughing. "Benton agreed to your material breach provision. He must have signed it without having Harvey Morgan review it. I'd say the only way Lauren could materially breach the design contract would be to not do the design."

"That was the main idea," Seth says. "Morgan's role is to crush those who stand against Robert Benton, making legal action too costly and too time-consuming to consider."

"They must be a terrible team to fight in court."

"Yes, they make quite a team. Benton is just as liberal as any Silicon Valley billionaire and generously supports liberal causes, including some of the most progressive prosecutors in cities nationwide. He doesn't put up with anyone challenging his business decisions or his politics."

Seth tells me. "There came a time when Lauren told Benton she was leaving to design golf courses for a competitive developer Benton was angry and wanted her to stay with him. Lauren demanded that she receive ten percent of the profits from real estate sales and golf course memberships in the Lake Tierra development. Benton agreed, but he added the word net to the profits and a non-compete clause in her contract. His way of getting back at her was to terminate her contract for cause to avoid paying the bonus and then claim he had designed it."

"Why did Benton agree to pay Lauren the bonus?"

"I assume he didn't want her to design golf courses for a competitor while never intending to pay her the bonus on the Lake Tierra Golf Course. Benton consistently refuses to fully pay contractors who work for him. He brags that his contractors should just be happy so they can say they did work for him."

"It was quite audacious of Benton to claim he's the designer," I say. "I saw on Lauren's website she claims to have designed the Lake Tierra Golf Course."

"By accusing Lauren of being transphobic and endangering transgender athletes, Benton is sending the message that suing him to claim credit for the design and recover her bonus will be a highly unpleasant and humiliating ordeal. Like countless others, Benton recognizes that repeatedly spreading the same lie on social media can be devastating for the person it targets."

Seth and I agree that Lauren's support of girls' and women's sports is not a material breach of the contract. It seems odd that Benton thinks Lauren will just take his stealing her golf course design idea and then trash her in the media. He must expect she'll sue him to get credit for the design, recover the ten percent bonus, and clear her name.

"Benton doesn't care about what's right. He has the money to make a lawsuit, a costly endeavor just to punish Lauren. He's counting on Lauren's strong desire to avoid the negative publicity barrage and the great expense he will make her face from the lawsuit and give up her ten percent profit bonus. Benton underestimates Lauren's resolve," Seth says. "But if you take her case, don't underestimate how Morgan and Benton will retaliate against the two of you."

Chapter 3

Luke

I wear my favorite power suit when I get dressed for the meeting. That includes my only Brioni blue pinstriped suit, my most expensive tie, a custom-made shirt, and my black alligator Lucchese cowboy boots. As I dress, I wonder if I am trying to impress a new client or my first celebrity client.

During my forty-five-minute flight, I quickly re-read Lauren's design contract. It allows Benton to terminate Lauren's contract at any time for any reason. But, he can only avoid paying her any bonus she may be due, or worse, claim credit to her design if she materially breaches the contract and fails to remedy the breach. Benton claims Lauren materially breached the contract by making comments about transgender athletes competing and girls' and women's sports. He claims credit for the design and refuses to pay her bonus as a result.

When my flight lands, I meet the limo, the law firm sent to pick me up. As we leave the airport, I look up at the fifty-six-story high-rise office building on Ross Avenue. It is an often-photographed building designed by a famous designer. When they remade Dallas, the building is featured in the opening credits.

Fifteen minutes later, I enter the building and give my name to the guard at the lobby counter. As I exit the elevator, I survey the palatial reception area with wood paneling, hardwood floors, and contemporary furniture. I've seen it many times, and I'm always amazed. I speculate again how much money McKenzie Simmons spent just for the wood and art in this one room. By extravagance, the law firm conveys to its potential clients that they are hiring successful and very expensive lawyers.

After sitting in the reception area for a few minutes, I see Seth, Ashley Shine, and Lauren. The first thing I notice is Lauren's smile. She's an attractive blond with radiant skin from years of playing golf. She's in great shape, with a solid athletic build. She's dressed in a fashionable neon blue suit with a tailored jacket, a white blouse, a short, tight-fitting skirt, and heels. She walks to greet me with the posture of a run-way model. As she draws close, I notice her perfume. It's Black Opium. I immediately recognize it because I had bought Black Opium for my wife, Allison.

I shake hands with my two law school classmates and turn toward Lauren. She smiles, looks deeply into my eyes, grabs my forearm with her left hand, and shakes my right hand. Her blue eyes are like the water of a lake I once fished in the Rockies, where I thought I could see all the way to the bottom. Lauren mastered the art of seduction without even trying. I look away.

She steps back and looks at me again. She says, "Luke, I remember you fighting against us at the zoning hearings."

All I can think of is her lingering eye contact and her perfume.

I'm at a loss. I need to put my lawyer's hat back on. I finally say, "Yes, I represented community members fighting you in the rezoning hearings."

"Since we prevailed, I won't hold that against you," Lauren says with a wry smile.

We spend a few minutes reliving the zoning meetings.

After we're seated in the conference room and served coffee, I say, "Tell me about your dealings..." I stop because I can't remember his name. I'm tongue-tied and not off to an impressive start. My hands are shaking, thankfully under the table and out of view.

She gives me a funny look. "Luke, his name is Robert Benton. He's the most narcissistic man you'll ever meet. He doesn't care whether people like him. Instead, he wants people to fear him. He's an overweight, slovenly looking guy. He once told me that if California women have to choose between a handsome man and a man with money, they'll go for the money every time."

I laugh.

"As you know, Benton never showed up to argue for the zoning of the Lake Tierra development. That would be beneath him. But, I can assure you he either bribed or dug up dirt on the board of supervisor members considering the rezoning request."

I had thought it was strange how the board of supervisors caved in so quickly, knowing the unanimous opposition by the Corona County residents, who were my clients.

Lauren continues. "When the county commissioners approved our zoning request, I went through all the steps to prepare a detailed golf design. I made several drawings. Benton built the golf course using my design. When he learned the Golf magazines planned to name the Lake Tierra Golf Course one of the top new courses in the United States, Benton terminated my contract and, claiming I materially breached the contract, he took credit for my design."

"He's claiming credit for your design because of the contract clause he included in the contract. But, you didn't materially breach the contract. So, he has no right to claim credit for the design."

"For Benton, there are no rules, only his rules. In his mind, he can claim credit for my design just because he wants to. He may even believe he designed the golf course. He's probably told enough people that he designed Lake Tierra that he believes he has the right to claim credit."

"Given how he treats people who do business with him, I'm surprised Benton can manipulate people who have succeeded in business.

"He's trading off my good name, reputation and my family-focused golf courses. No one building a second home in Lake Tierra is doing so because they think Benton designed the golf course."

I've seen some of the homes from the roadside. They stand tall and proud against the backdrop of the woods and the lake. The sprawling properties stretch out seemingly endlessly with the backdrop of the Hill Country. I've driven through Lake Tierra and noticed the manicured lawns and shrubs. The massive homes have at least three car garages and a separate space for the golf cart.

I'm unable to get in another word for the next ninety minutes, and I am listening intently. Lauren speaks with conviction and tells me about meeting Robert Benton at a pro-am LPGA event in California. During that first meeting, she shared with him her vision of golf course developments designed for the entire family; Lauren reconnected with him after she designed her first golf course in Dallas. "May I assume that you and Benton never discussed your different political views?" I ask.

Lauren chuckles and takes a sip of her coffee. "He knew we were at opposite ends of the political spectrum. He once told me he didn't care if I was a Republican as long as I made money for him. In the several years I designed golf courses for him, he never once mentioned transgender people, much less transgender athletes. On the contrary, Benton asked me to speak to groups about girls' and women's sports and to spend time with the families with daughters who came to hear me speak."

"You made lots of money for him," I say. "It sounds like his recent support of transgender athletes was a ploy to avoid paying your bonus and take credit for the design of a top-rated golf course."

"You bet. Benton didn't want to pay me the bonus, and taking the credit for the design of Lake Tierra Golf Course made him even more anxious to terminate my contract. I created the concept of developing luxury communities designed to engage the entire family. I found the land for each of his developments, and I'm the one who designed each of his top-rated golf courses. All Benton did was to put up the money and turn over his rich acquaintances to me. While he knows the potential wealthy clients, if you ask any of them, they will tell you they don't trust him. He has no friends, only people he can manipulate."

I nod, impressed. I can see that Lauren commands the respect of those with whom she interacts, and it's no wonder she's been so successful in a male-dominated industry.

Lauren continues. "Benton hates to lose, and he hates even more when people ignore him. Once, he made a golf match play wager with me, suggesting that the loser pays for a ski trip in Aspen for the winner. I agreed to play the tips, which were 7000 yards. I let him play the most forward tees. As we played, he lost his temper and threw his driver into the water. By the 15th hole, I had closed out the match. He lost his temper again and stormed off the course."

"How was the Aspen ski trip?"

"I'm still waiting to go to Aspen. Benton never pays off his losing bets. As I said, he hates being ignored even more. We once attended a charity event. As we went inside, people crowded around me, asking about the latest golf course I designed. No one even noticed Benton. He got mad and left the event, forcing me to get a ride home. Another time, he was mad as hell when he saw my photo on the cover of a golf real estate magazine. He called the editor to complain and then added his name to each of the developments and golf courses. Lake Tierra Golf Course is now called Benton Lake Tierra Golf Course."

"I'm fairly certain he will lose his case against you. You had a First Amendment right to offer your opinion on transgender athletes competing in girls' and women's sports. I don't understand why he didn't sit down with you and work something out."

"I wanted to reach an agreement and move on, but Benton never sits down to work out a dispute. Because he's wealthy, he can outspend and outlast his adversaries. He has a bully lawyer named Harvey Morgan. The two of them use the court as a weapon against enemies. He doesn't think I will have enough money to go all the way to trial and appeal when he loses."

"It reminds me of colleges who want to get rid of their football coach and not pay him for the balance of his term. They terminate the contract for cause to avoid making the payment. Then, they negotiate some far lesser sum and consider it a win."

Lauren shrugs and then explains that just like her trip to Aspen, Benton avoids fully paying anyone with whom he does business. "I thought I had negotiated a good deal on Lake Tierra, but I should have expected he'd find a way to not pay my bonus. But I never considered he'd use the same argument to claim that he designed the Lake Tierra Golf Course. When Benton called, he threatened to make my personal emails public."

"Did he tell you what was in those emails?"

"No, he didn't say, and I have no idea how he got access to my personal emails."

"Is there anything in those emails that could damage your case or make the jury dislike you if Benton goes public with them?"

Lauren pauses, thinking. "I've expressed concerns about transgender athletes competing against girls and women, but I can't think of anything else that might hurt my case."

"What exactly did you say about transgender athletes?"

"I never disparage transgender individuals, whether in public or in private. I've only ever said that it isn't right for them to compete in girls' and women's sports."

"Is there anything Benton has on you that would embarrass you or make you look bad to the jury?"

"No, Benton has nothing that would embarrass me or make me look bad to the jury."

Lauren takes another sip of coffee. Then, she asks, "Luke, are you the lawyer to fight Benton for me? Seth and Ashley tell me you are the most fearless lawyer they know and the top hill country trial lawyer. I've worked very hard to get where I am, and I'm not letting Robert Benton terminate my contract, take credit for my Lake Tierra Golf Course, and fail to pay me the bonus I deserve. You get what I'm saying?"

I understand what Lauren wants, and I know how contentious the litigation will be. It's one of the reasons I'm not sure I can successfully represent her. I know what it'll be like fighting Morgan and Benton. In the end, like most litigants, even when Lauren wins, she'll be unhappy for having spent all the time and money fighting Benton. "Yep. Lauren, I understand what you want," I reply. "But,…"

Lauren is quick to cut me off. "No buts. I want you to fight like hell for me. Harvey Morgan is the meanest and most ruthless lawyer you will ever go up against. Benton calls Morgan his bull, short for the bully. I want you to be as tough as Morgan, or maybe tougher. I will never settle this case, and I want you to aggressively fight Benton for me like Rambo and get our case to trial as soon as possible."

I had read a business article about Benton and Morgan. They had taken great pride in how they rarely settle a dispute, constantly attack the adversary, and are rarely forced to go to trial. Morgan, who other Los Angeles lawyers described as ruthless, told one reporter that his litigation strategy was to make the adversary's pain far greater than any potential gain from the litigation. He added that the more other lawyers describe him as ruthless, the more wealthy West Coast clients seek him out to represent them.

"I'm sorry," I reply. "I started to remind you that Morgan is Benton's legal hitman. Benton will fight you and make you give up instead of spending an ungodly amount of money putting up with every roadblock and every media attack he'll create. Morgan has made a name for himself, not because he's a brilliant trial lawyer, but because he does whatever it takes to win and subdue his opponent. Most people want to avoid litigation. Are you prepared for all that Morgan and Benton can throw…"

Before I can finish, Lauren says, "Damn Luke, unlike many others, I know what to expect, and I'm in the fight all the way. I've seen Benton file a lawsuit to get a headline and put the fear of God in others doing business with him, only to either drop the case or settle it before taking a loss. Even then, Benton claims victory. He's never acknowledged a loss. If we play nice, he'll walk all over us. I want to go after him and convince him that he will lose more than the bonus he owes me."

"I understand. Benton will do whatever is necessary for the public to perceive he was victorious. How much do you believe Benton owes you?" I ask.

"Somewhere around one million dollars, and it will increase as more people buy property at Lake Tierra," Lauren says.

I take a sip of water and choke as it goes down the wrong way. I frequently struggle with swallowing because my one vocal cord is paralyzed. I cough to clear my throat.

"Are you okay?" Lauren asks.

"Yes, sorry, I sometimes have difficulty swallowing."

I want to help Lauren. But I've never represented a client who wanted me to be "Rambo" in the courtroom. I've never had a case against someone who uses the legal system to punish their adversaries. Trying to out-bully Morgan in the courtroom makes no sense to me. It will run up the cost even more. Lauren will tell me how to represent her, and I'm not sure I can do it her way. I'm also still not sure I've recovered from my near-death experience in the hospital to take on what will undoubtedly be a very contentious case. I debate whether I should tell her that I am not at full strength physically or mentally. I decide against it.

If I agree to represent her, I'll be forced to combat Morgan delaying at every turn. He'll run up the costs and hide any documents that support Lauren's claim. A Corona County jury won't like Morgan or Benton. They'll like Lauren, and many who follow golf will know who she is. A Corona County jury will also find Benton had no right to terminate Lauren's contract because she advocated for girls' and women's sports. Judge Hawkins could rule as a matter of law that Benton violated Lauren's First Amendment Freedom of Speech rights. That said, most potential jurors know me or know of me, and they won't like me being a bully like Morgan in the courtroom.

I lean back in my chair and close my eyes momentarily, gathering my thoughts. I can feel the adrenaline pumping through my veins already. This is going to be a tough case. I don't know if I can do it. I decide I should get up to leave. I don't believe Lauren will let me be her lawyer and listen to my advice, and I know Morgan and Benton will attack her and me. I look across the table and see Lauren writing a check.

Lauren hands me the check and says, "Luke, here is a one hundred thousand dollar retainer to get you started filing suit against Benton to get me credit for my design and the bonus I'm entitled to receive."

I stare at the check for a moment. I've never been paid one hundred thousand dollars or anywhere close to that amount of money by other clients before I've done any work. My doubts about being able to represent Lauren quickly drift away. Then, they come back. I don't want to tell her I continue to suffer post-COVID side effects, and I'm not sure I can be a match for Morgan now. I come up with another response.

I hand the check back to her. "Lauren, I can't accept your check. I'm not the right lawyer to represent you. I'm not like Morgan. I can't out-bully Morgan. If Rambo is what you think you need and want, I recommend finding a big city lawyer from Houston or Dallas."

Lauren looks stunned and puzzled. "How can you turn down a one hundred thousand dollar retainer before you've done any work? No one has ever declined to work for me."

"Luke, what's the problem?" Ashley asks.

I want to help Lauren, and it's nice to have a client pay me one hundred thousand dollars upfront. But, I feel she's paying me to be her yes man, micromanage our legal strategy, and out-thug Morgan. I look at Ashley, and I turn back and say, "Lauren, I admire you and appreciate all that you have accomplished in your life and career and how you've brought inner-city children to golf. But as I told you, I'm not the right lawyer for you. Before I leave, would you allow me to make an observation for you to consider going forward?"

Lauren's forehead is wrinkled as if she is processing what I just told her. After a moment, she replies. "Yes, let me hear what you believe I should consider."

"Forgive me if this is more advice than you want to receive."

Before our meeting, I did some research on how Morgan operates. I had found pages of links to articles about Morgan and interviews that he had given. He's well-known for representing Hollywood stars in the most contentious divorces, including Benton's high-stakes divorce from a young Hollywood starlet. His wife had accused Benton of being a serial womanizer who had affairs with multiple women. Morgan smeared and slut shamed Benton's wife in court, calling her a gold digger who slept her way to the top and accusing her of crying crocodile tears to get sympathy. Opposing lawyers say that Morgan's intimidation tactics, including the way he treats women are improper and unethical.

"Based on what I've read, Morgan is cold and calculating and sees lawsuits as a chess match. When you file suit, he will stoop lower than you've imagined. He'll delay the trial for months, maybe years, run up your expenses, and launch a public relations campaign to malign you. You may have to spend five hundred thousand dollars to recover what Benton owes you."

"When we win, I'll get the legal fees, right?"

"Yes, but like I said, you could be out of pocket five hundred thousand or more just to get through the trial, and when Benton appeals the ruling against him, you will spend even more money. It will be a very long and expensive journey."

"I'll be able to cover the fees and expenses from my work for other developers," Lauren says.

I continue. "If Morgan and Benton want you to give up your case or settle it for next to nothing, they will use your fear of being publicly shamed from whatever you had on your computer to get what they want."

"I've already told you there's nothing they can do to make me settle my case. How can they publicly shame me?" Lauren asks.

"Benton has told you he copied everything on your computer. So, if there's anything that might embarrass you, they'll use it. Morgan and Benton will also have private investigators watch you full-time and dig into your past with the sole purpose of scandalizing you in some negative way. You may have someone tailing you now. Morgan and Benton may even make up stories about you. If you look back at scandals over the last twenty-five to thirty years, when a man is the subject of a scandal, he's made a comeback and rebuilt his reputation. Mentioning no names in each scandal involving a woman—especially a conservative, ambitious woman—the media condemned the woman involved, and she felt the brunt of their scorn. It's a double standard, and you risk the same thing happening to you. The sooner this can be out of the news, the better for you."

Lauren starts to respond and stops. She may have read accounts of the media mistreating successful women, but she may not believe the media could do that to her.

"You're telling me he and Morgan will have private investigators tail me, and they may make up lies about me? Can't you get a court order to make them stop?"

"I'd bet on it," I say. "And I'm not sure a judge will order Benton to stop."

"I appreciate how you feel. Don't give Morgan and Benton any ammunition to bring you down and force you to spend money on a PR firm to save your reputation."

"Are you saying I should stop speaking out for girls' and women's sports?"

"Not at all. But I'm saying the media will dissect each public word you utter. It's one thing to support girls' and women's sports. It's another thing to be labeled as someone who hates transgender people and puts them at risk. I hope you can find the lawyer you want, and he or she can take care of you," I say as I start for the door. I don't look back.

Chapter 4

Lauren

I'm frozen in my chair. I take a deep breath, trying to steady my racing heart. Luke Hartley may have walked out on me, but I'm not about to let him get the best of me. I stand up and smooth out my skirt, taking a moment to compose myself before turning to Ashley.

"Damn it!" I snap, my frustrations boiling over. "What just happened, Ashley? I want to know."

"I believe Luke wants to represent you and help you," Ashley replies. "I could see that in his eyes. But, after you told him you wanted a Rambo-like lawyer to represent you, Luke decided you want a lawyer you can control."

"But the most famous Texas trial lawyers have always been the most aggressive in the courtroom," I say. "And you told me Luke Hartley is the lawyer I should hire."

"Lauren, those great aggressive trial lawyers were from a different generation, and they were from Houston and Dallas. Luke Hartley told you Hill Country jurors don't like bullies in the courtroom. He told you he'd win your case by making Robert Benton and Harvey Morgan the bullies. Luke Hartley is the most pre-eminent trial lawyer you can hire to go toe-to-toe against Robert Benton and his lawyer. He's principled and ethical, and he'll be your zealous advocate, but he's not a Rambo-style lawyer. He can't become something he's not. That's why he turned you down."

"I don't think Luke understands how Benton operates. He thinks I will cut and run to avoid spending an ungodly amount of money and fighting his negative publicity campaign. I have enough money to fight him, and when we win, I should get my attorney's fees. I will pay Luke more money than he will earn in a year. I'll fight against his negative media campaign as well."

"Lauren, Luke is not motivated by money."

I understand money doesn't motivate Luke. If so, he wouldn't be a lawyer in a small Hill Country town. Ashley's right. He most likely felt offended when I handed him the one-hundred-thousand dollar check as a retainer. "What motivates him?" I ask.

"Winning in court for his clients and his reputation. But he told you he can't win if you are telling him what to do, and if he becomes the Rambo-like lawyer you want, it will hurt his reputation. Luke is undoubtedly the most exceptional trial lawyer in all of Texas Hill Country. He wins by out-preparing his adversaries, and local juries and judges love his gregarious personality. You've said Robert Benton makes life a living hell if one gets in his way. Luke tried to tell you what to expect and that he'd take care of you, but you cut him off."

I lean in closer, wanting to explain. "I know what to expect from Benton and his lawyer, but I have no choice. Benton stole my golf course design, took credit for it, and wrongfully terminated my contract to avoid paying me the substantial bonus he owes me. He thinks I'm afraid of what he can do to me. He may be right, but I won't let him get away with it."

I look over at Seth. "What do you think, Seth?"

"In the long run, you'll most likely win, but when you file suit against Benton, he will hire a media firm to destroy you online, in print, and on broadcast media for what they will claim is your transphobia and misgendering. It could really get mean and nasty. Do you want to not only fight Benton but also fight the TV news and the tabloids and social media trying to destroy you and your business?"

"Why would they be interested?"

“Because they’d like nothing better than to take you down because you vocally oppose the right of transgender athletes to compete in women’s sports.”

“That doesn’t mean I’ll compromise on what I know is right. Even though I wish I had not given Benton an excuse to terminate my contract, I’m not going to retract what I said. Women have fought too hard for too long to have opportunities to compete in high school and college. I will fight to not allow biological men to come in and dominate girls’ and women’s sports. It’s not fair.”

Ashley stares at me for a moment before speaking.

“I respect what you have accomplished in your career. It’s a refreshing change from the usual political correctness that is infecting the world. But, like it or not, after taking a stand on girls’ and women’s sports, you’re forever labeled a right-winger. Many in the media would like nothing more than to knock you off that pedestal.”

I stand up. I want to pound my fist on the table, but I restrain myself.

I look back at Seth Ashford. “I don’t want Luke Hartley. He walked out on me. I want you to find me another lawyer pronto.”

"Sorry, but Luke is the only lawyer I can recommend. He's far more talented in court than any lawyer in the Hill Country," Ashley says. "You better find him before he's gone. Tell him you want him to be your lawyer, and you accept that he is not a bully or the Rambo-type lawyer you described. Be open to listening and letting him take charge of your case."

"Damn," I mutter, "I'm not sure that is in my DNA to step back and let him take charge. It's my case, not his."

"I suspect Luke figured that out in our meeting, and that's why he left."

Ashley's right. I leave the McKenzie Simmons Dallas office, still reeling from being rejected and frustrated that Luke is the only lawyer Shine can recommend. I wonder why I care about what Luke Hartley thinks of me. He's just a small-town lawyer. But there's something about him. As best I can describe it, Luke Hartley inspires confidence without being cocky.

When I get downstairs, I spot Hartley waiting in the lobby for a car to pick him up. I lean in closely, subtly brushing against him. I look deep into his eyes. I reach to hold his arm. Luke pulls away. His eyes flicker as if I've taken him by surprise. He quickly gains his composure and stares at me.

I take a step back. “Luke,” I stammer. “I realize how I came across upstairs. I’m sorry. You know I’m angry about what Benton did to me. I want to get to know you better, and I want the chance to change your mind about representing me. Will you let me come down and spend the day with you?”

Luke’s eyes narrow, and I stand closer, invading his space, and I reach out for his hand again.

“Lauren, it’s far, far, far more complicated than me getting to know you. For now, let me help you find a lawyer to get what you deserve on the Lake Tierra project?”

“I want you to be my lawyer,” I say. “Spend the day with me. Get to know me.”

Luke knows what I’m doing, and I’m sure I’m not the first woman to put on the charm initiative.

“I don’t believe spending the day with you will change my decision about representing you,” he replies. “For things that matter in a lawsuit against Robert Benton. I don’t think I’m what you want in a lawyer.”

I’m shaking my head. Luke continues. “You’re a fighter, and I admire that. But, despite what you said, I don’t believe you are willing to listen to me. Instead, you want a lawyer who will let you direct him. I understand why you want that, but I'm not that lawyer."

"You're wrong about me," I say, my voice rising. I will listen to you, I won't direct you, I won't second guess you." I come close to telling him to go to hell and turn around and leave, but I need him. "Please spend a day with me, and you'll see what I am like when I am not venting."

Luke sighs heavily and runs his hand through his hair. As his eyes dart away from me, I notice the lines etched into his forehead and the tension in his jaw. He looks fatigued. "Okay, Lauren," he says, with reluctance in his voice, "I'll spend the day with you, but you likely won't change my decision. You need to find a lawyer who is willing to let you direct him or her."

"Is there anything wrong with you?" I ask. "You look like you have the weight of the world on your back."

"No, No. I'm tired from an early morning flight."

"Okay, I promise I'll listen to you. You'll see when I come to visit."

He rolls his eyes, undoubtedly thinking I'm trying to seduce him. "I have no free days during the week," he says. "I can meet you for breakfast on Saturday at the Corona Cafe and then go to my office. My daughter Megan has a soccer game Saturday afternoon."

"Sure. I'll see you Saturday morning," I reply. "I'll stay over on Friday night. We can talk while we eat breakfast and continue in your office."

There's a crease between Luke's eyes, which tells me there's something more than his not wanting to represent me than his not wanting to be a bully in the courtroom. I have no idea what else is standing in the way, but I hope to find out on Saturday when I'll have at least part of the day to work on him.

I nod, grateful that he's at least willing to give me a chance. I need his support in this fight. The silence is awkward, but I'm not sure what else to say to him.

I leave the McKenzie Simmons Dallas offices and take the elevator down to the parking garage. I get into my black Audi Q7 and exit the office on Fielder, heading towards the Dallas North Tollway. As I pull away, my eyes shift to the rearview mirror every few seconds. I can't shake the feeling of being watched. My office in the clubhouse of the Ember Ridge Country Club is only a fifteen-minute drive in light traffic.

It was the first golf course I designed with my mentor, Gene Wright. The course winds through the North Dallas Ember Ridge community. The clubhouse is uniquely western and has been showcased in the Dallas Fort Worth golf magazine. Everyone in the community knows me, so when I pass people who are outside, they each wave.

The greatest gift I had as a golfer was my father. He was named for Ben Hogan, and came close twice to qualifying for the PGA tour. Having not made it; he was determined that I would play professional golf. He wasn't just my coach; he was my rock and the guiding force in my life. From a young age, he told me I could be the best in the world if I believed in myself. I didn't fully understand what he meant at the time, but the look in his eyes made me believe it was possible.

I won the NCAA tournament in college, and when I turned pro, I went on to win sixteen tournaments, including two majors. Every victory felt like we were standing on that podium together like he was there lifting me higher than I ever thought possible. But when he got cancer and died, something in me shattered. I lost my drive, my mojo. It was a lonely road after that until I decided to design golf courses for families to enjoy.

A white Dodge Charger is lingering behind me since I pulled out of the parking garage. At first, I brush it off as a coincidence—this is Dallas, after all, and plenty of people drive from downtown on the Dallas North Tollway. But the Charger seems to change lanes when I do, maintaining a steady distance. When he pulls up next to me I see the driver, who appears to be a man in his late 40s wearing aviator sunglasses. He looks over at me and smiles while we are speeding along the tollway.

My heart races. Damn, Luke was right. Robert Benton has already hired a private investigator to follow me just close enough to be noticed, planting seeds of fear. Robert Benton wants me to know I'm being watched as a way to intimidate me.

I call Courtney Barr, and I tell her about my meeting with Luke Hartley and the man in the white Dodge Charger. She listens and offers her support.

Chapter 5

Luke

It's still dark as I drive from my home to the Corona Cafe. I arrive promptly at seven. It's a quaint spot frequented by lawyers, judges, business men and women. Several wooden tables and cozy armchairs make it an informal haven for countless conversations. Natural light pours through large windows, illuminating the room and highlighting the rich tones of the rustic wooden floors. The soft hum of espresso machines harmonizes with the gentle chatter of patrons, who sit at the same tables daily.

I order a latte for myself and a vanilla latte for Lauren, and I ask my friends to allow me to sit with my guests at our usual table while I wait for Lauren. Even though I may not be the right lawyer for her, I'm intrigued by the opportunity to spend time with her.

I played the Lake Tierra Golf Course with a client one early morning. From the zoning hearings, I knew that Lauren West had designed the course. When I drove through the gate, I passed the most prominent homes I had ever seen, all on oversized lots. Mansions lined either side of the fairway throughout the eighteen holes. My client told me that most people who belong to Lake

Tierra came from New York, Chicago, or Los Angeles. He was concerned if they all voted, then Corona County would become another liberal bastion like Austin.

"Luke."

I almost jump out of my chair.

When she sits down, she smiles, lifts her coffee, takes a sip, and says, "I see you remember what I like in my latte."

We each take slow sips of our coffee, our eyes fixed on the table. For what seemed like a long time, we don't continue our conversation.

Lauren sets down her cup and walks over to the window. She returns and tells me she was followed by Benton's private investigator. She says, if I look outside, I'll see a White Dodge Charger. So, I get up and go to the door. It's just light enough outside to see his car. He's standing outside the driver's side and smoking a cigarette. As he waves, I figure this is only the beginning of Benton's planned attacks to make Lauren's life miserable.

I don't confront him. Instead, I return to my chair and call Tommy Todd, the Corona Police Chief. When I go to the door five minutes later, the White Charger is gone.

After a minute of silence, I ask, “Why did you want to spend time with me?”

“May I assume that you’ve read *To Kill a Mockingbird*?” she folds her napkin and places it near her cup.

“Several times. Why?”

“You might recall reading the fatherly advice that Atticus gave Scout. He said, “You never really understand a person until you consider things from his point of view […] until you climb into his skin and walk around in it. I made a mistake with Robert Benton. I jumped into business with him before I knew him and against my father’s warning. I don’t want to make the same mistake with you. If you’re going to be my lawyer, I aim to learn as much as possible about you before we go into the battle together.”

I take another sip of my coffee. In my legal career, none of my clients have quoted from *To Kill a Mockingbird.* That said, in a small town like Corona, I’m friends with most of my clients. “I guess you can ask questions to help you see things from my point of view.”

“I’ll learn more about you later,” Lauren says. “For now, I want you to know more about me than you may have seen on TV or read about me.”

I suspect this is part of her plan to persuade me to represent her.

"Your college and LPGA tournament victories, along with how you encouraged the next generation of young girls to play golf, have been the subject of many golf magazine articles. I know your father left his job to become your caddie when you started on the tour. I also know it devastated you when doctors discovered your father had cancer and he passed away. More recently, your golf designs have been the subject of business magazine articles. I can't think of anything I don't already know."

She squeezes her eyes shut for a moment and takes a sip of her latte.

"My father loved golf, and he put a toy golf club in my hand as soon as I could walk. With all the lessons and competitions, I didn't have a normal high school life. I didn't date. I didn't go to the prom. I focused on getting good grades and improving my golf swing."

I ask, "I'm sure you were heavily recruited by the top college golf coaches. Why did you choose UT Austin?"

"I chose the University of Texas partly because it was an easy drive for my father to watch me compete. Years later, when my dad developed cancer, I didn't realize how much I depended on him until he was gone."

"What about your mother?" I ask.

Lauren sighs. "After my father died, my mother was depressed and retired from teaching. I convinced her to move in with me and travel with me to tournaments."

"I'm sure your mother appreciated being with you."

She sighs again and takes a deep breath before answering. "Yes, she was lonely. Heck, I was lonely, but we grew closer together in our loss."

I want to change the subject, so I ask, "What's it like to be on the LPGA tour?"

"First, playing professional golf is unlike a sport like football, basketball, or baseball. The athlete signs a contract in those sports before taking the field or court. Plus, those are team sports, where a player could be in a slump and still be paid. In professional golf, I didn't earn money until after I performed, and every swing or putt I made was on television. I felt more pressure to be successful, and in those days, we didn't have a sports psychologist traveling with us.

Second, unlike tennis, where women earn as much as men, there is an enormous difference in what PGA golfers earn compared to what I earned. If a PGA might earn two million dollars, or even more if he wins a tournament. When I won my sixteen tournaments, I earned maybe as much as three hundred thousand dollars. That's not chump change, but it is a fraction of what the PGA players earn."

She stops for a moment and takes the last sip of her latte. I can tell she'd like another cup.

"Can I get you another?" After she shakes her head, I say, "I'll be right back."

When I hand the latte to her, I sit back down. "I know there are great differences in prize money from reading tournament results in the newspaper."

"Many people do not know what it is like to be a professional golfer playing on the LPGA tour. Playing on the LPGA tour is a lonely experience. We train and practice constantly; therefore, we go from city to city each week. We play golf during the day and struggle to get a good night's sleep at night. We know our competitors, but they are not like having a close friend. When my father was alive, he kept me company as we traveled together from one tournament to another. When he passed away, I had my mother with me for a short time, and then I was on my own. I felt abandoned, and soon thereafter, I had anxiety and felt depressed. I couldn't focus on the course because of those feelings. Once I injured my back, I tried to come back. I thought I could make it to the top again, but I soon realized that, without my dad there to push me, I couldn't make it and keep the commitment to make a comeback. Thankfully, I could pursue a second career designing golf courses."

"I've watched you during many LPGA tournaments on television. I thought about the pressure professional golfers must contend with to win, or at least finish in the top ten, but I never considered the loneliness you described."

For the next couple of minutes, we sit in silence while we eat our breakfast. She's eating the Acai bowl, and I sense from the look on her face that she is fondly remembering her father. They clearly had a complex relationship. I suggested that we eat here because it is the only restaurant in Corona County with a healthy section on its menu. I had read that Lauren has always eaten only healthy foods. I'm eating the biscuits and gravy with eggs over easy and sausage. Lauren winces each time she sees me take a bite. I tell her I worked out from five to seven before I arrived at the cafe. That doesn't change how she looks at my plate. I smile.

Lauren's talking away between bites from her Acai bowl. Being fair to her, my listening and remembering what she tells me is far more important than eating my breakfast. I drop my knife and fork and motion Sandy to come over and take my plate. I ponder when to tell her I had COVID, was hospitalized and put on a ventilator two years ago, and I've still not fully recovered. My memory is still foggy, and I still have trouble concentrating for any appreciable length of time. I've been told that I have a long COVID. I should have told Lauren at the McKenzie offices in Dallas, but I didn't.

"When country clubs in the metroplex upgraded their golf courses, Gene Wright was the man they usually hired. Wright gave her the chance to get started, and she is forever in his debt.

I know of Wright for his golf course designs in Texas. I didn't know—he gave her the chance to design her first golf course in Dallas.

Lauren says, "There are so few women who have made a mark in golf course design. You can count them on one hand."

I wasn't aware. "Who are some of the women?"

“The first, and maybe best known, was Marion Hollins. She designed Cypress Point, one of the most iconic courses in the world.”

“Cypress Point is the course—the one with those breathtaking views along the Pacific, right?” I ask.

Lauren smiles. “I’ve played Cypress Point, and it’s a masterpiece. Back in the 1920s, Marion Hollins was a driving force behind the project. She identified the land, convinced Alister McKenzie to come on board, and even suggested some of the course’s most famous holes, including number 16, one of the most famous holes in golf. It’s a par-3, and the tee shot is over a cove to a green that’s perched on a rocky outcrop. It’s both beautiful and terrifying.”

Lauren grabs her phone and finds a photo she had taken from the 16th hole at Cypress Point. She tells me she read every article about Marion Hollins and considered her a role model.

I’m deeply impressed by the enthusiasm she has for her work, and interest in Marion Hollins. When I ask what she likes most, she surprises me.

"I meet highly successful people through my design of luxury golf courses. In every meeting, I learn something from them, including how they became so successful."

"I first met Robert Benton in a pro-am event in California. He loved golf and had become a billionaire in Silicon Valley. My father caught Benton cheating and told me if he cheated in golf, he was most likely dishonest in his business dealings. Years later, after I left the tour and started with Gene Wright, I called Benton and suggested that he develop high-end golf communities focused on families. Being a super-wealthy California liberal with many wealthy friends, Benton liked the idea, and we started working together."

After she describes each of her golf course designs, she says, "When I asked if you were a Rambo-type lawyer, I was venting my frustration and my experience watching what he and Morgan do to adversaries. I posted a photo of the Lake Tierra Golf Course award on my social media accounts and wrote that I was proud to be the designer. Robert Benton called and demanded that I remove the posts, but I refused. I didn't ask to be in this fight, but if I'm in one against Benton. I want a lawyer who will take him down."

I know what it's like going against men like Benton—men who think their money can silence the truth. I figure I must either say I will represent her against Benton or share with her that I'm not the lawyer I was before going into the hospital. I'm not sure I'll ever be that lawyer again or if I can match Harvey Morgan in court, I decide to bring that up later.

After we get up and walk to her car, she subtly turns her head and shifts her eyes toward me. There's something seductive about her. It's disarming. I catch her eyes and look away. I turn back and smile. She grins, signaling she's trying to entice me to take her case.

She says, "Let me follow you to your office."

"No need for you to drive. Come with me, and I'll take you there. We can't stay too long because of my daughter's soccer game."

We walk to my car, and I open the door for her. As Lauren slides in, she looks at me, smiles again, and then looks down at her phone and frowns.

"What is it?" I ask.

"Someone has posted my Dallas address, my phone number, my email address, and a photo of my mother and me."

Her phone rings. She looks and doesn't answer. Her phone rings again. This time, Lauren's hands are shaking as she turns it off.

Benton knows Lauren's address, phone number, and email address, and he has her laptop, which included photos. So, I'm sure Benton is behind the doxxing, but I have no way to prove it.

Chapter 6

Lauren

After arriving, I sit across from Luke in his office. It is the most organized and neat lawyer's office I have ever seen. I'm more accustomed to seeing files on the floor and a desk covered in papers. That's why Seth always meets me in one of the McKenzie Simmons conference rooms. Luke's L-shaped desk is immaculate, with only the essentials in place: a perfectly aligned Montblanc pen set, a crisp legal pad, and an iMac computer to his side.

Even though he's behind his bare desk, I smell the faint scent of Luke's cologne, a mix of sandalwood and musk. I like it. He speaks with a raspy voice, so I get up and pull my chair closer to him.

My thoughts are racing. How can I convince Luke Hartley to represent me? Once again, I smile warmly and gaze deeply into his eyes, trying to charm him. This time, he looks away. I talked about myself during coffee and breakfast. There are some things about me that I don't tell him. They will forever be my secret. I want to persuade him to represent me against Benton.

"Your reputation precedes you," I say. "Ashley Shine told me I'd never meet a lawyer more organized than you."

"It's all about not wasting time searching for things. I created a system that works well for me. Everything has a place, and I organize it so I can find what I'm looking for immediately."

"That's impressive," I say. "Seth and Ashley mentioned that you are the most skilled litigator in the Hill Country, and I witnessed your expertise during the zoning hearings, but my knowledge about you is limited."

"Okay, when I was at UT, I wanted to play major league baseball. If I couldn't make it to the major leagues, I wanted to either be a pilot or a coach."

"You're neither of those, so when and why did you decide to become a lawyer?"

Luke says. "I wanted to pitch in the major leagues, but I always had a Plan B."

He tells me he learned to fly in high school, and for a time, his "Plan B" was to become a pilot. He met Allison in his senior year and decided he did not want to be gone so much.

"After I decided that I wanted to build my life back in Corona, I realized I couldn't make any money coaching at the high school. I decided to go to UT law school. I applied, and they accepted me. In my first year, I almost quit, but after the first semester, I was ranked third in my law school class. I guess I had the interest and the ability to do well in law school."

"Was Allison the reason you wanted to come back to Corona?"

"Yes, Allison grew up a few miles from Austin, and she wanted to settle in the Hill Country."

"You made the right decision," I say. "My Dallas lawyers tell me that you're the best trial lawyer in the Hill Country. I thought you made a good argument in the zoning hearings."

Luke smiles.

"I don't know about that. But I fight for clients who can't fight for themselves. Winning is important to me, and losing, including my fight to stop your Lake Tierra development, hurts more than I can ever convey. I want to win, and I find meaning when representing the underdog. I take on cases others believe are hopeless. I get great satisfaction in proving them wrong."

"I have a question. It's more personal. Is that okay?" I ask.

"You told me you wanted to…," Luke replies.

"I want to climb in your skin and walk around in it. Isn't that what Atticus told Scout?"

"I'm sure it's close enough."

"I looked at your firm's web page and saw a photo of you and your girls. That prompted me to do a Google search, and I discovered your wife, Allison, and your son, Jack, died in a car accident. Having lost my father, I understand what it's like to lose a parent, But, losing your son and wife must be far more difficult."

Luke puts the palm of his right hand on the side of his head and then puts it over his chest. He tells me that what I read is true. His wife, Allison, and their son, Jack, died in a car crash in 2019. Since then, he's been raising their two daughters, Abby, who is eighteen and has autism, and Megan, who is sixteen and a top elite soccer player. He says Abby can be a handful. Her energy, her questions—they're relentless. He and Abby travel to watch Megan play soccer throughout Texas and other states.

"The top colleges in America are recruiting Megan," Luke says. "Abby has a lot of spirit. It's important to channel that kind of energy positively."

I nod in understanding. "Abby and Megan sound like wonderful girls. And I'm sure you are excited watching Megan become a soccer star. I can't imagine what it's been like for you and your girls. I'm so sorry. You have lost your wife, and they have lost their mother."

Luke takes a deep breath before continuing as if he's still feeling the weight of his loss heavy on his chest. "Allison's and Tom's death changed my priorities," he says. "I'm no longer focused primarily on my work. I cut back my hours to spend more time with my girls. Losing their mom and brother has been difficult for them. Then, being taken out of school in March 2020 for COVID-19 was an absolute disaster. Practicing soccer by yourself is not the best way to get better."

"I hadn't thought of that. It's understandable. Losing someone you love can be like losing a part of yourself. I appreciate your willingness to share that with me. Have you found anyone?"

"You mean, do I have a special lady in my life? No, I haven't tried. No one has told me when it would be appropriate. But in the meantime, I've received my share of casseroles from local divorced women."

I chuckle at his response, thinking he must have a bevy of divorced women seeking him out. I don't want him to think that I'm like those women.

"It's important to take your time and not rush into anything. But, sometimes, life surprises us in unexpected ways."

Luke swallows and shifts uncomfortably in his seat. "I'm not sure I would even recognize whatever life brings my way."

I ask Luke about Allison. He says Allison loved to travel and experience different cultures, and he spends the next twenty minutes reminiscing about his many family trips to Canada, Mexico, and Europe.

"You said that there is no one special in your life. Are you dating?" I ask.

"I don't date," Luke replies. "The girls would never approve if I brought another woman home, and I'm not comfortable sneaking around behind their backs."

Luke continues, "I miss being around people, but I'm devoting my time and attention to my girls. I spend time with Megan on her soccer and with Abby on her schoolwork. Abby is a 'high functioning autism spectrum disorder (ASD)' girl. She is brilliant in her own way, but the world can be overwhelming for her sometimes. The world is a blur of colors and movement for her, her eyes struggling to focus on one thing at a time. It took years and doctor after doctor before we realized she was autistic."

I want to learn more about Abby and how Luke and his wife ultimately learned she was autistic. He tells me that girls make up a much smaller percentage of autistic children than boys. They, including Abby, can mask their autism far better than boys. He says that as early as kindergarten, there seemed to be something that was off about Abby socializing with classmates. She had very few friends, and her best friend was a boy who came from a low-income family and whom the other kids ridiculed. When she was in third grade, we discovered she had little interest in team sports. She and Megan joined a soccer team. Megan was all in and loved it. During practice and when she got into games, Abby stayed off by herself on the field, and he could tell she was not enjoying playing on the team.

"That must have been a tough time for her," I say.

"You bet," Luke tells me. "We tried to get her involved in other team sports, and she was not interested. I understand why now. Over time, we discovered that children with autism do better with individual sports."

"I could teach her to play golf," I say as I reach across the table and lean in.

Luke pauses for a moment as if he is considering my offer.

I say, "Golf is a solitary sport and might be just what Abby needs."

"I'm not sure if golf is the right fit for her," he says. "I worry that it might be too difficult for her. She struggles with coordination and has a hard time staying focused for long periods of time. I don't want to set her up for failure."

"I'll do more research, can work with her and see if it's something she enjoys. And if not, maybe I can help find something else."

Luke nods. "Pediatricians told Allison and him repeatedly that Abby was just a late bloomer and Megan was an early bloomer. We could see there was more to it than that. There's lots more to Abby's story, but you have the idea. When Abby was in middle school, a doctor finally diagnosed her correctly. She occasionally has meltdowns, depression, and anxiety. Despite her disability, Abby's done well in school in every subject other than math, and she has been accepted by SMU."

"Wow, that's quite an accomplishment, given what she's gone through," I say.

"When she received the acceptance letter, she cried out loud with tears of joy. For the first time, she believed what I had been telling her for years and that she was an amazing young woman. I cried. I'm worried about how Abby will do having a roommate, either being alone in an apartment or having a roommate in the dorm. I want her to stay home and take courses at the community college for her first two years. Then, we can see if she is ready for SMU.

I look into his eyes. "As a widower. I'm sure you've had many stressful times. What it's like being a single father raising two teenage girls, one of whom is autistic?"

"Your ability to effortlessly engage with individuals you've just met and prompt them to share personal details that they wouldn't divulge to anyone else is truly remarkable."

I'm not sure he's complimenting me, but until I hear otherwise, I'll take it as one.

After a lengthy pause, he answers. "There's no manual on how a widower father is supposed to raise two daughters. There's also no manual on how to raise a teenage girl who is autistic. Experts only recently started writing about teenage girls with autism and how they differ from teenage boys. Abby and Megan were in middle school when their mother and brother died. They had never experienced death before, much less the death of their mother and brother. At first, they were angry and upset. So, the first thing I had to learn was how to nurture them as they experience grief for the first time."

"I'm sure that was difficult for you and your girls," I say.

"It was more than challenging. It's hard to describe it. I was experiencing grief myself. In addition to experiencing grief, the girls were going through adolescent development. I realized I didn't know all that I didn't know about raising teenage girls. I discovered what physical, emotional, and hormonal changes girls go through and how that differed from Abby's autism. I cut back on my work to spend more time with them and to be there for them. By trial and error, I found they wanted me to listen to them and understand them more than dictating what they should do. I understood, having spent my entire career listening to clients. Thankfully, they became passionate about soccer, Megan as a player and Abby as her biggest fan. I take Abby with me to every game. We've had great fun together on the soccer field."

Suddenly, Luke doesn't look well, and my hand brushes against his. "Are you all right?" I ask, searching for clues in his face.

"Yes, sorry. I was lost in thought for a moment," Luke says.

What thought? I wonder.

He tells me he has to go. "Megan's playing at one." He gets up. As he's leaving, I grab his arm again. "Can I come with you to watch Megan play before you take me to get my car?"

"Are you sure you have time to do that?" he asks.

"Yes, I'll spend another night here and drive back to Dallas tomorrow morning."

As I had hoped, we've spent our time together, not focused on my case. I've learned a great deal about Luke. More importantly, I believe I've persuaded him to represent me against Robert Benton.

He raises his eyebrows, looking surprised by my request to join him at the soccer game. That's for the best. I want to spend more time with him and get to know his girls.

"Why do you want to go to Megan's soccer game?" he asks.

"I enjoy watching young girls pushing themselves to become the best they can be in their sports. Is that okay?"

He glances at me and replies, "I get it. I'm sorry. I didn't ask that question very well."

Chapter 7

Luke

I'm not sure why she wants to hang around and watch Megan play soccer, but I'm enjoying her company.

"Since you're spending the night, I'll take you to dinner and then to my home, and we can continue our discussion."

After the game, I will tell her about my continuing side effects from COVID-19 and being on the ventilator for ten days.

"Sure," she answers. "That'll be fun."

Later that afternoon, I drive her to pick up Abby and Megan. When they come out of our home, I introduce them to Lauren. They both give me one of those looks that I interpret to mean they believe that she and I are a couple. I shake my head to convey we're not a couple, but I can tell they remain unconvinced.

When we arrive at the field, a young woman with a distinctive 'S' on her shirt greets me. She's the Stanford coach, and she's come to Corona to watch Megan. She is the first person to introduce herself to Megan. As we walk to the field, another young woman approaches us, wearing a UNC logo on her Carolina blue shirt. She introduces herself and tells Megan that she would love for her to visit Chapel Hill to see the University of North Carolina campus.

"Megan must be in high demand by the best college women's soccer programs in the country," Lauren says, her tone carrying a note of genuine admiration.

"She is indeed," I respond while feeling a swell of pride.

As we settle into the bleachers, Abby is practically bouncing with excitement, her eyes glued to the field. She's wearing a red, white, and black Rams shirt, just like the other parents, and her enthusiasm is infectious.

"Megan's going to score today; I just know it!" Abby exclaims.

Lauren smiles at her while leaning in slightly. "I bet you're her biggest fan. Aren't you, Abby?"

Abby nods vigorously. "Of course! Megan's the best! She says that 'I'm her lucky charm.'" She then glances at Lauren, her expression is serious. "You'll cheer with me, right?"

"Absolutely," Lauren replies, her tone is warm and encouraging. "I wouldn't miss it for the world."

Throughout the game, Abby's focus is entirely on Megan, her eyes tracking her sister's every move on the field. Whenever Megan makes a good play, Abby jumps to her feet, clapping her hands and cheering loudly.

"Go, Megan! That's my sister!" Abby shouts, her voice cutting through the noise of the crowd. She beams at Lauren, who mirrors her enthusiasm with cheers of her own.

As the game progresses, the tension builds. When Megan goes for a header and is called for a foul on the wet field, Abby's hands grip the edge of the bleacher seat, and her knuckles turning white. The stands fall silent as the Trinity kicker lines up for the penalty kick.

"Come on, Megan," Abby whispers, almost like a prayer. When the ball hits the crossbar and the crowd erupts, Abby jumps up and down, her relief and joy palpable. She looks at Lauren with a grin. "See, I told you she's the best!"

"You were right, Abby," Lauren responds, her smile wide. "Megan's amazing."

In the final minute, when Megan scores the unassisted winning goal, Abby nearly topples off the bleacher in her excitement, her cheers echoing around the field. “Yes! Megan did it! She did it!”

After the game, several parents come over to congratulate Megan. Abby, still buzzing with energy, runs up to her sister, glowing with pride.

“That goal was incredible, Megan!” Abby says, throwing her arms around her sister. Megan laughs and hugs her back; their bond is evident in the way they share the moment.

When they see Lauren and me standing nearby, Abby pulls Megan over to us. “Did you see, Dad? Lauren? Megan’s the best player ever!”

“We sure did,” I say, ruffling Abby’s hair. “You’re right, she was amazing.”

Lauren leans down to Abby’s level, her voice gentle. “I’m so glad I got to watch you cheer her on, Abby. You’re a big part of her success, you know that?”

Abby blushes, looking pleased. “Megan says I’m her good luck charm.”

"And I believe it," Lauren replies, her smile is full of warmth.

Lauren says that Natalie Hunter, one of the former top US women's soccer stars, belongs to a golf country club where Lauren designed the course. Abby and Megan both recognize her name immediately. She starred in two World Cup tournaments and two Olympic teams after playing college soccer at UNC in Chapel Hill. Abby, ever the sports encyclopedia, eagerly recites the names of players on those teams, impressing the soccer star.

Lauren, noticing the excitement on Megan's face, asks, "Would it be all right if I told my friend about you, Megan?"

Megan's face lights up with a mix of pride and anticipation. "Really? You'd do that?"

"Absolutely," Lauren says. "You've got a bright future ahead, and I think she'd love to hear about your game today."

Abby looks up at Megan, her eyes shining. "Lauren's right, Megan. You're going to be a star."

Megan smiles, clearly touched by her sister's confidence and Lauren's support. "Thanks, Abby, and thank you, Lauren."

As we leave the field, I notice Abby chatting animatedly with Lauren. Lauren glances over at me with a warm smile on her face.

"Abby really lights up when she talks about Megan, doesn't she?" she says, her voice filled with genuine affection.

I nod, feeling a surge of pride. "She does. Megan's always been her hero, and I think being out here, watching her sister play, really brings out the best in her."

Lauren's eyes soften as she looks at Abby. "It's amazing to see how close they are. You've done a great job with them, Luke."

"Thanks, Lauren," I reply. "Being out here with them, seeing them so happy... it's a nice break from everything else. The lawsuit feels a million miles away right now."

Lauren nods in agreement. "It's moments like these that remind us what really matters."

We walk on, the tension of the lawsuit fading into the background, replaced by the simple joy of family and the thrill of the game.

Megan joins her teammates on a visit to our local pizza parlor and takes Abby with her. After they leave, Lauren and I walk towards my car with my mind preoccupied with how I will tell Lauren about my illness and condition. Suddenly, out of nowhere, several people appear holding signs with Lauren's photo and Transphobe underneath. One of the young men with a megaphone shouts, "There's the bitch. Stop her!" I count five people carrying signs who surround us and stop us from getting to my car.

I stand firmly in front of Lauren, creating a physical barrier while maintaining a composed demeanor. I say, "Everyone, let's take a step back. We're not here to engage in conflict. We just want to leave peacefully."

They start towards Lauren. I shift my body to block any aggressive movement toward Lauren while still addressing the group calmly.

By this time, the parents of Megan's teammates step in. One man steps forward. "Hey, leave them alone and get out of here." I fear there's going to be a fight until one of my friends, who is a police officer, breaks it up and directs the protestors to leave.

Lauren is breathless and shaken. When we finally reach my car, we sit for what seems like fifteen minutes. Finally, we calm down and start for my favorite Mexican restaurant in the same strip shopping center—the restaurant where the girls are eating. I'm thankful that they left before the bru ha ha and uproar.

After dinner, we all ride together, and once we reach home, the girls go inside while I stay in the car with Lauren. It is time for me to tell her. Before I can start, Lauren says, "I appreciate you standing up for me."

I feel certain it will not be the last time that protestors confront us. I assure her that we'll be okay and say that I have something I want to say to her. Lauren's phone rings. She takes a deep breath as she turns off her cell phone and puts it away.

I say, "In Seth and Ashley's office, I said I wasn't the right lawyer for you because I am not the Rambo type.

"And I told you I was venting about what an attack dog Morgan is when I suggested you needed to be that type."

Before sharing my condition, I tell her a few things first. I start, "I wanted to tell you that when a lawyer represents a client in a trial, they each have a role. It's the client's case. As such, the client decides what her goals are and what she wants to do. A lawyer's job is to give the client his best advice, and then when the client decides what she wants, it's the lawyer's job to develop the strategy and implement it to get there. You're very independent and strong-willed…"

She interrupts, "I have to be. I played a sport where I had to be independent and strong-willed. Now, I'm a woman trying to succeed in a world dominated by men. But, working with you, we'll be a team, and you'll be the leader. I value your judgment and I want you to represent me."

"I want to remind you what I said when we met. Whoever represents you, Robert Benton will make it as expensive as possible. That's how he runs over contractors who challenge him in court."

"And I told you that I have other developers willing to pay me even more than Benton paid for my golf course designs."

I squirm in my seat. I must tell Lauren now, "Okay, I was not candid with you when I said I'm not the right lawyer for you."

Lauren frowns, and I continue. "There's a far more compelling reason that I'm not the right lawyer for you to fight Benton in court."

Her eyebrows furrow, meaning she doesn't understand what could be the more compelling reason I don't want to represent her.

"I'm not going to sugarcoat this. I had COVID-19 in 2021, and I was on a ventilator for ten days. I haven't fully recovered yet."

"From COVID-19?" Lauren asks. "How could that be? I thought everybody who had it and didn't die had recovered. I had it and have had no problems afterward."

"I've never completely recovered from COVID or being in ICU," I reply. When I came home from the hospital, I had lost twenty pounds, and my legs were so weak that I couldn't walk. When I got up from the wheelchair, I fell, and Abby and Megan helped me get up from the floor. After that, my mom came and became my nurse while the girls were in school. She helped me get up from the wheelchair until I could use a walker."

"You're walking fine now," Lauren says.

"Yes, I've come a long way from where I started, but I'm still a long way from where I was before being on the ventilator. When I first came home from the hospital, I could manage only about eight hundred steps a day using a walker. When I watched football games, I walked around my house during commercials. I feel better now, but I'm still not back to normal. I've gone through extensive therapy to strengthen my arms and legs. I can walk, so that's the least of my current problems. It's the mental issues that make me not the best lawyer for you. It's been eighteen months since I came home from the hospital. I never thought about how a ventilator works and what are the side effects I would encounter from being on one for several days. My memory is a disaster. I meet people, and five minutes later, I've already forgotten their names."

"I didn't know that was one of the COVID-19 and ventilator side effects," she says.

"There are more. When I was in the hospital, I had vivid hallucinations from the pain medicine. I thought that the nurses were trying to kill me. I thought they sent someone to kill my girls. I dreamed that a client I had defended was facing the death penalty, and it was all my fault. I'm still trying to sort through what was real and what was one of my many hallucinations. When I shared these problems with my primary care doctor, he told me that surviving COVID-19 was just the start of what might be a new normal for me. Part of that new normal is symptoms I'm wrestling with—they're unpredictable. I feel well one day, and the next day, I can't work the entire day."

I know that Lauren wants to pursue the litigation against Robert Benton to the very end. I'm not sure that I can successfully fight the bully and his lawyer to the end. I'm also not sure whether, during the course of the long fight, Lauren will want to hang in there until the end.

Chapter 8

Lauren

I see an old Mercedes sports car, when we walk into the garage. It looks like it's in disrepair.

"Tell me about your car," I say.

"It's a Mercedes 300SL, Gullwing. Mercedes only produced a few thousand of those cars between 1954 and 1957. If I can restore this one, it will be worth a lot of money."

"You restore cars?" I ask.

"Yes," he says.

"What do you enjoy about restoring cars? Is it the money?"

He chuckles and shakes his head. "No, it's not about the money. It's about the challenge and the satisfaction of bringing something back to life. Plus, it helps me clear my mind. With Abby's autism and my health issues," he gestures towards his chest, "Working on the cars helps me put my mind on something else."

I nod, understanding. “That makes sense, and it’s impressive that you can do it with everything else you are facing.”

I’m interested in learning more. “I’ve watched you following Megan’s soccer, and now you’ve shared with me that you restore cars. What else do you do when you are not working?”

He pauses for a few seconds as if he’s unsure how to answer my question.

“I enjoy hunting and fishing, and I can take Abby fishing and spend the day with her. Being able to hunt and fish without driving for miles is one of the many reasons I love living here. “Oh, and one other thing,” Luke says with a sparkle in his eye. “I enjoy barbecuing and smoking brisket. Abby pitches in to help. If you like brisket, you’ll love ours.”

That one takes me by surprise. I decide Luke is both a true Renaissance man and a family man, even though I remind myself to look up what Renaissance means. I admire him. He’s charismatic, confident, and self-assured. Yet there’s a tenderness in his voice when he talks about what makes him all the more attractive.

“When do you find time for all these outside interests?” I ask, genuinely curious because I’ve never found time to pursue outside interests.

He takes a deep breath before answering. “I have very little time for anything other than work and caring for my daughters. Abby needs attention because of her autism, and Megan’s soccer schedule also keeps me busy. But I try to squeeze in some hunting and fishing trips whenever it’s possible. However, it’s a good way to clear my head and relax. I’ve taken too much of your time talking about myself.”

“Not at all,” I reply, leaning in slightly. “I’m really interested in learning more about Abby. You seem to have such a strong bond with her. How does she handle being out on the water when you fish together?”

Luke’s face softens as he talks about Abby. “She loves it, actually. There’s something about the rhythm of fishing, the casting, the waiting—that really calms her. She’s more focused, and I think it gives her a sense of peace. So, when she catches a fish, the joy on her face is priceless.”

“I’d love to see that sometime,” I say, smiling at the thought. “It sounds like you’ve found some great ways to connect with her.”

Luke smiles back, clearly pleased. "I try. Abby has her own way of interacting with the world, and it's taught me a lot about patience and understanding. She made me a better person."

"That's really wonderful, Luke," I say, feeling a deepening respect for him. "I'd like to get to know her better, too. She seems like such a special girl."

"She is," Luke agrees, his voice filled with quiet pride. "And she's already taken a liking to you. That means a lot."

We both fall silent for a moment, the conversation lingering in the air, making me feel more connected to Luke and his family. There's a lot more to him than just the confident lawyer I've seen in the courtroom. He's a devoted father, someone who's deeply engaged in his daughters' lives, and that makes him all the more compelling.

"I've enjoyed learning more about you," I tell him. "You have an interesting life." I'm thinking about what his life was like when he was married with three children and how that terrible accident, taking his wife and son, changed his life. "I've also enjoyed spending time watching Megan play soccer. I enjoyed meeting Abby. I want to teach her to play golf while I'm here."

"That's nice of you," Luke says.

"I'd love to work with Abby. I've very rarely spent a whole day cooped up inside. I need to spend time outside for my own mental health, and helping Abby learn to play golf gives me another goal to pursue."

With that, Megan and Abby come back into the house with their golden retriever.

"What's her name?"

"Bella," he says. "We bought Bella when I was recovering from my trip to the hospital, and the girls were in school."

"How did you manage to care for Bella when you could hardly walk after coming home from the hospital?"

He smiles. "I was forced to get out of my chair or off my bed and let Bella go outside. After a few weeks, I walked her in our neighborhood as therapy for me."

We spend another hour chatting about his hobbies and interests while watching Bella. I find myself feeling more and more drawn to him, not just because of his accomplishments but also his passion, his drive, and how he stood up for me when the protestors surrounded us. As we say our goodbyes, I head back to my car.

"I've enjoyed spending the day with you," I tell him again. "I look forward to spending time with Abby."

When I get home, I open my laptop and search for "Renaissance Men in 2022." I find an article listing the characteristics. The writer says that Leonardo da Vinci was a role model for future Renaissance men. He was arguably the most remarkable creative genius in history. I read each characteristic and decide that Luke Hartley is a Renaissance man masquerading as a lawyer. I like being around him since he has charisma and charm. But I have no idea what he is going through with the loss of his wife and son and the side effects of his COVID-19 treatment.

I start reading the documents he gave me to learn more about his condition. Not having been on a ventilator when I had COVID-19 or knowing anyone who was hospitalized and put on a ventilator, I'm still trying to understand how being in the hospital on a ventilator could impact the patient's physical and mental health. Reading the articles, I understand for the first time why he's reluctant to represent me against Benton.

Ironically, when I open the Dallas newspaper on my iPad in the morning, I see the headline, 'Evidence Is Mounting That COVID-19 Is Bad For The Brain.' I read the first sentence, and I'm horrified when I discover that a COVID-19 infection can potentially damage your brain. The writer portrays survivors who face challenges in working due to brain fog, fatigue, and depression. Reading the article makes me more worried about his health. I call Luke.

"I understand why you're worried; you may not be the right lawyer to represent me if we have to go to trial," I tell him. "I have a question for you."

"Ask away," he replies.

"In my trial, will it be more important to remember all the facts or to connect emotionally with the jury?"

Luke replies, "That's a great question. It's more important to present a persuasive story that will emotionally connect with the jurors. Many, if not most, cases are won or lost after the opening statements. Jurors form their initial impressions about the case. I want it to be the foundation upon which we build and persuade the jurors. Just like the ongoing division in our society, it is incredibly tough to sway jurors into changing their mindset once they have picked a side."

"I suspected that to be the case." He confirmed what I had expected. "You said it's up to me to decide what I want. Like if he has treated others, Benton won't settle the case with me. So, I'm prepared to fight like hell to get credit for the design, keep my reputation, and receive my bonus. I'm prepared to face whatever he may do to destroy my business. I want you to take on my case against Benton."

"Are you sure you want to take a chance? I tire easily. I have a raspy voice, and I become winded just by talking. I'm not the lawyer that I was before my hospital stay."

"I understand. I am counting on you to do everything possible to overcome those challenges. I'm confident you'll pick the right jurors and connect with them as you have connected with me."

"Fasten your seatbelt because we are going to ride like being on the wildest roller coaster you've ever ridden. You said that Benton won't settle with you. We're prepared to fight him relentlessly, and he'll stop at nothing to make your life a living hell."

As I carefully push the button to end the call, my phone buzzes incessantly with notifications. My posts about the Lake Tierra Golf Course and a statement that I was proud to be the designer are inundated with comments. "You're a disgrace!" one comment reads, while another spats, "Bigot! Crawl back into your hole."

More follow: "I hope you lose everything," "Transphobic scum," "Die, you hateful bitch."

I also find social media posts with fake news shared by accounts with suspiciously similar usernames and profiles. One headline reads, "Lauren West Funded Anti-Trans Groups," while another falsely claims, "Lauren West Kicked Out of LPGA for Bigotry." Each lie spreads rapidly, reshared, and retweeted thousands of times, further tarnishing my reputation.

I stare at my phone, trying to figure out what I can do. I knew combatting Benton would be bad, but I underestimated his hatred and power. I find Luke's number and call. It rings twice before his calm, steady voice answers.

I say hello, and Luke senses something is wrong. He asks what's wrong, and I begin, then after a few words, I'm out of breath.

"Take a deep breath, Lauren. I'm here to help you."

I take a deep breath. "It feels like they're everywhere, Luke. The threats, the lies...I can't even use my social media accounts."

Luke's tone turns resolute. "First, we're going to make sure you're safe. Have you noticed any unusual activity around your home or when you're out?"

“Not yet, but I’m scared, Luke. They said they know where I live.”

“Okay. I’ll arrange for a security company to install surveillance cameras at your home and hire a private security firm to keep an eye on you for the next few weeks. Your safety is our top priority.”

I feel a small measure of relief. “Thank you, Luke. But what about the social media attacks?”

“I’ll call in some favors. I know a cyber-security expert who can track down these bots and trolls. We’ll compile evidence and present it to the social media platforms. They have mechanisms for dealing with coordinated harassment.”

Chapter 9

Luke

As I had promised Lauren, I contact my law school friend, Jock Powell. Over the last few years, Jock has become one of the top cybersecurity lawyers in Texas. After a few days, Jock tells me his investigator is using web scraping tools and APIs provided by social media platforms to collect data from Lauren's social media accounts. He says this includes posts, comments, messages, and user accounts interacting with her content. He says that's the first step, and his investigator is analyzing the data.

I tell Lauren and assure her even though I'm not sure what it means, Jock will take good care of her. Thankfully, she's ready to get back to work on her case.

Over the week, Lauren and I meet at my office. It's nothing like the palatial McKenzie Simmons offices in the Dallas high-rise. I prefer the view of the wooded Hill Country out my window. Lauren provides the information I need to file the Petition to begin her suit against Benton Land Company, Robert Benton, and the Lake Tierra Development LLC. She once again shares her history with Benton, going back to the first golf course design she did for him. It is in Dallas, with tree-lined fairways and a creek that runs through the course and provides a hazard on several holes.

I'm eager to learn as much as I can about him, so I ask Lauren to tell me more about Benton.

She says he's a short, overweight man who, to make up for his rotund figure, dresses in high-end custom-made clothing and prominently displays his gaudy Rolex watch. She says he claims to have a twelve handicap, but he routinely cheats by hitting a second ball and moving his ball out of trouble. He stiffs his contractors, claiming their work has defects as an excuse for not fully paying them. According to her, Benton utilizes his wealth and power to suppress critics, finding joy in tormenting adversaries in legal battles and mocking them through media platforms. "He once told me anyone who dares to take him on in court will soon regret it."

I'm not surprised. I've known men like Benton before. Thankfully, none have been my clients. "I'm not letting him torment you," I say.

I ask Lauren if there is anything negative in her history I need to know that Benton and Morgan might bring up during a deposition or during the trial.

She pauses as if thinking about it. She looks up and says, "There is one thing Benton knows about my time on the LPGA tour. During one charity event he sponsored, there was a huge mix-up. Some of his folks accused me of redirecting a donation without permission. It was a nightmare, but I was eventually cleared."

"Is there anything else?"

"No, I have no skeletons in my closet," Lauren says.

To start, I send Benton a demand letter, telling him I represent Lauren West and West Design Company regarding Benton's breach of Lauren's design contract and his misappropriation of West Design Company's Lake Tierra golf course design. I lay out Lauren's case over the following seven pages of the letter, including showing Lauren's drawing of the Lake Tierra Golf Course holes compared to the as-built layout. I give Benton a week to reply.

The following day, I receive a phone call. As I reach to answer, I see my hands trembling, a residual effect of long COVID-19 serves as a cruel reminder of my vulnerability. After Harvey Morgan introduces himself, he says, "Do you know who I am?"

I say, "Yes. I've come across articles about you."

"I couldn't hear you. Is there something wrong with your voice?"

My raspy voice results from my right vocal cord not closing correctly. I say it again, this time louder, "Yes, I've read articles about you."

"Then, you know what it will be like to go up against me. Robert Benton has no interest in making a settlement. But if I were in your shoes, I'd make sure your client knows what she can expect if she sues Robert."

Morgan is like the bully on the playground in first grade. I don't want to bend down to his level. I say, "Mr. Morgan, I think we'll be seeing a lot of each other over the next several months. I look forward to it, and so does Lauren."

As I hang up the phone, my stomach churns, thinking about battling Morgan in court when I'm not in top form. Lisa, my trusty assistant, notices and asks if I'm okay. I say, "Yes," to ease her concern, but I'm struggling.

I take a moment to catch my breath, one of the side effects of the damage to my vocal cord, and then I call Lauren and tell her about my phone call with Morgan. She's more upset than ever. I tell her again that I'm not myself and she should find another lawyer. She says, "I'm the only lawyer she wants," which shows me she doesn't fully comprehend the effects long COVID-19 has had on my brain.

As she instructs me, I file our Petition in the Corona County Court. I allege Benton and his companies breached the Lake Tierra Development LLC contract with Lauren; they tortuously terminated the contract, breached their duty of good faith and fair dealing, falsely and fraudulently claimed to have designed the Lake Tierra Golf Course, and a host of other technical legal misdeeds. I also allege Robert Benton has defamed Lauren by claiming she hates transgender people who identify as women. I ask for an injunction to prevent Robert Benton from representing that he designed the Lake Tierra Golf Course. I also ask for the amount of bonus Lauren is entitled to receive now, as well as in the future, punitive damages, and attorney fees.

The next day, the Dallas Morning News publishes a first-page article under a headline reading, "Former LPGA Golf Star Beauty Says Robert Benton Stole Her Golf Course Design." In the article, the writer quotes from our petition at length, including my assertion that Benton had nothing to do with the design of the Lake Tierra Golf Course, but in marketing material for the development, he claims he designed the golf course.

The newspaper includes my quote in the article. West attorney Luke Hartley said in a statement, "Lauren West is one of North America's most recognized and talented golf course designers. Her golf courses have brought great joy to families throughout the United States and Canada. We intend to prove Lauren designed the award-winning Lake Tierra Golf Course and she is entitled to a bonus based on the record sales of the Lake Tierra Hill Country Development properties. Robert Benton wrongfully terminated Lauren's consulting contract after she stood up for the rights of girls and women to compete against one another fairly."

The lawsuit grabs the attention of the national television news media. Television networks call both Lauren and me, asking for interviews. I tell Lauren to hold back from the interviews, but she ignores my advice.

The story changes the next day. Robert Benton has hired a PR firm to vilify Lauren for filing a suit against him. Every Dallas television station ran stories featuring the spokesman for the Benton camp, berating Lauren and painting her as a greedy opportunist. The spokesman called Lauren's lawsuit a "Frivolous attempt by a loser to extort money from a successful businessman," with no evidence to back up her claims. The print and television media pick up on the greedy opportunist theme.

Lauren says a sports network has interviewed Lisa McIntyre, a former LPGA golfer. I find the interview and watch.

"Lisa, you've had a storied career on the LPGA Tour, and you've been a strong advocate for inclusivity in sports," the broadcaster says. "What are your thoughts on the recent controversy surrounding Lauren West's comments about transgender athletes?"

"You know, I have a lot of respect for what Lauren has accomplished on the golf course," McIntyre responds. "She's an incredible talent, and I don't want to take anything away from that. But when it comes to her stance on transgender athletes, I disagree with Lauren. I believe sports should be a place where everyone feels welcome and where everyone has a chance to compete fairly."

"Do you think Miss' West's views could harm the inclusivity in sports?"

"I do," McIntyre says. "We're living in a time where understanding and acceptance are more important than ever. Transgender athletes face enough challenges as it is, and I think it's important that we support their right to compete. Lauren's comments—while I'm sure they're coming from a place of concern, could be seen as excluding a group of people who just want the same opportunities we all had."

Lauren tells me she's devastated by the overnight change in tone by the media, and by Lisa McIntyre, who she always considered a friend. She hopes Robin Howell can counter the slander hurled at her. She calls the Dallas newspaper reporter, and I listen to the call. Robin promises to write another positive story about Lauren and says she's poking around trying to learn more about Robert Benton.

Several days later, Benton and his companies file a motion to remove the case to the Federal Court for the Western District, Austin Division. Dallas lawyer, Andy Johnson, signs the motion, but Morgan is clearly calling the shots. Morgan and Benton don't want to try the case in Corona County. Instead, they want a more liberal jury pool. However, to remove a case from federal court, there must be complete diversity, meaning all defendants are from a different state. Thankfully, the Lake Tierra Development LLC is a Texas Limited Liability Corporation. When I make that point in my reply to the motion, Judge Hawkins rules in our favor and directs Benton and Lake Tierra LLC to answer our Petition.

The motion to remove the case is the first of many efforts by Benton, Johnson, and Morgan to delay any trial and run up the expenses to prosecute Lauren's claim. They will delay the trial as long as possible while attacking Lauren in a daily barrage on social media sites. The trial will be delayed anyway because of the backlog of trials delayed by the Texas courts being closed during COVID-19. A week later. Morgan files an Answer and, as Lauren had predicted, a Counterclaim for breach of the consulting contract and defamation.

Both the Answer and the Counterclaim allege Lauren breached the Morals Clause of the consulting contract when she unethically and without permission, stated repeatedly in the media that states should only permit biological girls and women to play high school girls' and college women's sports. According to Benton, Lauren's transphobic, misgendering, and hateful statements made Benton Land Company clients uncomfortable. Benton further alleges Lauren defamed him when she claimed he had stolen her Lake Tierra Golf Course design. In his Counterclaim, Benton asks for one million dollars in damages.

The headline, the day after Morgan files Benton's Answer and Counterclaim, reads, "Benton Claims Lauren West is Transphobic and Defamed Him." That gains even more attention from the national television news media while sensing a red-hot issue. The media quotes Benton at length, including his statement, "Several of our potential development clients came to me complaining about

Miss West's hateful comments about transgender athletes. They told me they'd not buy land or build a second home in any development with a golf course designed by Lauren West. I replied I had designed the award-winning Lake Tierra Golf Course. What Miss West claims to be her right of free speech does not apply to her hate speech against transgender athletes."

I receive a phone call from Robin Howell, who promises to publish our side of the story. "How do you respond to allegations against Miss West by Robert Benton and his lawyer?" she asks.

"Those allegations are unfounded," I say while hoping she can hear my raspy voice. "I can assure you that Miss West has said nothing that could be construed as transphobic, and she's never defamed Robert Benton. Miss West will not let Robert Benton spread lies about her. She will continue to fight for her fair compensation."

Fox News asks Lauren to be a guest on one of its evening shows. Lauren wants to appear, partly because the legislature in Texas is considering a bill to limit participation in high school and college sports to biological females. The Fox News interview goes well. The anchor and others firmly back Lauren's claim that only biological girls and women should compete in girls and women's golf in high school, college and the LPGA.

Her bold stance draws more criticism from the transgender community. In the days following the Fox News interview, Lauren finds herself the target of relentless social media harassment. One well-known female athlete accuses her of being transphobic, hateful, and discriminatory. I'm convinced that Benton, Morgan, or someone on their behalf is paying social media users to post or repost negative comments about Lauren. I can't figure out any way to prove it.

Lauren tells me she's receiving death threats. That makes her even more determined not to back down from her stance, arguing that allowing transgender women to compete in women's sports creates an unfair advantage due to their biological makeup. She also asserts that her opinion is not motivated by hatred or bigotry but rather a desire to protect the integrity of girls' and women's sports.

Lauren continues to speak out in support of girls' and women's sports. She tells reporters she cannot sit back and stay silent while biological men are changing from losing in men's sports to winning in women's sports and using women's locker rooms and showers.

Morgan has to know that his breach of Morals Clause argument is a sham. I doubt Benton can bring forward one potential client who truthfully declined to purchase land and join the Lake Tierra Country Club when they learned the proposed course designer supported girls and women playing high school and college sports. But raising the issue has diverted the attention away from Lauren getting credit for the design of the Lake Tierra Golf Course and receiving ten percent of the net profits the Lake Tierra Development LLC has earned on the development.

Lauren's support of girls' and women's sports has become the story. That is exactly what Benton and Morgan planned. They've changed the narrative by lying and repeating it, and Lauren's original claim to the design of the Lake Tierra Golf Course and her demanding ten percent of the net profits per her contract as a bonus receives no mention on television or the print media.

Benton is a guest on several television news networks. Hosts ask him to explain why he terminated Lauren's contract during the construction of the Lake Tierra Golf Course. Morgan explains that the future of girls' and women's sports in America includes transgender women and girls. He states contrary to that fact, Lauren West has rallied ultra conservatives and some other hate groups in efforts to pass legislation that would limit the rights of transgender girls and women. Benton claims that is hateful speech and it violates the morals clause in Lauren's golf design contracts.

The same television networks ask Lauren to appear. I advise her to decline, as I can see no good coming out of it and even more attention being taken away from Lauren's case, and instead, given to Lauren's position on women's sports. After several calls, Lauren, despite my warnings, agrees to appear. She suggests I go with her to New York.

As Lauren prepares for her appearance on the network, I can see her nerves creeping up on her.

I stand behind the curtain to watch the interview. I sense the emotions similar to that of the father of a teenage gymnast during the Olympic trials, hoping for a score as close to ten as possible to secure her spot on the team. Only in this case, Lauren is not on a balance beam, and she's relinquished control to the anchor.

The interview starts as expected, with the news host asking Lauren about her controversial statements. But Lauren is prepared and explains her viewpoint calmly and rationally. She says, "People will not consider it controversial if the news host considers simple biology." Lauren describes the physical differences between biological men and women and how allowing trans women to compete in women's sports can give them an unfair advantage.

But the host isn't satisfied with her answer, and she pressures Lauren, accusing her of being discriminatory and hateful. I know

Lauren won't back down. She takes another deep breath and responds with conviction.

"I'm not transphobic," Lauren says firmly. "I have nothing against trans individuals. My concern is about fair competition in sports. Women athletes have fought long and hard for their right to compete on a level playing field, and allowing biological men to compete with them undermines that progress."

The host tries to interrupt her, but Lauren continues. "I firmly support equal rights for all individuals, including trans individuals," she says. "But when it comes to sports, we need to ensure there are separate categories for biological men and women. It's not discriminatory to support women's sports. All women who have competed in sports should be speaking out. We've come too far since Title IX to let biological men spoil it now."

The tension rises as the interview ends, but Lauren tells me she feels a sense of pride for standing up for what she believes in. As we leave the studio, I realize this fight is far from over and may be more contentious and bitter than the lawsuit.

Chapter 10

Luke

I don't want to spend any more time than necessary on Benton's bogus transphobia issue. Instead, I hope to put pressure on Benton by demanding a long list of Benton's financial records, including, among others monthly, quarterly, and annual income statements showing revenue, expenses, and profits on all the golf courses Lauren designed. The Tierra Hill Country project is by far the most profitable of all the Benton Land Company luxury golf course developments. Still, I want to see the records of every development.

If I can get Benton's shady accounting formula to the jury, they, and the public reading or hearing about the case, will think Benton is taking advantage of Lauren. If people label him as someone who cheated on Lauren, then it will tarnish his reputation.

I've been analyzing Benton to figure out how best to attack him. He's both a brilliant man and an intimidator. I've learned he helped fund protests in Seattle and Portland. He's a guy who has never admitted he was wrong and insists on his way, even when it is clear it's not the best way. I also learn he consistently disparages women.

As I delve deeper into Benton's actions, I can't help but feel a profound sense of moral outrage. How could someone treat others with such disdain, particularly a woman, solely based on her gender? It's utterly unacceptable. As a lawyer, it's my duty to expose Benton to the Corona County jury for the tyrant he truly is.

When I discuss everything I've learned about Benton with Lauren, she makes one additional point. She says, "In all our time together, Robert Benton never once spoke out on behalf of transgender people until he decided to use them as an excuse to avoid paying the bonus I earned.

I suspected as much.

I know how Judge Hawkins operates. Before, the parties spend tons of money on discovery, and before he sets the case for trial, he convenes a conference to discuss how the parties might resolve the case without a trial. I meet Harvey Morgan for the first time. He looks like he came straight from Hollywood. He's physically fit. His hair is neatly styled, with streaks of gray running through it. He is dressed impeccably in a well-tailored navy suit. He carries himself like a lawyer who has never lost a case.

When the settlement discussion goes nowhere, Judge Hawkins orders us to mediate our case and appoints Jack Williams, one of the top mediators in the Hill Country.

***

Two weeks later, Lauren and I are seated in Williams' waiting room. We've been waiting for over an hour when Robert Benton and Harvey Morgan finally arrive with a young man carrying their briefcases. When Benton strolls in, he barely acknowledges Lauren or me, his eyes already scanning the room for an escape route. Morgan apologizes for being late and tells us Mr. Benton's jet had to make an aborted landing had delayed them. Benton looks at Lauren and sarcastically asks, "Do you miss flying in my jet, Lauren?"

When she starts to reply, Benton dismissively cuts her off. "Let's cut to the chase. I don't have all day for this," he says.

I had expected Benton to be a real piece of work, but seeing how he treats Lauren..., he's an even bigger asshole than I imagined.

Lauren takes a deep breath and responds, "Actually, Robert, I don't miss one moment of flying with you. I don't miss spending time with you."

Benton says, "Nothing," and looks away. Morgan, Benton, and the young lawyer take seats, then Lauren leans over and whispers to me, "I told you he was arrogant."

Benton glares at her. Jack Williams is a well-known, gifted mediator, but I can't picture him bringing Benton and Lauren to a settlement. Both Benton and Lauren realize this is a waste of time, but it delays dealing with a trial, so, for Benton, it's worth the trouble.

As the mediation session commences, the tension in the room is palpable. Benton and Lauren refuse to even make eye contact with each other, setting the stage for a dramatic confrontation. Williams, the mediator, begins by inviting each lawyer to state their position and desired outcome while adding to the anticipation of the proceedings.

I speak first. "Lauren West, a key figure in the Lake Tierra Hill Country Development, found the land and prepared several preliminary designs for the Lake Tierra Golf Course. Her contract with Benton entitles her to a bonus based on ten percent of the net profits from the land sales and the country club initiation fees. When Benton realized the potential of the Lake Tierra Hill Country Development, he terminated her contract and took credit for the Lake Tierra Golf Course design. It's crucial to note that Miss

West's design of the Lake Tierra Golf Course is what attracted families to buy multimillion-dollar homes in the Lake Tierra Development."

I carefully set my pen next to my notepad and look at Williams. "Lauren wants credit for the golf course design and ten percent of the profits from the land sales and country club initiation fees."

Morgan tells Williams that Robert Benton learned Lauren was spewing hate against transgender athletes in the media. Benton claims when two well-known Hollywood celebrities, a Broadway star, and a top recording artist threatened to cancel their contract to purchase property and join the country club unless Benton terminated West's contract and did not use her preliminary design for the golf course. This is the first time Benton has suggested he could prove Lauren's position on transgender sports participation would cause him to lose sales and country club members. Morgan says his client wants a ruling that he had the right to terminate Lauren's contract, wants the credit for the golf course design, and wants recognition that the Lake Tierra Hill Country Development has no profits.

After our opening statements, Williams tells Lauren and me to stay in the conference room, and he shows Morgan, Benton, and the young lawyer to another conference room. I explain to Lauren that this stage of the mediation is when Williams uses shuttle diplomacy, going back and forth trying to persuade each side that their case is weak and they should settle today.

Williams is gone for forty-five minutes. When he returns to our conference room, he stands at the whiteboard. "Miss West, I'm sure, you know, Luke is one of the most respected lawyers in the Hill Country. If you decide to proceed with this case, you've got the best lawyer you can have. But here is the problem you're going to face. A Corona County jury will be wowed by the celebrities Mr. Benton can bring in to say they would not go forward with their land purchases and country club memberships if you had anything to do with the Lake Tierra Golf Course. The celebrities will accuse you of spewing hate, endangering transgender athletes, and making baseless claims about girls and women being unfairly denied opportunities to compete in sports."

Lauren and I exchange looks, both of us are well aware of the uphill battle we could be facing. Williams continues, "Now, I'm not saying that any of the celebrities' allegations are true, but it's all about perception. Perception is a reality in the eyes of the jury. The celebrities will make you out to be a bigot who hates trans people and wants to deny opportunities to those who identify as girls and women. That's not a good look."

Lauren takes a deep breath and speaks softly. "Mr. Williams, that's not who I am. I'm not a bigot, and I don't hate trans people, but girls and women should compete in sports on a level playing field."

"I understand, Miss West, and I have no offer to settle from Mr. Benton. What if I tell him you'd be willing to come back and design golf courses for his future developments?"

"There's no way Lauren will come back and design golf courses for Mr. Benton," I say. "He's mistreated her both privately and publicly."

"How so?" Williams asks.

"Benton launched a social media campaign that resulted in protestors in front of her house nightly, with professionally made signs, shouting obscenities, death threats, and other public harassment. He's mistreated her in other ways."

"Other ways, what other ways?" Williams asks.

Lauren shakes her head.

"I'm not at liberty to say. I understand there's more to the story than we've covered in the lawsuit and our statement today."

Williams clears his throat and shifts in his seat, his eyes darting between Lauren and me. "I see," he says slowly. "Well, I can relay your concerns to Mr. Benton, but I'm afraid that he has no plans to settle. Do you care to make an offer? I'll leave so you can talk it over."

Fifteen minutes later, we bring Williams back into the conference room. "You can tell Benton and his lawyer that Lauren will agree to settle if Benton gives her credit for the golf course design, immediately stops his media campaign impugning her, and pays her a one-million-dollar bonus."

As expected, Benton turns our offer down.

"Mr. Williams," Lauren says with her voice shaking, "then, why are we wasting our time? I could have told you at the start that Benton wouldn't settle the case with me. He uses his wealth to punish adversaries in court, and sadly, in our country, he can get away with it."

"I agree," Williams says. "I'll go back and tell Mr. Morgan and Mr. Benton that, given their refusal to make an offer, we have nothing to discuss."

Once again, Robert Benton has capitalized on the opportunity to waste our time and run up Lauren's cost. He's more interested in causing Lauren pain than he is in settling with Lauren and moving on.

As we get up to leave, Lauren says, "Luke, we need to hit Benton hard from the start. Let's go public with his shady business deals with the contractors who built the Corona Golf Course. We can get the media involved and pressure him into a corner."

"Lauren, that might feel good in the short term, but it's not the best strategy to win a case in Corona County."

"But potential jurors need to know what kind of person he is! How can we win if we're always holding back?"

"We win by being smart and methodical. A media blitz will only invite Bennett to get nastier. Trust me, I'll dismantle his case piece by piece. He won't even see it coming."

Lauren sighs. "I just hate what he's doing to win the media war."

"I understand how you feel. But I'm convinced the best strategy to win your case is to avoid coming across as bombastic as Benton. I promise you; we're going to make Benton pay for every bit of suffering he caused you. Trust me to handle Benton my way."

Chapter 11

Lauren

It's been several months since I became a news item for supporting women's sports. I'm going crazy from not being able to work. It's the first time I've had nothing to keep me busy since I was a young kid.

The Lake Tierra Golf Course is built and has already been named one of the top new golf courses in the United States. I sense my position on women's sports, which was originally thought to be controversial, is now old news. Then, out of the blue, I'm back in the news and discover social media influencers are calling me out for my views on transgender athletes. I didn't know exactly what canceling meant until it happened to me. I know Robert Benton is behind it, but I have no way to prove it.

It all starts when a Dallas television reporter interviews me. Before the interview, she explained to me that she plans to ask me about my girls in golf initiative. I think this will help me raise attention to my desire to encourage girls to become active in sports. So, contrary to Luke's advice, I agree to do the interview.

The reporter asks why I focus on encouraging girls to learn how to play golf.

"That's a great question. Thank you for asking. Over time, I learned about the challenges preteens and teenage girls face. They are more likely to commit suicide. They are more likely to have mental illness. Sadly, they are encountering sexual violence and slut shaming. Knowing what young girls face inspired me to design a golf course in Dallas where they can flourish and enjoy learning life lessons through golf."

The interview is going well until she asks me one final question. "Why did you decide to testify before the Texas senate to support a bill banning transgender athletes from competing in college sports designated for the biological sex of the athletes?"

I take a sip of water and reply, "Transgender girls and women have inherent competitive advantages over biological females in high school and college. Allowing transgender girls and women to compete against biological girls and women will be the worst thing that has happened to girls' and women's sports after decades of hard-won opportunities."

I keep talking and say, "I had never imagined that biological boys and men would be competing against girls and women, and most certainly never imagined that the President of the United States would fully support it."

I say each state and the federal government should ban transgender athletes from competing with girls and women. I had taken the reporter's bait. I spend the next ten minutes listening to her, deriding my opinion that allowing transgender athletes to compete against girls and women is destroying girls' and women's sports. I tell her I began competing in women's golf tournaments and started winning tournaments when I was twelve years old. I can't imagine what would have happened if I was defeated in a city or state tournament by a biological man who transitioned to be a woman. I share with her that I had read a story of a biological male winning a woman's golf tournament in Australia. More recently, two biological males eliminated two biological girls in a state tennis tournament. I conclude by saying my support of girls' and women's sports should not be controversial. It is common sense, and I don't understand why women known for fighting for women's rights are now fighting to make girl's and women's sports open to biological males.

On my way home, Courtney calls me. She tells me she watched the interview. She urges me to keep on speaking out in support of girls' and women's sports. I thank her for continuing to support me. She asks if she can do anything to help me, and I suggest she join me in speaking out on the fairness issue,

That evening, the Dallas television station that had interviewed me posts the interview on YouTube. They also publish an article titled: “Former LPGA Golfer’s Argument to Ban Trans Athletes Invalid.”

The writer claims that my arguments during the interview, if supported, will discriminate against transgender athletes. They quote a so-called expert doctor who claims my argument that trans athletes have an advantage over what he refers to as cisgender athletes, those who identify with the sex assigned to them at birth, is not supported by the science. He says, “There is no good-faith reason to deny transgender athletes the right to compete against cisgender athletes, as there is no evidence that men are born more athletic than women.” I’m certain Morgan and Benton’s liberal PR team is responsible for the expert doctor’s quote, and once again, Benton has launched a crusade to cancel me on social media.

It’s not just social media. One week after the interview, I’m scheduled to play in a charity golf event to raise money for a well-known Dallas charity. The day before the event, the spokesperson for the charity calls me. She says, “They’ve been told protestors plan to disrupt the event by blocking the street leading to the golf course." Therefore, she asks me to forego playing in the event and let her make the announcement on social media sites. I'm surprised, given the time and monetary contributions I had made over the years to the charity.

The following week, I'm scheduled to speak to MBA students at a local university. I think it is odd when, instead of the dean of the business school introducing me, the Diversity, Equity, and Inclusion dean introduces me and makes snide remarks that I want to deny transgender athletes the right to compete in sports.

I stand at the podium, hoping my tall and athletic stature commands attention, even from the naysayers in the audience. The bright lights blare in my eyes, making it challenging to see who is in the audience. All I can see are photographers, television cameras, and people holding up their phones and shooting video. I pick up on murmurs in the crowd as I start to speak.

After thanking the university for giving me the opportunity to speak, I start. "Girls and women in sports deserve fair competition, equal opportunities, and most of all, safety," I declare, my voice rising as I become aware of the hecklers in the audience.

I scan the room, looking for supporters. There are several, but they are outnumbered by the protestors.

"As a former LPGA golfer and now a golf course designer, I've dedicated my life to breaking barriers and advocating for those who need it most."

Someone shouts, "Transgender athletes need it most, you bigoted bitch." Several in the audience cheer.

As I continue, there are a handful of students who disrupt my speaking by shouting me down each time I start a sentence. They claim, among other things, that I am transphobic and a hypocrite for being against trans athletes competing against biological girls and women but denying a woman a choice when it comes to abortion.

After a few minutes, I had enough, and I walk out of the room. After learning that some of the students who disrupted my presentation had been paid, I send an email to the dean of the business school asking when the university stopped allowing free speech on its campus.

After the articles about my speech being disrupted, I'm trending on social media, not for any of my LPGA wins, not for any of my golf course designs, and not for what I have done to promote girls playing golf, but for being transphobic.

I'm called a bigot, Karen, and worse. I'm accused of endangering transgender young athletes. Critics claim I must apologize for my statements denying transgender athletes the right to compete, and they are trying to silence my views. They say I represent a cruel effort to stigmatize and discriminate against LGBTQ+ people across the country.

While trying to digest all of this, I sit at the kitchen counter, a glass of wine in my hand and the bottle on the counter. I'm drinking to get my mind off everything that is happening. The vibration of my phone on the table pulls me out of my thoughts. I glance at the screen and see Courtney Barr's name.

I hesitate for a moment before picking up. "Hey, Courtney," I say, trying to keep my voice steady.

"Lauren," she says, and I can hear the concern in her voice, "I hate to bring this up, but I thought you should know. Natalie Brooks just posted something on Twitter. She's speaking out against your stance on transgender athletes."

I close my eyes for a moment, feeling the weight of it all pressing down on me. "What did she say?"

"She was respectful, but it's clear she doesn't agree with you," Courtney replies. "She mentioned that golf should be open to everyone and that we need to focus on inclusivity."

I sigh, running a hand through my hair. "I expected pushback, but not from people I considered friends. First, Lisa McIntyre, and now Natalie. That's two of them, Courtney. Two people I thought understood where I was coming from."

"I know," Courtney says softly. "It's a tough situation. People are picking sides, and it's not fair to you. I can't imagine how overwhelming this must be."

"It is," I admit, my voice is quieter now. "It feels like everything is closing in on me. The media, social media, even people I thought were in my corner... they're all turning against me."

"Lauren, you need to remember that not everyone sees the bigger picture," Courtney says gently. "They don't understand the pressure you're under or the principles you're standing up for. But I do, and I'm here for you."

I feel a wave of gratitude but also a deep sense of isolation. "Thanks, Courtney. It means a lot to know I still have your support. I just... I never thought it would come to this."

"Neither did I," Courtney agrees. "But listen, don't let this tear you down. You're strong, Lauren. You've faced tougher battles before, and you've come out on top. This is just another challenge."

I take a deep breath, trying to steady myself. "You're right. I've worked too hard to let this break me. I'll get through it."

"And remember," Courtney adds, "the people who really know you, the ones who matter, they'll stand by you. This will pass, Lauren. You just have to hold on."

"I will," I say, my resolve slowly returning. "Thanks for the heads-up, Courtney. And thanks for being there."

"Always," she replies. "Take care of yourself, okay? I'm just a call away."

"Will do," I say, ending the call and setting the phone down. I stare out the window as the setting sun casts long shadows across the room. I see protestors marching and holding signs in front of my house. Each night, the crowd gets larger. They trample on my front lawn and even ring my doorbell. I discover that activists have posted my address and a photo of my home on many social media sites, encouraging followers to come to my house and rape both my mother and me. I learn that sharing someone's personal information online is called "doxxing."

The World Athletics Council, the international track and field governing body, bars transgender women athletes from elite competitions for women. I had nothing to do with their decision, and I didn't even know of the decision until I read about it, but I'm one of many blamed for denying transgender athletes the right to compete. Because I have spoken in several state legislatures, activists blame partly for the nineteen states that have banned transgender athletes from playing on girls' or women's sports teams. They claim I am one of the movement leaders.

When another biological male wins a women's golf tournament, and few in the media make note of that fact, one asks me to comment. "I believe that allowing biological men to compete in women's sports will ruin all that we've accomplished. Country clubs and golf courses sure as hell should not allow a biological male to compete in the women's club championship."

When I post my comments on Twitter, I include the hashtags #Disgrace and #SaveWomensSports.

My comment goes viral on Twitter, and retweeters call me more bad names than I've ever heard before. I receive at least a dozen more death threats.

Then, upon arriving home from dinner, the piercing sounds of car horns parked on my block and the shrill voices of protestors blocking my driveway stop me in my tracks. I don't want to hit them, so I don't open my garage door. My heart races as I think about how my mother is coping inside my home. I call her. When she answers, my mother's voice is shaking when she asks, "What is going on." I try to explain that the people outside honking or chanting are protestors.

"How can they invade your property like that?" she asks.

"They shouldn't be doing that," I say.

I dial Luke's number. When he answers, I tell him what is happening to my mother and me. He says he can make out the shouts in the background.

I tell him I'm back in the news after my stand against transgender individuals competing in girls' and women's sports. Only this time, protestors are in front of my house, blocking my driveway, and some are threatening to hurt me or kill me and hurt my mother.

He reminds me that, contrary to what Benton claims, most, if not all, of the golfers who are purchasing homes and joining any luxury golf courses I designed, agree with me. So, the haters may be trying to take me down, but they won't succeed in canceling my development business.

That comment makes no sense to me, given my circumstances. I say, "I'm not worried about Benton's accusations. I'm more worried about the death threats I've received, how they are terrifying my mother, and the doxxing that has appeared on social media in the last twenty-four hours."

"Oh, I'm sorry," Luke says. "I wasn't trying to trivialize what you and your mom are experiencing. What can I do to help?" he asks.

"I don't think you can do anything legally other than winning our lawsuit," I respond. "You can be my friend, my lawyer, and help me reassure my mom. That's what you can do. I have nothing against transgender people. They should be able to live the life they choose and be happy. I support girls' and women's sports and want them to have a fair opportunity to compete."

"Maybe you and your mom should come down and stay in Corona. Because of the court's order, you can't work for another developer, and the trial is only a few weeks from now. I can find you a house to rent in a gated community, and you'll be safer here."

"That may be a good idea," I reply. "I'm suffering by not being able to work. Maybe getting away from my home and office will lessen my anxiety. I can hang out in Corona until this blows over or until we finish our trial."

If it ever blows over.

I debate on whether to call the police. Instead, I go through the mass of people and open and close my door before any of them enter my house. I see my mom. She's as white as a ghost. I tell her it'll be okay and she should ignore what's going on outside. She gives me a hug.

For the first time, I ask myself why I had answered the question about biological boys competing in girls' and women's sports. I thought, at the time, I was doing the right thing, or more accurately, I was too naive to anticipate the blowback that would put my mother and me in danger. I wish now I had answered that I didn't have enough information to offer an opinion. I realize I've never said those words in response to any question. So, it's wishful thinking now.

An hour later, it's raining, and most of the protestors have left. My phone rings. I see the number is from the 212 area code. I let it ring without answering. Later, I see the caller left me a message. She says that she is from Fox News, and she wants to schedule several more appearances for me to speak out on not allowing biological men to compete in high school and college women's sports. She says I've become the voice of women across America who are afraid of speaking up. Then, she offers to pay for me to fly to New York or to set up interviews from my home.

I am deeply passionate about this issue. I'm standing firm and fighting publicly for women's sports.

I tell her, "I'm interested in doing more interviews and speaking out about the importance of fair competition in women's sports."

"That's great to hear," she responds. "We're looking for another guest to speak on this topic next week, and we'd love for you to join us."

I agree to participate, and we discuss the details of the show. I learn the other guest will argue against my point of view. She says, "This is all part of Fox's commitment to be fair and balanced." I feel a renewed sense of purpose as I hang up the phone. I can make a difference and stand up for my beliefs.

The next week, I fly to New York for the guest appearance. When I step onto the set, I become aware of the intense glare of the studio lighting, and I sense the tension in the air. As the caller explained in our phone call, I am one of two guests. Sheila Sutherland advocates for trans rights and has been vocal about her opposition to my argument that no biological males should be allowed to compete in high school girls, college women, or professional women's sports.

While we are on live television, Sutherland reminds the audience of a time when, during match play, my opponent was a woman who was six feet two inches tall and had to weigh over two hundred and twenty-five pounds. The network shows a video of a par five hole when my large and strong opponent hit an iron onto the green, while I hit a fairway wood short of the green and hit a wedge onto the green on my third shot. The video stops there, not showing that my hefty opponent three-putted, and I sank my putt for a birdie to win the hole.

Sutherland asks, "If I thought it was unfair when I competed against a woman several inches taller than me and almost a hundred pounds heavier than me." I say, "No, because she was a female at birth."

Sutherland shakes her head. "But what if she wasn't?" she asks, and the audience leans forward in their seats.

I feel my palms sweating as I realize where this conversation is heading. But I know I must stand my ground.

"Look, I understand that people should have the right to identify as they choose, but when it comes to sports, biology matters," I say firmly. "It's just not fair to have someone who was born male competing against women in sports. The physical advantages are too great."

Sutherland bristles at my words, and her eyes flashing with anger. "You're just trying to exclude trans women from sports," she says. "You're denying them the right to participate in something they love."

"That's not what I'm saying at all," I protest. "I just think that there should be a level playing field, and that means separating sports by biological sex."

Sutherland scoffs at my words. "Do you even know how hard it is for trans women to compete in sports? They face discrimination and bigotry every step of the way. And now you want to take away their right to compete? That's just cruel."

I take a deep breath, trying to remain calm. "I'm not trying to take away anyone's rights. I'm advocating for fairness in sports. It's not fair for someone who was born male to compete against women who were born female. The physical differences are just too great."

"But what about hormone therapy?" Sutherland asks. "Trans women have to undergo hormone therapy to compete in women's sports, and that levels the playing field."

I shake my head. "Hormone therapy doesn't change everything. It can't change the fact that someone born male has greater muscle mass and bone density than someone who was born female. It's unfair and puts female athletes at a disadvantage. Plus, in some sports, like boxing, a transgender boxer could severely injure a girl or woman boxer."

My tension is palpable as I respond to each of Sutherland's arguments. Finally, the host says, "We have to take a break now. We'd love to have the two of you back to continue this debate."

I'm ready to go back to my Corona rental home. I'm tired of being attacked for something so obviously fair and reasonable, but I won't back down.

Chapter 12

Luke

Following Lauren's television interview, public outrage escalates. She plays in a Dallas charity event, and there are widespread protests outside the country club, as well as calls for boycotts against any events hosted there. Lauren's reputation takes a significant hit, impacting not only our lawsuit but also her and her mother's personal life as they face the relentless backlash. I have to stay focused on her case against Benton, and I have to keep Lauren focused.

I'm in my office and thinking about how we can prove that Benton lied about who designed the Lake Tierra Golf course, which was recently named one of the top golf courses in America. Benton has been on TV, claiming he designed the golf course.

In my years of trying cases, finding a 'smoking gun' that completely undermines my adversary's case is a rare occurrence. I've rarely, if ever, found a smoking gun that torpedoes my adversary's argument. Therefore, I'm taken aback when Lauren informs me that Steven Strong, a California printer, could potentially provide us with such evidence. He claims that Robert

Benton wrongfully took credit for Lauren's design of the Lake Tierra Golf Course.

After terminating Lauren's design contract, Benton audaciously emailed Strong, instructing him to halt the printing of the Lake Tierra Development brochure and replace Lauren as the golf course designer with himself. This blatant act of injustice is a testament to Benton's deceitful nature.

Dear Steve,

Please change our marketing brochures. I've terminated Lauren West's golf course design contract because she has wrongfully misgendered and disparaged girls and women transgender athletes. Destroy any brochures you printed showing Miss West as the designer of the Lake Tierra Golf Course and instead show me as the designer on the brochures and the scorecards.

Sincerely,
Robert E. Benton

"Why did Strong contact you?"

"You're going to like this one. Strong told me that Benton refused to pay him for the over one thousand brochures he had printed, reflecting that I designed the golf course. He saved a dozen of them and is sending those to me."

My initial inclination is to contact Morgan and tell him that even Benton has acknowledged both in the mediation and email to Strong that Lauren designed the Lake Tierra Golf Course. So, the only thing in dispute is the amount of your bonus Benton owes. But I know the bonus amount will make no difference to Benton. He'll lie about designing the golf course. I tell Lauren, "I can use it to destroy Benton's credibility at the trial."

"Won't Benton know we have the email and the original brochure he approved?" Lauren asks.

"I will request any correspondence related to the Lake Tierra Golf Course design. When he fails to produce the email, we can assume he is unaware that we already have it."

I spend the next couple of hours meticulously rehearsing how I will dismantle Benton's credibility during cross-examination.

I prepare a Request for Production of Documents while asking Benton and Benton Land Company to produce any and all documents related or pertaining in any way to the Lake Tierra Hill Country Development project. As I expect, Benton's Los Angeles lawyer, Harvey Morgan, demands that we sign a confidentiality agreement. I tell Lauren that Benton doesn't want anyone in the media to know how much money he's made on his Lake Tierra development.

It takes time to agree on what the confidentiality agreement covers, but we eventually work it out. Morgan proposes that I come to Dallas to review the files and copy whatever is relevant. I meet Clark Mitchell, an accounting expert I've hired, in Dallas and drive to Benton's office. As I anticipated, Morgan's team has stacked several hundred boxes of documents along the wall six feet high. I'm sure at least ninety percent of the documents are irrelevant.

"Can they bury us any deeper in documents?"

"Reams of irrelevant nonsense. I'm sure that anything that would help our case is not here, or Benton's team strategically placed relevant documents where we are most likely to miss them," I reply while tossing a flyer for a fishing tournament in California. "I would expect nothing less from Harvey Morgan."

After hours, I tell myself to stay focused. It's a challenge since the COVID-19 and ventilator have reduced my attention span. I step outside and walk around the building to breathe some fresh air. I dive back in when I return.

We dedicate days to meticulously reviewing the documents, taking a break every hour to ensure our focus remains sharp. This thorough process instills confidence in the quality of our investigation. We then take a well-deserved break for the weekend, spending two enjoyable days with our loved ones, and our minds temporarily freed from the burden of Benton's documents.

We return on Monday to continue our review. Among other things, I'm looking for the letter or email Benton sent to the brochure printer. Unless we missed it, the letter is not among the thousands of documents that Clark and I review. That means Benton or Morgan removed the letter from Benton's files, thinking we would never know it existed. Benton is even more of a scoundrel than I expected.

Judge Cedric Hawkins calls for a status conference. Born in Corona, Judge Hawkins returned to his hometown after graduation from UT Law School in 1978. Hawkins has been on the bench for the last thirty years. He's a difficult judge to try a case before. The Hill Country lawyers say Judge Hawkins takes a side early in a trial and conveys to the jury how they should decide the case by his response to objections and his questions for witnesses. I hesitate to agree to arbitration because I'm counting on Judge Hawkins to take our side and convey it to the jury.

"Tell me what Lauren West is complaining about," Judge Hawkins asks me.

"Your Honor, Miss West spent months preparing a design for the Lake Tierra Golf Course, which is part of Mr. Benton's Lake Tierra Hill Country Development. Before the construction of the golf course, Mr. Benton terminated Miss West's contract, stole her golf course design and took credit for it, and failed to pay her ten percent of the net profits from sales on homes, lots, and golf course memberships. Mr. Benton falsely claims he designed the golf course on the Lake Tierra Golf Course scorecards and the Lake Tierra marketing material."

"Okay, Mr. Morgan, what does your client say?"

"This case has no merit," Morgan tells the judge. "Miss West started designing the golf course, but there is far more to designing a golf course than what she accomplished. We'll present evidence of all the work that Mr. Benton did in designing and monitoring the construction of the golf course. Regarding the bonus, Mr. Benton terminated Miss West's contract for cause. She created hatred towards transgender athletes that brought great embarrassment to Mr. Benton and caused a loss of sales at all of his developments. Even if Miss West convinces a jury that she designed the golf course, she's not entitled to recover any money."

"Why did Mr. Benton terminate Miss West's design contract?" Judge Hawkins asks.

"Miss West breached her contract when she made transphobic comments arguing that trans athletes should not be able to compete in women's sports. Most home and real estate buyers and country club members believe Miss West has endangered transgender people with her hate speech. Many complained to Mr. Benton and told him they would not buy property in a development with a golf course designed by Miss West."

"I understand you didn't settle the case in mediation. Do you have any other ideas that might take the case off my docket?" Judge Hawkins asks.

"I've offered to arbitrate the case," Morgan replies, sitting erect in his seat. "We feel it is far better to have an arbitrator who is an expert on golf course design decide the issues in the case than to present the complicated facts to a jury and have them decide."

"What do you say about arbitration, Mr. Hartley?"

"We understand Mr. Benton wants to keep this case out of the public eye. He wants to sweep it all under the rug. A Corona County jury can listen to testimony, study the exhibits, and come to a reasonable conclusion."

Judge Hawkins shoots me a stern look. I've seen it too many times to count. He doesn't want to try a relatively complicated case for two weeks or more.

"Your Honor," Morgan says. "There's one more thing I want you to rule on. Miss West's contract included a non-compete clause. We understand she has been designing a golf course for one of Mr. Benton's competitors. I've made a motion not to allow her to work for another developer while this lawsuit is pending."

I'm thinking, *what the heck? Lauren is only happy when she's working. She's obsessive about her work. Plus, she needs the money to live on and fund her lawsuit against Benton.*

"Do you have anything to say, Mr. Hartley?"

"Your Honor, it is blatantly unjust to allow Mr. Benton to breach Miss West's contract and then not allow her to work. Mr. Benton is using his wealth and your court as a weapon against Miss West. At every turn he's prolonged this legal battle. He filed a spurious counter-claim to increase Miss West's legal expenses. I'm sure you can see he's delaying the trial and running up the legal fees and other expenses."

"Mr. Morgan, I'm not fond of what you are asking me to do. I don't like your client using my court as a weapon against Miss

West. But I'll grant your motion until the trial date, which I'm setting for eight weeks from today. I will also order you to finish all your depositions and document discovery six weeks from today."

"Your Honor, we need more time than that to get through discovery and prepare for trial," Morgan says.

"Mr. Morgan," Judge Hawkins says with a sly grin. "You've delayed this trial at every turn. I suggest you persuade Mr. Hartley to settle the case if you need more time. If you cause a delay in the trial, I will not limit Miss West's ability to work."

"Damn," I hear Morgan say under his breath. He must know that Judge Hawkins isn't wearing his hearing aids. "Your Honor, Mr. Benton has no interest in settling this case with Miss West. He's fighting for the rights of transgender people."

"Okay. Prepare for the trial that will be eight weeks from today."

I call Lauren. "Morgan filed a motion to enforce the non-compete clause in your contract. He told Judge Hawkins that Benton has no interest in settling the case with you. I believe he wants to keep going with his effort to smear you on social media."

"He can't do that. I'm already designing a golf course. I can't just call the developer and tell him I can't work for him."

"I'm afraid you're going to have to make that call," I say,

Lauren continues, "We're spending my life savings at a record pace. Where am I supposed to get the money for my mother and me to live on and for me to pay you?" Lauren sighs. "If I can't work, I can't pay you. What do I do now? I can't believe I cannot work for another developer."

That's not good news for me either. It's not like I'm a lawyer at a big firm that will continue to pay me even though Lauren's not paying the firm. I have my own law firm, and I'm only working on Lauren's case. I have no other source of income.

I say, "We have a trial date. It's eight weeks from today. Somehow, we'll press on.

"I sense the last thing Morgan wants to do is try this case in Corona County. Judge Hawkins doesn't appreciate Morgan filing a motion to enforce the non-compete clause in your contract. That's why he set an early trial date.

"It's not early enough for me."

Chapter 13

Luke

I find talking to Lauren about anything other than her case with Benton, is awkward. But, sometimes, we need a break from that work. I want to see more of her, but I'm not sure what else we can discuss.

Lauren had told me she loves coffee shops, so I suggest, we meet at Coffee Bean, another one of my favorite Corona coffee shops in an old restored building on Main Street.

I arrive first and greet many friends seated around the coffee shop. The coffee shop is buzzing with the hum of casual conversation, the scent of freshly brewed coffee mixing with the aroma of baked goods. The rich smell of roasted coffee and soft jazz background music is warm and welcoming. I secure a corner table so we can have some privacy and order a vanilla latte for her and an americano for me. When I see Lauren, I lead her to our table. I catch myself with my hand on her elbow and pull it away. I'm certain Lauren doesn't want to talk about what haters are trying to do to her on social media.

I lamely ask, "So what do you think of the PGA's decision to merge with the Saudi's LIV golf tour?"

Lauren looks at me, and her expression conveys that she's also struggling to come up with topics for our coffee discussion. She replies, "I believe the merger announcement surprised many of the PGA players, and they were not happy. They had passed up millions of dollars to stay with the PGA. Now they, or at least I, would feel betrayed for being loyal to the PGA. Before the shocking merger announcement, the PGA had made an enormous increase in the prize money. I'm sure the PGA golfers were happy about that. I only wish we could raise the pay of LPGA golfers. An LPGA tournament winner may earn about the same as a PGA golfer who finished thirtieth or worse."

"Have you watched a LIV tournament?" I ask.

"So far, hardly anyone is watching the LIV tournaments on television, including me. It's on some obscure cable station. The mediocre golfers who signed with the Saudis are happy because they made a ton of money when they signed to play. There are only a handful of top players signed, but the number has increased over time. Most of them say they moved to LIV golf partly because they can spend more time with their families."

While she answers, I'm trying to come up with another topic for our discussion. "Would you like me to tell you about the restaurants in the Corona area?" I ask.

Lauren takes another sip of her latte and puts her cup down. "Sure," she says. "I'm not sure I'll dine out very often. I hate going to a restaurant alone."

I spend ten minutes telling her about my favorite restaurants. In a small town like Corona, the restaurant owners build relationships with their diners, which makes the experience more enjoyable. "Our most expensive and up-scale restaurant is a steakhouse on a cattle ranch about five miles out of town. It is worth the trip." Having heard what she had said about eating alone, I say, "I'd love to take you some time."

Lauren's face lights up. "That would be nice," she says.

"Our best family-owned Mexican restaurant is one block from our town square," I say. "If you dine at their restaurant, you'll likely meet the whole family."

Just as Lauren is about to respond, a loud, cheerful voice interrupts her.

"Well, well, if it isn't Luke Hartley," Rhonda Rose's voice chimes as she approaches our table, her eyes solely focused on me.

Without a glance at Lauren, she leans in a little too close, her hand resting on the back of my chair. “Fancy seeing you here. I've been thinking, it’s been too long since we spent time together.”

I politely smile, though my eyes are flickering with discomfort. We haven’t spent time together, at least not alone. “Hey, Rhonda.” I start to introduce her to Lauren, but Rhonda continues.

“I was just saying to myself the other day, ‘Why haven't I seen that handsome face around lately?’ Maybe we should fix that. How about dinner sometime? Just you and me.”

I see Lauren raise an eyebrow.

I clear my throat, eager to steer her away from us. “Rhonda, let me introduce you to Lauren West,” I say, motioning to Lauren. “She's a client of mine, and we're discussing something important.”

For the first time, Rhonda's eyes shift, her gaze finally landing on Lauren. Her smile falters, and a faint blush colors her cheeks as she realizes her mistake. “Oh, I... I didn't see you, Lauren,” she stammers, straightening up.

“Well, I should let you two get back to your discussion,” Rhonda says. “Maybe another time, Luke.”

Rhonda turns and makes a hasty return to her seat.

When Rhonda is gone, Lauren takes a sip of her coffee. She sets the cup down and leans back in her chair, giving me a playful look.

"No," I say in a low voice. "Nothing is going on between us."

Lauren smiles. "Seems like Rhonda thinks there's a bit more going on between you two."

I explain further. "There's nothing between us, Lauren. Rhonda's just... persistent."

Lauren leans in, lowering her voice conspiratorially. "Well, if that's how she acts when nothing's going on between you, I'd hate to see what she'd do if something actually was."

She's enjoying this, and I want to change the subject. I ask, "Have any other large golf course development companies tried to hire your design company?"

"I get at least one call a month from a large golf course development company wanting me to help design a family-friendly golf course in their development. For now, I must tell them Benton is not allowing me to work for a competing developer. I can't work with them until we resolve my dispute with Benton."

"Have you considered working with any of them after the trial?" I ask.

"I haven't pursued any of them because of the non-compete. Contrary to what they say to me; the larger development companies aren't meeting the needs of the entire family. My work for Benton's developments put the family first. I persuaded him to compete by having far more recreational activities than golf available to families. I told him to keep creating a unique family experience. That has become the Benton Land Company brand. Even if we win my case against Benton, he may sue me for recreating what I did for his developments. On the other hand, if I don't work for another luxury golf community developer, what will I do with the rest of my life? I'm too young to retire."

I appreciate her point. She's focused her life after playing on the tour to creating family-oriented luxury golf development. I ask, "What will it be like to live in a town where you designed an award-winning golf course without being allowed to see it?"

"The Lake Tierra home buyers built their homes because Benton showed them drawings and renditions with my name on them, showing I would design the golf course. They're nice to me and introduce themselves when they see me in town. I don't have a social life here, but I didn't have one in Dallas either. I was on the road too often to make friends."

Lauren finishes her coffee and goes to the counter to order a second cup of coffee. When she comes back, she hands me a pastry. She catches me smiling and winks at me.

Lauren's phone makes the sound of an incoming call. She glances at the caller ID, answers the call, and speaks in a hushed tone, clearly annoyed. She walks outside to talk.

Lauren returns and tells me, "The caller was Thomas Caldwell, one of the top golf course developers in the world, with far more money than Benton. Caldwell wants me to design a golf course for his new development project in California. Supposedly, no other golf course architect has provided him with a plan that will create a unique family experience as I have done for each of Benton's developments. He tried to persuade me to violate the non-compete order and design a golf course for him."

"What?"

I told him I couldn't and I was about to finish the conversation, but, Thomas Caldwell is smooth and persuasive over the phone. He said it would be a once-in-a-lifetime opportunity and that with him bankrolling it, I could redefine the family-friendly golfing experience.

“How did Caldwell plan for you to get around the non-compete court order?”

“He claimed he’d find there’s a way around it. He suggested that we could keep everything under wraps until the case is resolved. He said I could start on preliminary sketches and concept ideas in my own time without formally committing to the project. This way, I’d not be directly working on the project, but you’re still moving forward with your ideas. I told him I was worried I’d get caught.”

“With good reason. Benton has private investigators looking at your every move.”

“I told him Benton would find out. He said that if I was worried about getting caught, he’d use an intermediary to handle the initial discussions and paperwork. That way, I’d remain at arm’s length, and nothing gets tied directly back to me. He said it’s about working smart, not breaking the law.”

I’m concerned by the look on Lauren’s face that she is considering it. “Lauren, you can either give up getting the million-dollar bonus and see if Benton will drop his counterclaim so you can go to work for Caldwell, or you must wait until the trial is over. You can't do both."

"I know," she says unconvincingly. "Part of me wants to go to trial and kick Benton's rear end. But the other part of me...well, the other part of me just wants to move on. Benton won't agree to give up his counterclaim so I can work with Caldwell."

"I guess I'm stuck. We have to win," Lauren says.

No pressure, I'm thinking. I must win this case. I hope my continuing side effects don't make that more difficult. The usual confidence I have is overshadowed by this nagging concern. My health has been playing tricks on me—my energy wanes faster than it ever has, and my memory isn't as sharp. It's like trying to juggle with one hand tied behind my back. I just hope these side effects don't make this already tough battle even harder.

Chapter 14

Luke

After spending over a month with Clark Mitchell, our expert accountant, while reviewing Benton Land Company files, I receive a notice that Morgan wants to take Lauren's deposition in his office sometime agreeable in the next month. I call and agree on a date and that he can take Lauren's deposition in Morgan's Dallas office.

Over the next two weeks, I rehearse Lauren's deposition every day. Each day, Lauren's attention span is only about an hour. I say, "Pretend this is like practicing golf. I'm sure you did that for hours, hitting likely more than one thousand shots a day."

Lauren grins, "But that was outside, and I was doing something I enjoyed. Preparing for this deposition keeps me from being outside, and I can't even begin to tell you how much I hate doing it."

We keep preparing in an odd way. I work with her for an hour, and then she has free time. I have a fair idea what Morgan will ask, and Lauren will be ready by the date set for the deposition.

She asks what she should wear, and I suggest a business suit with a skirt, jacket and a white blouse. I drive to Dallas the night before Lauren's deposition. In the morning, I pick her up from her house. Lauren dressed just as I advised. She looks both professional and confident, ready to face whatever questions Morgan may have in store for her.

We arrive at Andy Johnson's Dallas office promptly at 10:00 AM. After a few minutes, the receptionist escorts us to a conference room. As we enter, I notice Morgan sitting on one side of the table with a sly smile on his face. I can tell he's been waiting for this moment, eager to question Lauren. A court reporter with a video camera is at the end of the conference room. Morgan asks Lauren to sit at the head of the table so the video camera will catch her face as she testifies.

"Good morning, Miss West," Morgan's voice drips with false sincerity. "I'm sure Mr. Hartley has explained to you in great detail what we are doing today."

Lauren nods, her eyes fixed on Morgan. "Yes, he has. I know why we're here."

"Well then, let's get started, shall we?" Morgan says, leaning back in his chair. He spends the entire morning asking biographical questions, starting with her first memories as an infant and concluding with her experience as a student-athlete at the University of Texas. I object on the grounds of relevance about every fifteen minutes, hoping Lauren will take it as a clue not to tell Morgan her life story.

If Morgan's strategy is to get Lauren talking, it's working. Morgan asks when she became interested in golf, and Lauren replies that her father both pushed and encouraged her to take up golf at an early age. She says he bought her a children's plastic golf club and ball when she was three years old. When she was five, her father cut off a seven iron, put a grip on it, and took her to the local driving range to hit balls. At the range, a golf pro took an interest in teaching her, much to her father's delight. Lauren tells him her father gave her a whole set of golf clubs when she was seven, and she would carry them to the golf course five blocks away from her home.

Lauren also mentions that her father gave up an opportunity to become a bank manager because he preferred to spend hours and hours teaching and coaching her on the driving range and traveling with her to junior golf tournaments throughout the country. Her mother, Kelly, taught school. Lauren traveled with her father to the junior tournaments. She tells Morgan that her father never pushed her. Instead, he taught her to love the game and constantly strive to be the best she can be, and importantly, he made it fun for her.

"I owe my success to my father's relentless efforts to teach me to be mentally tough and physically fit and my mother's undying support." Lauren's eyes mist over.

"Morgan, move on and focus on the matters in the lawsuit."

Morgan grins. "Describe your teenage years playing competitive golf."

"Relevance, Morgan."

Morgan again grins and continues. "How did you end up at the University of Texas?"

Lauren says that in high school junior year, she received college scholarship offers from Stanford, UCLA, Arizona, and other well-known colleges. She says she accepted the offer from the University of Texas, so her mother and father could watch her play in tournaments in Austin.

Lauren testifies that she knew that accepting the offer from the University of Texas would not only bring her closer to her mother and father and also put her on one of the top college golf teams in the country. Lauren says she was determined to become the team's number one player, and by her junior year, she accomplished that goal.

She continues discussing her college golf career, telling Morgan that in her sophomore year, she was invited to play in the LPGA event in Dallas. She says she had never been so nervous on a golf course as when she hit her driver on the first tee with hundreds watching her in person and who knows how many watching her on television.

I know from having gone to the Dallas tournament why she was nervous on the first tee. The tee box is a massive stage. A huge gallery of spectators is waiting for the players. Spectators hold up their phones shooting video, and the television cameras capture every angle and a player's golf ball is tracked on television using a technology called Toptracer.

Lauren's face lights up as she describes her performance at the event. "I was nervous, but I overcame it and shot one under seventy -one on the first day. I was a little less nervous the second day and played well enough to make the cut and continue playing on Saturday and Sunday. I finished the twentieth and was proud to have accomplished that. The experience was a turning point for me. I knew then I had what it would take to become a professional golfer."

Why is Morgan spending time on Lauren's background and career, which have nothing to do with the issues in the case? Sadly, he goes on asking Lauren more questions about her golf and academic experience at UT and her grades. He pulls out copies of her report cards and continues questioning.

With flushed cheeks, she says, "Golf practices or matches year-round made it hard to maintain my GPA. I spent hours before classes on the course and practice areas."

Morgan smirks and continues to drag out the deposition, and at one o'clock, he suggests we break for lunch. He's only now started asking her about qualifying to play on the LPGA tour.

I shake my head, trying to give Morgan the hint that I think he's a jerk. He blows it off.

When we are seated for lunch, I remind Lauren that she should not give long, detailed answers. I say that Morgan's strategy is to get her talking at length about herself.

I pause when the waitress arrives and takes our order. I order a Reuben sandwich, and Lauren orders tuna salad. We sit silently, eating. I know Lauren is nervous about what Morgan will ask in the afternoon. When our waitress clears our dishes, and hands me the check, I assure Lauren that she will handle Morgan's questions as we have prepared.

After we return from lunch, Morgan spends two hours asking about specific golf tournaments. None of his questions are relevant, but all I can do is object to the form of the question and let him continue. After asking about many tournaments while showing Lauren videos taken from television broadcasts, Morgan turns to asking Lauren about her earnings on the tour, about her friends on the tour, who caddied for her, and details about each of the sixteen tournaments she won, including the two majors, her injuries, and more LPGA trivia.

Lauren takes a long breath. "When I started, it was more fun. American golfers supported each other. Some girls had a support system. Either they had married, or their parent or parents came to tournaments and supported them. I was single, and that was okay when my father caddied for me, and my mother, who taught school, came to the tournaments in the US to walk the course, watching me on Saturday and Sunday. We were one happy family. But then my father was diagnosed with cancer, and our lives were turned upside down. After he passed away, my mother was lost and depressed. I spent several months with her before returning to the tour."

"And the pressure affected your career, right?" Morgan asks.

Lauren makes steady eye contact with Morgan and speaks through gritted teeth. "Mr. Morgan, those of us who play or played college and professional golf have devoted our lives to golf, to our family, and in my case, to supporting young girls who want to participate in golf and other sports."

Morgan asks if Lauren sought help to deal with the pressure. Once again, I object and state that Lauren's health has nothing to do with any issue in the lawsuit. Morgan ignores me and directs Lauren to answer his questions. So, she's stuck answering. I learn from her testimony that Lauren regularly saw a sports psychologist while she was on the tour.

Lauren loosens her top collar and removes her jacket. She narrows her eyes at him, takes a deep breath, and says, "Mr. Morgan, will you eventually ask me a question that has anything to do with this lawsuit? I realize Benton is paying you by the hour, but Mr. Hartley and I could be doing far more productive things."

Morgan has a wicked grin on his face and tells Lauren that he'll ask the questions and not answer hers. Then, he surprises her by switching gears and asking her what I consider to be the first relevant question. It's now three fifteen.

"Miss West, when did you first meet Robert Benton?"

"I first met him at the Dallas LPGA tournament when he played with our group in the Wednesday Pro-Am. He was our amateur."

Morgan continues by asking repeatedly when Lauren next saw Robert Benton.

Lauren speaks from her memory, but we've reviewed those questions and her answers.

Morgan asks when Benton first gave Lauren a break, hiring her as a golf course architect for his first golf course development.

As we had practiced, Lauren corrects Morgan. "Benton didn't give me a break," she says. "I gave him a break when I first shared with him my idea of building luxury golf course developments with a golf course design and amenities in the development that would appeal to the whole family. I found the land to develop Benton's first luxury golf course community in Scottsdale."

"Why did you agree to design golf courses for Robert Benton's luxury golf developments?"

"Because I had a unique idea for high-end golf course developments, and Mr. Benton told me he wanted to diversify his real estate portfolio and had the money to make it happen. He also initially supported my idea of building golf courses in less affluent neighborhoods and encouraging children in those neighborhoods to take up golf."

Toward the end of the day, Lauren goes over each golf course she designed for Benton Land Company. She explains, why she demanded ten percent of the net profits in the Lake Tierra Golf Course Design Contract.

"Many purchasers at other Benton Land Company developments told me the only reason they bought a home or lot and paid to join the golf course was because of my family-friendly design. For Lake Tierra, I negotiated the share of profits clause, expecting him to pay me the bonus. He agreed, and I took him at his word. Now, he claims he doesn't have to pay me a bonus."

At five-thirty, Morgan says he has one last question before adjourning for the day and coming back tomorrow.

"Miss West, while you were designing golf courses for Mr. Benton. Did you have any personal or business relationships with any other real estate developers?"

"I'm not sure I understand what you are asking, but if you want to know if I offered to design a golf course for another developer, the answer is no."

"Have you been approached by any other developers since you filed this lawsuit?"

Lauren looks at me, and then she lies. "No, Mr. Morgan."

Morgan asks if I agree to adjourn for the day, and I agree, noting that Lauren appears exhausted from talking all day. I'm also exhausted and a bit confused by her reaction to Morgan's last question.

Lauren packs up her belongings and prepares to leave. I can see her sense of dread. She knows from our discussions that Morgan will ask her about what he and Benton believe are her controversial views on trans athletes tomorrow. We've talked about whether she's ready for the backlash that will follow and how important it will be to stay calm when responding.

As we leave the conference room, Lauren pulls me aside and asks if we can chat privately. I nod and follow her to a quiet corner of the hallway.

"Listen, I know I've been talking a lot today. But there's something else I need to tell you," she says, her voice barely above a whisper.

I can sense the urgency in her tone and gesture for her to continue.

"During a break, Benton stopped and talked to me. He warned me that if I didn't withdraw my lawsuit, my reputation would be severely damaged. He said there are audio and videos of me on the internet spewing hate against transgender individuals, and told me he'd go to bat for me if I withdrew the lawsuit."

"How can there be an internet audio and video of me? I never said what he claimed I said in the videos."

"Did he have someone post them?" I ask.

Lauren's expression shows her disdain as she divulges, "He claimed he had nothing to do with it, but I told him if that was true, one of his many followers got the idea that posting audio and videos would hurt my case against him. He's telling me he can embarrass me. I've never said what he claims are on the audio and videos someone has posted. How could audio and videos of me saying things I never said be posted on the internet?"

My heart sinks as I hear her words. Benton didn't post the audio and videos. But I'm sure he paid someone connected with him to post them. They are designed to damage Lauren's reputation and make her look like a bigot and hypocrite. I always thought he was a sleazy businessman, but I never thought he would stoop this low.

I explain to Lauren about the creation of audio recordings, photos, and videos through artificial intelligence, known as deepfake porn. Teenage boys mainly do it to embarrass girls, using a method called deep learning to swap faces in images and videos. But, it has also been used in political campaigns to disparage the candidate.

“Isn't that illegal?” she asks.

“It’s not a federal or state crime, but the Texas legislature is working on a bill to make it a crime. The issue is proving who made the fake content. Can you listen to the audios posted, look at the videos, and see if anything can help us?”

“I’ll listen to the audio recordings people have posted, and I’ll watch the videos, but I want to make sure you know I didn’t say what has been posted. Benton likes to have leverage on his business partners, and I’m no exception. He probably showed me these to throw me off guard. Can't we get Judge Hawkins to order the social media sites to remove them?”

“I will report this to the police,” I say.

“But in the meantime, people will believe I spewed that hatred. My reputation will be ruined, and my mother will be devastated,” Lauren frets.

I understand how she feels. That may be only a part of the problem. The other part is how potential jurors will judge Lauren when they learn about the audio recordings and videos.

Chapter 15

Lauren

As we make our way to my house, I ask Luke how I had done in the deposition. He tells me I did well but warns me to avoid giving long and detailed answers to Morgan's questions. Morgan asked straightforward questions to lull me into a false sense of security.

"Harvey Morgan is not your friend," Luke says. "I expect tomorrow he'll ask about the golf courses you designed, and at some point, he'll attack you based on your public statements that transgender athletes should not be allowed to compete in women's sports. I've worked as hard as you'd let me, preparing you for the onslaught. Just remember not to lose your temper."

I'm still getting over the pressure from having been in the hottest all day. I wish Luke had more confidence in me.

"I know, Luke," I reply. "You've drilled it into my head a hundred times. But I refuse to sit there and let him twist my words or make me look like some kind of villain for speaking my mind. I'm not just going to roll over."

"I'm not suggesting you should roll over," Luke says.

"You keep telling me not to lose my temper, but what about defending myself? I'm not going to let Morgan walk all over me tomorrow. He's out to ruin me, and I won't make it easy for him."

Luke holds my gaze for a moment, then gives a slight nod without saying more. Finally, he lets out a quiet sigh, signaling that he disagrees with me, but he's choosing not to push the issue further—for now.

I decide to stop arguing. I thank Luke for his advice. He nods and reminds me to get some rest. Morgan will make tomorrow another long day.

I walk into my house and head straight to the kitchen. I open the freezer and stare at the Bombay Sapphire bottle I keep there. I reach to grab it. I contemplate for a moment, close the freezer, open the refrigerator, and grab a bottle of water instead. I add a powdered hydration packet. I need a clear head for tomorrow's deposition.

I'm parched from all the talking I did today. As I'm drinking from the water bottle, I sense my nerves settle down a bit. But it's only temporary. Tomorrow is going to be a long day.

I try to sleep, but I keep playing questions and my answers in my head. I take a sleeping pill and finally fall asleep. At two, I wake up and turn over. I lay in bed for what feels like an eternity, staring blankly at the ceiling. I can't stop thinking about the deposition and what could go wrong tomorrow. I toss and turn, hoping to find a comfortable position to help me drift off to sleep. But no matter what I do, I can't shake the anxiety that's been building up inside of me.

Damn. Go to sleep now.

Finally, I get up and walk to the kitchen, hoping drinking more water will help me calm down and get back to sleep. But as I walk through the silent house, a shadow moving outside my window catches my eye. I freeze, wondering if it's just my imagination. But then I see a silhouette of a man standing in my backyard. Looking out in front, I see at least a dozen protestors in my front yard chanting. A man with a mask shouts into a megaphone that I am a transphobic bitch.

My heart pounds so loudly that it drowns out the protestors. I grab my phone and call 911. I hear a click, and a calm voice says, “911, what’s your emergency?” I can barely find my voice to respond.

"There are people outside my house," I say while trying to keep my voice steady. "Protestors in my yard. And... I think there's a man in my backyard. He's just standing there, watching. I'm afraid of what he might do."

"Stay on the line with me," the dispatcher says firmly. "Officers are on their way."

The shadows outside seem to twist and move with a life of their own, each flicker of light casting eerie shapes on the walls. The silence between the shouts feels charged with a menacing tension that wraps around me like a suffocating cloak. I strain to hear any sound that might signal the police's arrival, but the outside noises seem to close in on me."

"They're closing in. What should I do?" I ask the dispatcher.

"Can you get to a safe place inside your home?"

"Yes, I can lock myself in my bedroom." I hurry up the stairs, her heart pounding in my chest, hoping not to wake my mother. The chants from the protestors grow louder, and my mother comes out of her bedroom.

Every second feels like an eternity. I wait for twenty minutes, and from my bedroom window, I finally see flashing lights on the street in front of my house. After a few minutes, the crowd has gone, and my doorbell rings.

I rush to the door and open it to find a tall and broad-shouldered police officer in front of me. He looks stern, but there's a hint of sympathy in his eyes. “Ma'am, are you okay?” he asks.

“I’m better now that you are here. But the protestors have scared the bejabbers out of my mother.”

“We'll keep an eye out for any other troublemakers. I think you and she will be all right the rest of the night, ma’am. Call us if they come back.”

“Thank you, officer,” I say. I’m grateful for him breaking up the crowd, but I struggle to get my mother back to sleep. This is far from over.

Luke picks me up in the morning. When I get in the car, he asks if I had a restful night. I tell him what happened.

“We’re not doing your deposition today,” he says.

“I’m fine,” I say.

“That’s what you say, but it’s not how you look. Your puffy eyelids and dark circles under your eyes tell a different story.”

Luke's right. I want to get the deposition over with, but today is not the day.

He calls Harvey Morgan and puts the call on the speakerphone. After a couple of minutes on hold, Luke tells Morgan what happened and that we won't be showing up today for the deposition. Morgan says he and Benton had nothing to do with the protestors and that we should appear as agreed. Luke reiterates protestors harassed my mother and me all last night. I got little to no sleep, and I'm not physically and mentally ready to answer his questions. Morgan makes one more attempt to change our minds. Luke says that if he doesn't like our decision, he should take it up with Judge Hawkins.

"Let me know if you want to bother the judge with this issue. Alternatively, let me know when you want to reschedule day two of Lauren's deposition."

When we get in his car, Luke asks if I want to go home and sleep. I'm exhausted, but I want to know what we can do to stop protestors from coming to my house.

"Doxing is against the law in Texas," Luke says. "Can we prove Benton is behind what happened to you? I doubt it."

Hearing him say that makes me realize I'm in for more taunting. "Benton's smart enough to leave nothing that can be tracked back to him."

Luke's expression softens. "Listen, Lauren, I'm not just going to sit back and let this happen. I'll follow up with the police. I'll make sure they're taking this seriously. I can also hire private security if it makes you and your mother feel safer. I want you to know that I'll do everything I can to keep you and your mother protected."

I take a deep breath and thank him. Luke reminds me of my father. He has a strength that's hard to ignore, a quiet confidence that draws me in. I can't help but wonder if there's more to this than just his role as my lawyer. But I push the thought aside. There's too much at stake and too many battles to fight. Still, I can't deny the flicker of something more every time he's looking after me.

Thankfully, when I return to my bed, I'm able to fall back asleep.

I wake up when my phone buzzes on the nightstand, and I see Courtney's name flash across the screen. I hesitate for a moment before answering, still shaken from the night's events and struggling to wake up.

“Courtney, hey,” I say, trying to sound more alert than I feel.

“Em, I just heard what happened. Are you okay?” Courtney asks.

“I’m fine, just a little rattled,” I admit. “The protestors were in my yard, and someone was creeping around outside. It scared my mother to death.”

I hear Courtney sigh sympathetically. “That’s horrible. I can’t believe they’d go that far. I heard they put your address online, too. Are you sure you’re safe?”

I freeze for a second, my heart skipping a beat. “Wait, how did you know they doxxed me? I didn’t mention that part.”

Courtney quickly responds; her tone is light. “Oh, one of the girls from the tour texted me about it earlier. She’s been keeping tabs on everything going on with you. I figured she saw it on social media or something.”

I’m at a loss, who might have been keeping tabs on me, but I have much more on my mind.” Right, yeah… I guess that makes sense.”

“Anyway, you just focus on staying safe, okay? Don’t let those idiots get to you,” Courtney says, her voice is warm again. “If you need anything, I’m here.”

“Thanks, Court. I appreciate you,” I say, now fully awake.

After we hang up, I call Luke. He tells me the police called him an hour ago.

“What did they say? I ask.

“They tell me they questioned one protestor from last night. He admitted he was paid by a third party to cause a disturbance outside your house. He says he saw your name, address, and phone number on a website with the suggestion that people protest because you hate the LGBTQ community.”

My heart sinks. “Who would do that? Can we trace it back to Benton?”

Luke pauses. “The protestor they questioned didn’t know the original source of the payment. He was paid through a third-party app, something like Venmo or Cash App, by someone who contacted him anonymously through social media.”

I take a deep breath, gripping the phone tighter. “So, we can’t prove Benton funded the protest?”

"No," Luke says. "The police said the protestor mentioned that the message he received directing him to your house came from an account that was created recently with no real identifying information. The account had a generic profile picture and a username that didn't give anything away. It's likely a burner account."

I sigh, frustrated. "So, we're back to square one."

"Not entirely," Luke reassures me. "The fact that this protestor admitted to being paid is a lead. It's also clear now that whoever's behind this is targeting you specifically, using these tactics to try to shake you. The police are looking into other recent protests to see if they find any similarities—same methods of payment, similar messaging, anything that might connect the dots."

Morgan reschedules my deposition. Two weeks later, I drive back to Dallas. At Luke's suggestion, my mother and I stay in the hotel he had chosen for us a block from Morgan's office. Thankfully, none of the protestors find us there, but in the middle of the night, I hear a knock on my door. I get up, go to the door and a police officer is standing there. He says, "The police received a call from a female complaining someone was trying to break into this hotel room."

I tell him that no one has tried to break into our room, and I didn't call the police. He asks that I wait a couple of minutes while he reaches out to the dispatcher who took the call. When he returns, the officer says, "It was a SWAT call. Someone called with a fake emergency to draw armed officers to your home. I'm sorry to have awakened you, but since someone is trying to harass you, this may not be your last incident."

I'm once again not able to get a good night's sleep.

The following morning, we make our way to Morgan's office. As before, I am seated at the end of a conference room table. At the other end of the table, the court reporter's camera is already focused on me. The camera's presence was a constant, unyielding reminder that there would be no room for error, no escape from the scrutiny I'm about to face. That camera will capture every gesture and facial expression I make while answering Morgan's questions.

Across the table Morgan's seat is empty for now, but I see his neatly arranged folders that I assume are the notes and potential documents for me to review. Luke tells me, "Morgan left the notes and folders to intimidate me."

We wait and wait with the court reporter. I look over at Luke. He's tapping his pen on his legal pad. My mouth is dry as a result of my nervous anticipation. I had faced being nervous on the golf course many times, but my nervousness now was different.

Finally, Morgan walks in and takes his seat across the table from Luke and close to me. I wonder why Benton isn't with him. I look at Morgan and he makes a brief insincere smile. Before we start, I ask for a glass of water. Morgan goes to a portable refrigerator, brings out a bottle of water and pours it into a glass stored in a cabinet next to the refrigerator. I take a sip of the water and wait for him to start. Morgan sits again. This time, poised and ready to start. Morgan asks the court reporter to start the video camera, and he says, "Let's get started, shall we?" I want to say it's about time, but I smile for the camera, and we finally begin.

After some preliminary discussions off the record, Morgan says, "This is a continuation of the video deposition of the plaintiff, Miss Lauren West. Miss West, the instructions I previously gave you still apply. Do you need me to repeat any of those instructions?"

Morgan's gaze is hard and unblinking, a deliberate attempt to unsettle me. I can almost feel the weight of his stare, but I don't look away. Instead, I sit up a little straighter, my posture calm and steady. My eyes lock onto his, holding firm, a silent message that I won't be easily shaken.

I take a deep breath, trying to steady my nerves. "No," I reply. "But I want you to tell me whom you paid to make the fake emergency call, which resulted in an armed police officer knocking furiously on my door in the middle of the night and meeting me at the door with his pistol drawn. Is there no boundary too low for your harassing me?"

"Miss West, now that you made your speech on camera, first let me make clear that I know nothing about a call to the police, and I deeply resent your accusation. Second, I'd like to ask you to stop making false accusations so we can continue your deposition. Mr. Hartley, will you instruct your client to keep her accusations to herself?"

"Mr. Morgan, just go ahead with your questions."

"Okay, Miss West, tell us the steps to design a golf course." I assume Morgan eventually wants to show that I hadn't taken sufficient steps to have designed the Lake Tierra Golf Course before Benton terminated my contract.

I remember Luke wanted me to keep my answers short, but I want to use this time to convince Morgan that I designed the Lake Tierra Golf Course, and his client stole my design and took credit for it.

I begin. "Mr. Morgan, a golf course design is like a work of art. What makes it unique is that no two golf courses are alike. I start by selecting the right piece of land. Selecting the right land for the golf course can make or break a project. While I designed golf courses for your client, he twice selected land that almost made it impossible for me to design a championship golf course. In one case, the soil was not suitable for a golf course, and the challenge for me was figuring out how to create appropriate drainage. Your client selected land for the second golf course, where the rock under the surface made it too costly to build the golf course." I add, "The American Society of Golf Course Architects, of which I am a member, says that a golf course site should be at least one hundred and seventy-five acres."

"Who selected the land for the Lake Tierra Golf Course?"

"I did."

"How did you select the Lake Tierra Golf Course site?"

"I had hiked in that area when I was in college. I remembered the area. What struck me was being able to have tree-lined fairways. Many courses today have wide fairways. They are less picturesque, and they are easier to play. The Lake Tierra land allowed me to design wide fairways for amateurs to keep their drives in, but visually striking because there would be trees on each side. I could also use the creek that runs through the property on several holes."

"Explain the steps you made to design the golf course."

I take a sip of my water and wonder why Morgan is asking me questions that essentially will prove I designed the Lake Tierra Golf Course. "Are you sure you want me to explain each step?" I look over at Luke. He nods.

"You can just summarize what you did."

"Okay," I say. "The first thing I did was a feasibility study. Earlier, I told you about some of the challenges of selecting the land. I wasn't sure at the outset we could build an award-winning course at a reasonable price. I determined we needed two hundred acres of useable land to build a luxury golf course. Before we could go any further, I had to acquire the land and get it rezoned."

I testify at length about the rezoning hearings that Benton never attended. Morgan cuts me off.

"What did you do after the Corona County Zoning Board approved the rezoning?"

I take another sip of my water before responding. “I made rough drawings of the layout and estimated the earth moving costs.”

Morgan asks how long it took me to develop a preliminary design.

I tell him it took me several weeks.

Then, Morgan asks me to describe each stage of a golf course design and then asks at what stage Benton terminated my contract. I tell him that it was after I obtained all the agency approvals and completed the conceptional design.

Over the next two hours, Morgan asks me about the conceptional design of each of the eighteen holes. I assume, at some point, he wants to show the differences between my conceptual design and the final design. There are very few. During my testimony, I explain how I incorporated views of Lake Tierra in the design, making it a hazard on two holes.

Finally, we break for lunch. I’ve been in my element with Morgan’s softball questions all morning. I expect Morgan will ask contentious questions about transgender athletes competing against girls and women during the afternoon deposition session. I take a deep breath and try to push the uncomfortable sensation in my stomach aside.

Chapter 16

Luke

We sit silently, eating lunch before returning to Andy Johnson's Dallas office. Lauren eats only half of her tuna salad and pushes her plate away.

"Are you okay?"

Lauren rubs her stomach. "I'm not hungry. Maybe just another Coke Zero. I'll need caffeine this afternoon."

Thirty minutes later, when we enter the conference room, I see Andy Johnson talking to Robert Benton. He's attending Lauren's deposition for the first time. I suspect he's there to intimidate her. Benton stands up and walks towards us with a smug look. I can tell he's feeling confident, probably because he believes he has the upper hand in this case. But I am well aware that Lauren is not one to back down easily, and I have a hunch that Benton will soon understand that.

When we are all seated, Johnson departs. Morgan and Benton shuffle papers and drink from their water bottles. Benton fixes his piercing gaze on Lauren.

Unlike his previous questions, Morgan's voice is accusatory. "Do you contend that transgender girls and transgender women cannot be considered girls and women?"

"I've never said that."

"That wasn't my question. I'm asking if it's your contention."

Lauren's jaw clenches, her knuckles turning white as she grips the chair's armrests. She begins the answer as we had rehearsed it. "In my view, everyone should have the right to identify as they choose, and everyone deserves respect and equality, regardless of sex or gender. But that doesn't mean we should permit biological men to play against biological women." Lauren told me she had read dozens of articles on how Title IX transformed girls' and women's sports. She started to explain how girls and women benefited from Title IX when Morgan cuts her off.

"When did you go public with your anti-trans messaging?"

"I'm not anti-trans," Lauren answers as we've rehearsed. "I've testified that I support a person's right to live the life they choose. I hold the view that biological men, regardless of how they identify, should not compete against girls and women in sports. It's unfair, and in many cases, it's unsafe. "

“Okay, then,” Morgan says. “When did you go public wanting to deny trans athletes the right to compete against their chosen gender?”

Lauren pauses as if she doesn’t like how Morgan posed the question.

“I can’t tell you exactly when a Dallas reporter first asked what I thought about biological males competing in women’s sports. She asked me to comment after the college swimmer who had competed in the men’s swimming competition was allowed to compete against women the following year. I had the opinion, and still maintain, that the NCAA’s decision to permit a swimmer who had previously competed as a man to compete against women the next year was illogical and unjust to the women swimmers who had dedicated countless hours to their sport. The media applauded the biological man who competed in the women's swimming competition.”

“Did you speak with Mr. Benton before you came out against trans athletes?”

“No, if my support of women’s sports had any bearing on my golf course designs for Mr. Benton’s developments, it was positive. I’m known for designing golf courses with the whole family in mind. In the past, we referred to the forward tees as women's tees, but the designers placed those tees as an afterthought and built and maintained them accordingly."

"Some experts say that allowing trans athletes to compete in women's sports will benefit everyone. Why do you disagree?"

"Can you let me look at anything you claim shows experts say allowing trans athletes to compete in women's sports will benefit everyone?"

Morgan's eyes widen.

"Who are these experts, and tell me their claimed expertise?" Lauren says.

Morgan shows me a document and then shows Lauren.

"One expert is Doctor Lewis Dawson. As you will see in this article, he claims a person's genetic makeup and internal and external reproductive anatomy are not useful indicators of athletic performance. We should not treat her physiological characteristics related to athletic performance differently from the physiological characteristics of a non-transgender woman. Isn't it true that you competed against women golfers who were bigger, stronger, and hit their tee shots further than you?"

"Yes."

Morgan takes the article back and changes the question.

"You gained a great deal by competing in sports. Isn't that true?"

"I owe my career and enjoyment in life to competing in golf from when I was a young girl?"

"But you want to deny trans athletes the same life-changing opportunities."

Lauren takes a deep breath. "They can continue to compete against men. If there are enough trans athletes in a given sport, we can create a new category and have men's, women's, and trans competitions."

"So, as Dr. Dawson has found, what difference does it make if that person transitions to becoming a woman and wants the opportunity to compete in sports?"

Lauren takes a moment to gather her thoughts, shifting in her seat before answering. "I understand the argument, but there are physical differences between male and female athletes that no one can ignore. Testosterone levels, bone density, muscle mass, and lung capacity contribute to athletic performance. And while a trans woman may undergo hormone therapy to lower their testosterone levels, it doesn't completely erase the advantages they may have gained during puberty."

Morgan leans forward towards Lauren. His eyes narrowed as he speaks. "Are you aware that studies have shown that hormone therapy reduces muscle mass and strength, which would put trans athletes at a disadvantage?"

Lauren refuses to waver from her position.

"Wouldn't you agree that transgender athletes vary in athletic ability like cisgender athletes?"

"Yes," Lauren answers.

"Are you aware that trans people, particularly trans women, face disproportionate rates of violence?"

"I read that, and my heart goes out to anyone who faces violence. But that doesn't mean I support trans women competing in women's sports."

Morgan's voice is crisp. "When you spoke out against trans athletes competing against women, did you give any thought to how your public statements might impact Benton Land Company sales?"

"If anything, Benton Land Company would experience a positive impact because my golf course designs and other ideas make the Benton Land Company developments appealing to families. The families buying properties in Benton Land Company developments agree with my support of women's sports. Those families know my work and the money I have donated to encourage girls to participate in golf and other sports."

I glance over at Robert Benton. I notice that Robert Benton's jaw is clenched, and I see a muscle twitching in his temple. He drums his fingers impatiently on the table. He wasn't expecting Lauren to defend her position so effectively. I give Lauren a reassuring smile.

Morgan suggests we take a fifteen-minute break. When we step into the hall, Lauren's shoulders sag. She rubs her temples as if trying to fend off a headache; her movements slow and deliberate.

"I know you're feeling worn out, Lauren," I begin, placing a reassuring hand on her shoulder. "But remember why you're here. You've got the expertise and the strength to match wits with Morgan. Focus on each question he asks. Just breathe and take it slow. We've prepared for this, and you're ready. You've faced tougher challenges before and come out on top. Just stay centered. You've got this."

Lauren grins and grabs my hand.

When we reconvene, Morgan is even more aggressive than before. He hammers away at Lauren, questioning her motives and twisting her words, apparently putting on a show for his client. But Lauren remains steadfast, never once losing her composure.

He inquires, "Miss West, don't you think a person should have the freedom to select their gender and pursue the sexual lifestyle of their choice without facing any criticism?"

Lauren says, "A person should be able to choose without criticism from others, but that has nothing to do with whether a biological male should be able to compete in women's sports."

Morgan smirks, "Oh, but it does, Miss West. It has everything to do with it. If a person identifies as a woman, then they should be allowed to compete as a woman, regardless of their biological sex. To deny them that right is discrimination."

"Mr. Morgan, is there a question somewhere in your diatribe?"

Morgan could turn what he said into a question by adding, 'isn't it?' at the end of his statement. That would make Lauren answer why it's not discrimination. Morgan decides to leave his statement as is with no answer from Lauren.

After what feels like hours, Morgan ends the deposition. Lauren and I file out of the conference room. Lauren's eyes have dark circles under them. Lauren doesn't ask, and I don't volunteer that I am mentally exhausted. I am deeply worried about my ability to perform as Lauren's lawyer in a two-week trial if I'm already this exhausted after just one day of her deposition.

We walk in silence for a few moments before Lauren speaks up. "Can we stop here and grab a drink?"

We stop at Sam's Bar and Grill. The atmosphere is electric as people flock to the downtown Dallas bar for happy hour. We find a quiet booth in the corner and sit close together, facing out. Lauren orders a glass of white wine, and I order a beer.

When the waitress brings our drinks, I ask, "Are you okay?"

Lauren looks at me and says, "Sometimes I think it would have been better if I had never offered my opinion when the reporter first asked about transgender athletes competing in women's sports. I could have said I hadn't studied enough to have an answer, and I'm confident the trans supporters would have left me alone."

"I understand. Don't beat yourself up. You handled yourself well today. It may not have been easiest, but you did the right thing when you supported women's sports. Hopefully, because of your good work, Megan won't be competing against biological men when she plays soccer in college."

"The one thing I've learned from this experience is Robert Benton loves conflict, and he'll never admit he made a mistake. He's weaponized the media to attack me and to silence me. His surrogates in the media question every statement I've made and twist what I have said supporting girls and women athletes. I'm tired from the fight. Heck, half of our country believes I'm a folk hero, and the other half believes I'm a bigot, hates me, and wants to harm me. I don't want to let the haters bring me down. But I'd prefer to go forward without having people who hate me, want to harass me, and some that even do me harm."

"You are wrong on the percentages," I say. "It's far more than half of the country that holds you in high regard as a hero, and it's far less than half of the country views you as a bigot. But it sounds like you've given this much thought."

"I have. I don't appreciate that some percentage of people in this country hate me. Many people who admire me think I had a wonderful life playing on the LPGA tour. I never told the interviewer what I was going through when she interviewed me. I often felt lonely and depressed. I had one close friend, Courtney Barr. Looking back, I realize my most enjoyable times playing golf were as part of my high school team and the UT team, and the highlight of my career was playing with US golfers twice in the Solheim Cup. Courtney Barr was my partner, and we won all the team matches."

"I've watched the Solheim Cup matches when you teamed with Courtney Barr," I say. "You played well together."

As Lauren reminisced, I noticed her eyes soften and a tender smile forming on her lips. She looks distant, lost in the memories of the competition, pride evident in the slight lift of her chin and the spark that lit up her gaze. I decide to change the subject.

"Tell me why you chose to design golf courses for Robert Benton."

"Benton is a narcissist. But he allowed me to build golf course developments for families to enjoy, paid me well, and for the most part, left me alone. I can't begin to tell you how much it meant when a mom or dad told me they and their kids love coming to our golf course development because it is their happy place."

Lauren shakes her head. "I'm getting sick of this case and being unable to work. Thomas Caldwell is offering me top dollar to work for him. I want to settle with Benton right now. I want to get back to the feeling I had creating something families will enjoy. Beat up Benton in his deposition and make him squirm like I did. Then, meet with Morgan about a settlement."

I ask, "You said that Benton won't settle with you because he wants to prevent you from working with Caldwell? What makes you think differently now?"

"There's nothing different. But we never approached him to find out. Maybe he's also tired of fighting."

"Benton is counting on you being desperate."

"I don't care. For me, the money is less important now than my mental health."

"Okay, there's only one way to find out. I'll schedule Benton's deposition. Then, I'll approach Morgan and see if Benton will reasonably settle your case."

Lauren takes a slow and deliberate sip of her wine. Setting her glass down, she lightly brushes her fingers over the back of my hand, the touch lingering long enough to be suggestive.

I’m not sure how I should respond.

She looks at me and says, “I’ve been so stressed out about this case and facing Morgan today, I’ve found it almost impossible to relax. Let’s order another drink and take it easy.” I call the server over. When she arrives, Lauren orders a Bombay Sapphire Martini up, with an olive and no vermouth.

“Are you sure you want to go from wine to a martini?”

“Yes, I need a martini after what I went through today.”

After our server brings our second round of drinks, Lauren takes a few sips of her Bombay Sapphire. “I needed this,” she says, leaning in closer, placing her hand on my knee, and moving it slowly up my thigh.

I've had numerous explicit thoughts about her. I’m feeling it, and I smell that Black Opium perfume. But it's been so long that I'm worried about humiliating myself. I’ve lost my mojo.

I reach down and touch her hand. I can’t tell her I’m worried about humiliating myself. Instead, I say, “Lauren, we are at a point when you need me to be your lawyer and maintain our professional relationship. I’ve thought about having a personal relationship with you, and I know it would be special, but like I said, you need me to be your lawyer now.”

Lauren looks at me. Her gaze wavers. She bites her lower lip and pulls her hand from my thigh. She takes a deep breath. When she speaks, her voice is soft and strained. “You’re right, Luke. I’m sorry. I want you to be my lawyer. I think I let my emotions get the best of me.”

I want to tell her there’s no reason to be sorry, but I can’t find the right words to follow after saying that. She takes another sip of her martini and glances at me again. I want to lean in and kiss her, but I don’t.

After I pay the check and we leave the bar, my eyes are drawn to the White Dodge Charger parked a half block away. The same man from before is leaning against the car, his camera hanging at his side. I see what looks to be a woman in the passenger seat. Lauren, unaware, chats animatedly about our case and the upcoming celebration.

She pauses, turning to me with a warm smile. Before I can say anything, she leans in, kisses me on the cheek, and hugs me tightly. Her embrace is reassuring, but my gaze shifts back to the man, who now appears to be adjusting his camera.

Lauren waves goodbye and heads to her car, oblivious to the scene unfolding behind her. I’m uneasy as I watch the man open his car door, slide inside, and say something to his passenger.

Once I'm in my own car and pulling out of the parking lot, my phone buzzes with a new text from Lauren. I park in my garage and pull out my phone, heart pounding, to read: 'Let's win our case against Benton, and after that, celebrate. Have you ever been to Paris?'

I stare at the message; the weight of the photo Benton's private investigator just took of us hangs heavy in my mind. I won't spoil her mood. Not now. I slide the phone back into my pocket, resolving to keep this unsettling detail to myself.

Chapter 17

Lauren

Several conservative media outlets ask me to appear on their shows or offer a comment for an article they are doing about the states legislating to deny transgender athletes' participation in high school girls' and college women's sports. Having walked through gauntlets of protestors yelling obscenities at me and throwing objects at me, I tell them I've made my position on girl's and women's sports clear, and I have no further comments.

I want to move on until I read a headline from a national sports network. It reads, "Why Lauren West's Support of Women's Sports is Both Ignorant and Bigoted." Among other things, the writer makes the point that there are only a handful of trans girls and women competing, and if I deny them the right to compete, they will have no options. The female sportscaster calls me a bigoted snob and somehow claims that not only am I transphobic, but I am also a racist.

I couldn't believe what I was reading. How could someone twist my words so far out of context? I never meant to exclude anyone, including trans girls and women. They should be allowed to compete against each other or continue competing against boys and men. I support girls and women. I felt hurt and angry, but mostly, I wanted to set the record straight.

I contact the network, hoping to speak with the writer or the sportscaster who had accused me of such horrible things. But instead, no one responds. They have no interest in hearing my side of the story.

So, I took matters into my own hands. I wrote a blog post detailing my views on women's sports and how I do not discriminate against anyone, regardless of their gender identity. I spoke about the importance of creating a level playing field for all athletes while also acknowledging the unique challenges that trans athletes may face.

To my surprise, my response went viral. People who had never heard of me before were sharing it, and I received messages of support from high school girls, college women athletes, and parents alike. I even got invited to speak on a panel about women's sports at a national conference.

With one blog response to a misleading article, I was back in the news and the subject of well-organized protests.

A week later, Luke will take Robert Benton's deposition. After spending days being grilled by Harvey Morgan, I can take my mind off of the social media attacks.

Like my deposition, Benton's will be captured on video by a court reporter. On the scheduled day for Robert Benton's deposition, I watch from the window of Luke's Hill Country office as Benton arrives in his sleek Mercedes, a stark contrast to the rustic charm of the office's surroundings. Harvey Morgan is by his side, both men radiating an aura of superiority. A lady who I've never seen before is with them.

The warm glow of the Hill Country sunlight pours through the conference room windows, casting long, dramatic shadows across the room. Benton strides in; his presence is deliberately inflated, his attempts to dominate the space evident in his puffed chest and haughty posture. Yet, his stubby legs and stout physique only serve to highlight the incongruity between his self-important air and his actual physicality. His eyes are sharp and calculating while scanning the room with the predatory intensity of a hunter assessing his prey. The smirk on his lips is both arrogant and chilling, a clear display of his confidence and contempt. Morgan follows along with the lady.

I gaze at her and then back at Luke. I can almost feel the room grow colder despite the sunlight streaming in, the tension palpable as Benton and Morgan settle into their seats, ready for the battle of wills that is about to unfold.

Luke straightens up and clears his throat, his eyes locked on Morgan. With a firm, authoritative tone, he says, “Who is accompanying you and Mr. Benton?”

Morgan introduces her with a practiced nonchalance. “This is Carlotta Hampton, our trial consultant,” he says, clearly enjoying the surprise on our faces.

Luke raises an eyebrow and meets my gaze. His look says it all: this doesn’t add up.

Carlotta extends a hand to Luke, her smile both charming and calculated. “It’s a pleasure to meet you, Mr. Hartley. I’ve heard great things about you.”

Luke takes her hand, momentarily distracted by her presence. “Likewise, Ms. Hampton,” he replies.

She turns her attention to me; her gaze is sharp and assessing. “And you must be Lauren West. I followed your impressive career on the LPGA tour.”

I nod, trying to keep myself cool. There's something disarming about her. "Thank you, Ms. Hampton."

As we sit in the worn leather chairs on one side of the conference table, a charged silence fills the room. Benton, Morgan, and Hampton take their seats with an air of confidence. Benton sits at the end of the antique wooden table, Morgan across from Luke. Hampton, with a slow, deliberate grace, settles into the chair next to Morgan. Luke glances in her direction, clearly affected by her presence.

As Luke shuffles papers, preparing to start, a palpable tension lingers in the air. I have a feeling that this deposition will be anything but routine. The deposition begins, and while Luke's questions are sharp and precise, I notice his eyes flickering toward Carlotta every now and then as if trying to gauge her reactions. Her calm and inscrutable expression never wavers, adding to the unease.

A videographer is recording the deposition. Benton sits straight up in his chair. I can see from the corner of my eye that his right foot is rapidly tapping up and down under the table. I write a note on the legal pad in front of me and show it to Luke.

Luke nods, and I continue watching Benton's right foot shake under the table. I notice a smirk on his face as if he was about to come out fighting for the first round of a boxing match.

Luke clears his throat and leans forward, placing his hands on the table. "Mr. Benton, thank you for coming in today," Luke begins; his voice is even and professional. "Before we begin, I'd like to remind you that your deposition is being recorded, and you are under oath. Please answer all questions truthfully and to the best of your ability."

Benton nods, his eyes avoiding mine as he fidgets with his hands in his lap. Benton glares at Luke and snaps, "This isn't my first deposition, Mr. Hartley. I'm a busy man, so do get on with it."

I laugh when Luke replies, "But, Mr. Benton, it's your first rodeo in Corona County, Texas."

Benton doesn't laugh. "Then, get on with it," he says.

"Okay, Mr. Benton," Luke starts, "could you please state your name and occupation for the record?"

Benton leans forward, adjusting his tie, and hesitates momentarily before replying, "Robert Michael Benton. I'm a real estate developer, and I created a software company that I sold in 2010."

As the deposition begins, I can sense the tension in the room. Luke asks Benton about his background and education. Benton answers them curtly, in monosyllabic replies, clearly uninterested in making small talk. I learn for the first time that Benton dropped out of college.

Morgan objects to each question. He's determined to make Benton's deposition as difficult as possible. Luke remains calm and continues to ask basic questions about Benton's Silicon Valley business dealings. After Morgan objects, Benton answers curtly and dismissively, clearly not amused by the process.

That said, Benton appears eager to brag about himself and how he grew up in a middle-class family but became wealthy during the technology boom. His arrogance is showing through with each answer. The smirk on his face gives him away. He thinks he's the smartest person in the room and can easily handle Luke.

"And when did you first meet Lauren West?"

"I first met Miss West when I played golf in an LPGA Pro-Am event."

Benton coughs to clear his throat and then continues. "During the round, I told Miss West I was interested in luxury home developments. At the time, the Silicon Valley economy was on fire.

Many successful entrepreneurs were looking to build second homes in luxury developments. After the event, your client approached me and shared her idea of developing luxury golf course communities where golf was only one of the features appealing to wealthy young families. She also told me that most golf courses, even ones the LPGA played on, were designed with women as an afterthought."

"What happened after that?" Luke asks.

"Lauren continued playing on the LPGA Golf Tour, and I started looking for land to develop golf course communities."

"When did you next have a conversation with Miss West?"

I look over at Spade. He's staring at me.

"It was after she retired from the tour and had gone back and got her master's in landscape architecture. I believe that was about five years after we first met. I reached out to her because I had only been moderately successful in implementing her vision of family-oriented and luxury golf courses."

Luke asks Benton about my contract to design golf courses. Benton tells Luke I demanded a share of the net profits as part of my contract. Benton says I claimed that he was making money because I had the original concept of a family-oriented development, and I found the land and made the most of it in my golf course designs.

Luke asks if Benton believes what I claimed is true.

Benton nods, a smug expression on his face. “That's correct,” he says. “I may have hired Miss West, but she was only one piece of the puzzle. The golf course wasn't the only thing that made these developments successful. Many other factors were at play, and I was responsible for all of them.” Benton leans back in his chair with that same smirk as he finishes his last sentence.

Luke raises an eyebrow; his gaze is steady. “Interesting,” he says softly. “And what, exactly, were these other factors?”

For me, it’s funny. Like every conversation I had with him, Benton can’t keep his hands by his side or below the table. With each answer, he waves his arms to emphasize his points. “Among other things,” Benton says, “I have contacts with most of the wealthy clients who bought the property, built homes, and joined the country clubs. You could have the best-designed golf course in the world, but it's worthless if no one buys land and homes.”

“Why is there a morals clause in the design contracts?”

Morgan objects, saying Benton’s reason is irrelevant, and Luke instructs Benton to answer the question.

Benton says, “It serves to protect Benton Land Company's investment, allowing Benton Land Company to separate itself if Miss West engages in bad behavior and prevents her from obtaining any more money from the company.”

“What caused you to believe that your conclusion that Miss West had breached the morals clause of the design contract was a material breach of contract?”

Benton raises his eyebrows and widens his eyes. He opens his mouth to speak, then closes it again, his gaze darting from Luke to Morgan. He shifts in his seat. Finally, he says, “I’m sorry, Mr. Hartley. I’m not a lawyer, and I don’t understand your question.”

Luke shows Benton the design contract language, stating that Benton Land Company could terminate my design contract and avoid paying the bonus if I materially breached the contract.

“What makes you believe that Miss West’s support of girls’ and women’s sports is a material breach of her golf design contract?”

Benton reads the provision and looks at Morgan for help. He must not have thoroughly read the Lake Tierra Golf Course Design Contract, and Morgan must not have reviewed the material breach provision with him before the deposition.

Morgan objects, saying that a material breach of contract is a question of law, not fact.

Luke tells Benton to answer the question.

"Making hateful comments against transgender athletes in the media is a material breach of contract because those comments caused Benton Land Company to lose sales."

Over the next hour, Luke asks Benton specific questions about each luxury development. I assume Luke will revisit the morals and material breach clauses in cross-examination at the trial. Luke has Benton describe each golf course I designed for him. Benton describes his luxury golf course developments throughout the United States, Canada, and Mexico. I nod several times while jotting down notes.

As Benton speaks about his luxurious golf course developments, I know my golf course design was the reason each development attracted wealthy people who got to experience such luxury. The way he describes the lush greens, the sparkling lakes, the creeks, and the tree-lined fairways, I take pride in what I had created. I feel like an artist whose canvas was one hundred fifty to two hundred acres.

At this point, Morgan suggests we take a break for lunch. Luke agrees. As Morgan, Benton, and Hampton head towards the door, I watch them intently. They file out of the office, and I see them get into Benton's Mercedes. Hampton pauses before entering the passenger door. Her gaze lingers on me, sharp and unyielding, like a predator assessing its prey. I turn away from the window, unsettled by the intensity of her stare.

I turn to Luke. "Hampton's staring at me. It's like she's sizing me up or something."

Luke's eyes narrow as he takes in my expression. "What do you mean?"

"She's just watching me, and her eyes are rarely leaving my face. It's like she's trying to stare me down to intimidate me."

"Do you want me to tell Morgan to instruct Hampton to stop staring at you?"

"No, that would just reaffirm that she's intimidating me. Where are we going for lunch?"

Luke tells me he ordered lunch for us to eat in the office so we can talk freely. When Luke's receptionist brings us lunch, I see Luke has ordered a veggie sub for me with a side of fruit. As I eat, I can't shake the feeling of Carlotta's eyes on me. Her presence is a constant reminder of the calculated mind games at play, adding another layer of tension to an already stressful situation.

Luke leans back in his chair and runs his fingers through his hair. "I'm convinced Morgan brought Hampton to evaluate Benton's answers to my questions and adjust them before the trial."

"Then, why is she staring at me?"

"She's probably evaluating how jurors might perceive you." He takes a bite from his panini. "How would you feel if I bring up Benton's sexual harassment history during questions this afternoon? That would give Hampton something to think about."

"No, don't you dare," I reply, my voice is sharp with anxiety. "Benton threatened to ruin me if I ever brought up his sexual harassment. Morgan has destroyed women who have accused Benton. He's notorious for tearing apart women's lives in court, making them look like liars and opportunists. Morgan would do the same to me."

Luke's expression hardens. "I understand your concern, Lauren. But we need to expose him for what he is."

"I get that, but not this way. Bringing it up now could backfire. Morgan will twist everything I say and make it look like I'm trying to defame him out of spite. Morgan will dredge up every personal detail about me to discredit my character. I've seen him do it to other women, and I don't want him to do it to me."

Benton's threat wasn't just an empty boast. In the tightly knit world of luxury golf community developers and golf course designers, a single smear on my name could be catastrophic. Benton knows that if he can embarrass and ruin me, he can effectively forever tarnish my reputation. He has the connections and the influence to spread damaging rumors, undermine my credibility, and push me out of the industry. He's holding this threat over me, knowing that the fear of losing everything might be enough to keep me silent.

Benton wants to keep his proclivities secret. That's why each of his young women victims has signed a non-disclosure agreement. As far as the public knows, Benton is a squeaky clean gentleman. So, it's important to him that I keep it a secret.

Luke nods understandingly. "I see your point. It's your privacy and your reputation at stake here," he says. "Alright, Lauren. I won't bring it up. We'll focus on the contract and the unpaid bonus. Based on his testimony this morning, I have the sense that he doesn't remember or believes we don't know about the original marketing brochures and scorecards and the email he sent to Steven Strong."

I nod, appreciating his support. "Thank you, Luke. I just don't want to give them any more ammunition."

While I continue eating, my cell phone rings, and I see the call is from New York. It's a liberal news network calling again. "Miss West, would you care to comment on the federal appeals court decision dismissing the case brought by high school girls challenging trans athletes competing against them?"

I feel a surge of unease. She's blindsiding me. "I don't know anything about the case, so I can't comment on it."

The journalist's tone becomes sharper. "The girls filed a lawsuit in 2020 claiming their state's trans-inclusive sports policy violated their civil rights and violated Title IX. The court of appeals ruled there was no basis for the girls' claim that transgender athletes put the girls at a competitive disadvantage. That's directly in conflict with what you have been advocating in states passing laws banning trans athletes from competing against girls."

I feel my jaw tightening. "I told you I'm not familiar with the case. As you know, all that I am advocating is that girls and women deserve the right to compete fairly and not to have naked men in their locker rooms. I will continue to support girls and women in their right to compete in sports fairly. If you do your research, you'll find many examples of trans athletes taking away victories and top finishes by biological girls. Some girls are the very best in their sport until they must compete against a trans athlete."

The reporter presses further. "Miss West, are you aware that the federal government has issued a rule that declares that it's unlawful discrimination to treat transgender students differently from their classmates, including by restricting bathroom access."

I'm getting frustrated now. I want to blow her off. "Yes, and how stupid and how dangerous could that be? I wouldn't want a daughter to be exposed to a naked teenage boy in a girl's locker room. It's also a ruse to require states to allow transgender athletes to compete against high school girls and college women. I'm also aware that the rule has been successfully challenged in a number of states and cannot be enforced in those states."

"Well, Miss West, we know you've taken it from the far right's playbook. Do you even know how many transgender athletes are competing against girls and women? Did you know that the percentage of adults who identify as transgender is less than one percent?"

I'm angry now.

"I don't believe the number of transgender athletes or the percentage of adults who identify as transgender is relevant. If only one high school girl loses the opportunity to qualify for a championship, or one college woman finishes second in a race against a transgender swimmer or track and field athlete, in each case, that is one too many. If one female athlete is hurt, or one young girl is confronted in a locker room by a naked biological male who says he is a girl, in each case, that is one too many."

"So, it's okay with you if boys and men who identify as girls and women are not allowed to compete in girls' and women's sports even if they become victims of hate crimes?"

"You know that is not okay with me. Biological boys and men who identify as girls and women can compete against other biological males or other transgender individuals who identify as girls and women. It's never okay for anyone to harm or threaten to harm any person who identifies as a girl or man. I understand your points, and even though I'm afraid I have to disagree, I believe it is important to have a civil debate on the issue and not call people with whom you disagree unflattering names."

"Then, I assume you aren't aware of the trans golfer who won a golf tournament and received death threats. She was forced to delete her social media accounts."

"No, I was not aware. But, I suspect you are aware that I've received dozens of death threats, not only for me but also for my mother."

I could hear her hang up before I finished my sentence. I sit there for a moment, trying to get over my upset. The tension lingers, leaving me feeling vulnerable. The media scrutiny is relentless, and every word I say seems to ripple outward, affecting not just the case but my public image and advocacy. I should have refused to answer when I saw the area code.

Chapter 18

Luke

Lauren returns to our table, her face pale and eyes wide. She takes a deep breath before speaking. “I just got off the phone,” she says. “It's starting again. The protestors... they're planning to show up at my house tonight. They’ve been leaving threatening messages on my phone. Some of them are really disturbing.”

I lean forward, concerned. “What kind of threats?”

Lauren swallows hard as she places her phone on the table. “One of them said they know where I live, and they’re going to make sure I regret speaking out. Another message mentioned my family and said they hope I enjoy living in fear.” She pauses, glancing around the room as if expecting danger. “They said they'll be outside my door with signs and megaphones. They plan to make a scene, get the neighbors involved, and ruin any sense of peace I have left.”

I feel a surge of anger mixed with a protective instinct. “Lauren, I'm so sorry you're going through this. We need to make sure you're safe. Have you contacted the police?”

She nods. “Yes, they said they'd increase patrols, but... you know how it is. They can't be there all the time. I just don't understand why people are so cruel. I'm only trying to stand up for what I believe in.”

“Focus on Benton for the rest of the day,” I suggest, trying to steady her nerves. “We'll deal with the protestors and threats later. Right now, we need to stay focused on your case.”

Lauren nods, taking a deep breath to steady herself. “You're right. We need to take Benton down.”

We return to the conference room. I’m even more determined to win Lauren’s case. The videographer starts recording the deposition. I look directly at Benton and ask, “How do the sales of the developments where Lauren designed the golf course compare to those designed by others?”

Benton says he’s not sure, which prompts me to bring out the financial records for each development and get Benton to admit that the developments where Lauren designed the golf course sold dozens more lots and gained almost one hundred more golf course memberships than the other developments.

While showing Benton his financial records, I point out that each project where Lauren designed the golf course made a substantial profit.

I've caught Benton a little off balance. After spending hours bragging about himself, Benton's answers to my deposition questions regarding the profits of his developments are far more evasive. "That was the gross profit," Benton says. "From the gross profit, you must deduct the advertising cost, Benton Land Company management fees, and other miscellaneous costs."

"Mr. Benton, is the Lake Tierra development your most profitable?"

Benton pauses for a moment and looks over at his lawyer.

"I'm not sure."

I lean forward across the table and lock eyes with Benton's. "Mr. Benton, I have here an article from the California Business Journal where you mentioned that the Lake Tierra Hill Country Development is, and I quote, 'by far my most successful venture.'" I slide the printed article across the table towards Benton.

Benton glances at the article; his expression unreadable. He then slowly lifts his eyes to meet, a slight smirk forming on his lips. He shrugs his shoulders as if he's blowing off my question.

"Mr. Hartley, I'm in real estate. We want to create sales by bragging about our properties. I wanted Californians reading the article to come look at my Lake Tierra development."

His nonchalance annoys me.

"Mr. Benton, what made you believe that Lauren West's support of girls' and women's sports gave you the right to terminate her design contract?"

Benton leans back in his chair, exuding an air of superiority. "Mr. Hartley, living and working in your small world, you obviously do not know that many wealthy people support the right of transgender athletes to compete in sports," he replies in a condescending voice. "I terminated her contract because her campaign against those children and adults caused a substantial loss in my sales."

I nod, feigning I believe him while knowing Benton's response is bullshit. I know Benton is holding back and hiding something from me. But I'm not letting him get away with it. I lean forward again, staring intently into Benton's eyes. He stares back at me.

I take a sip of water before returning my look at Robert Benton. "Mr. Benton, how do you know you lost sales?" I ask.

Benton's smirk widens. He likes this. “Potential Lake Tierra clients told me they would not buy a lot in a community where Miss West designed the golf course. I also read interviews in the news and saw interviews of potential buyers.”

I believe Robert Benton or Harvey Morgan paid people to go public with those statements. Before he can go further, I ask. “And how did you determine how much in sales you lost?”

Benton leans forward. His eyes are cold. “I made an estimate based partly on the percentage of people in the US who support the right of transgender athletes to play sports.”

“How did you determine how much in sales you lost?” I ask.

“I made an estimate based partly on the percentage of people in the US who support the right of transgender athletes to play sports.”

Benton had just explained how he had denied Lauren’s bonus on Lake Tierra. I go over his estimate of lost sales. It is nothing but a wild guess at best. I conclude he made up a big number to scare Lauren and bolster his termination for cause argument.

I’m shocked by Benton’s audacity in claiming his company lost sales because of Lauren. If anything, his company had increased sales because of Lauren.

By this time, I'm tired. I can't let Benton see it in my eyes. I'm worried he'll think he's wearing me down.

I tap my pen on the table in a slow and deliberate rhythm. "So, you're saying you terminated Lauren's contract because you lost sales, and you base that on an estimate? Not on actual figures?"

Benton's eyes flicker with irritation. "I made a reasonable projection based on the data available."

"Mr. Benton, do you have any proof that a potential client declined to buy property in any of your golf course developments because Miss West designed the golf course?"

"Several of my clients, including famous athletes and celebrities, complained about Miss West's discriminatory and hateful statements about transgender athletes."

"Who were the celebrities and athletes?"

Benton looks over at his lawyer. Morgan nods.

"I'm not at liberty to say."

"Mr. Benton, if you claim you terminated Miss West's contract because your clients Complained about her statements about transgender athletes competing against girls and women, you can't refuse to identify those clients."

Morgan interjects, “We don’t plan to call any celebrities as witnesses.”

Benton raises a hand to silence his lawyer. “I’ll answer your question,” he says. “Two of my clients complained about Miss West’s statements. I won’t tell you who they are, but I will say that they are both very influential people in the entertainment industry.”

I raise an eyebrow. “Mr. Benton, answer the question.”

“I don’t remember which celebrities refused to buy land and golf membership at Lake Tierra, but I know it was several people.”

“And what did they say?”

Benton’s voice is strong and decisive, and our eyes meet. I don’t flinch. “They said that because of Miss West’s transphobic statements, trans athletes have faced prejudice, discrimination, misgendering, death threats, and violence.”

“Did any of your clients express their concerns in writing?”

“No, but thousands of people commented on Twitter and other social media sites.”

Thousands of negative comments, I bet. Any negative social media comments have Robert Benton's fingerprints all over them—a dirty trick he would pull without batting an eye. Those comments weren't a grassroots backlash—Benton most likely paid bots and trolls to flood social media, creating an illusion of widespread outrage. He likely laughed like hell thinking of when Lauren discovered what he'd made look like public opinion.

I type a note on my laptop: "Investigate the source of social media comments." It would unmask Benton's charade and show the court just how low this man will go to crush anyone who dared to oppose him.

"When did you decide that Miss West's position on women in sports had hurt your sales?"

"Almost immediately after she first made the comments. Twitter and other social media sites pushed back."

"And after Miss West offered her opinion that women should be allowed to compete in sports fairly, you terminated her design contract on the Lake Tierra project and took credit for her design of the Lake Tierra Golf Course. Isn't that what happened?"

"I made dramatic changes to her design before construction."

For the next thirty minutes, I get Benton to admit that Lauren found the land and created the initial drawings for each of the eighteen holes. I ask how the contractor constructed each hole differently than what Lauren designed. His testimony reflects the contractor made only minor changes. Lauren's design matches Which holes the contractor constructed as par threes, par fours, and par fives. The signature hole is the same as the one Lauren designed. The water is on the same holes as those that Lauren designed. He can only highlight minor changes he made, which are no more significant than the ones Lauren would have made if she had overseen the construction of the golf course.

I ask Benton if any other golf course architects approached him about designing the Lake Tierra golf course after he terminated Lauren's contract.

Benton flashes a cold smile and answers, "No, Mr. Hartley, I changed your client's design. I didn't need any help from another designer."

I'm inclined to ask him to describe each step of the design, but I decide to save it for the trial.

"What other golf courses have you designed?"

"Mr. Hartley, I never said I designed the golf courses. What I said is I fixed many errors your client made in her design. That's why I deserve the credit for the design of all of my Benton golf courses."

I feel like we've accomplished as much as we can, so I adjourn the deposition.

I ask Harvey Morgan to sit back down as we pick up to leave. When we are alone, I say, "Mr. Morgan, you know Benton will lose this case. Lauren designed the Lake Tierra Golf Course. Your client made no meaningful changes. Your client's claim that Lauren's stand in favor of girls' and women's sports is not a material breach of contract. To avoid Mr. Benton's embarrassment, your client names her as the designer and pays the bonus she has earned."

Morgan gives me a dismissive nod and waves his hand in dismissal. I've seen it in many photos before.

"Mr. Hartley, Robert Benton told me Lauren wants to be done with this."

How would Robert Benton know that?

Morgan continues, "She's very impatient, isn't she? Robert knows your client cannot afford to fight as long as she needs to get what you say she's entitled to. Robert will never say your client designed Lake Tierra Golf Course, and he's not paying her the bonus. Take that back to her and let her know the battle will only get worse for her. I will test your client's will and her patience every step along the way. You may win with a jury in your hick town, but I guarantee you we'll have grounds for appeal, and we can drag this case out for years."

Getting up from my chair I stumble slightly as I get to my feet. My breath catches, a shallow wheeze escaping before I can steady myself. Morgan's eyes narrow; his expression shifting from its usual sharpness to something almost resembling concern. He steps forward, his hand reaches for my arm.

"Are you sure you're okay?" His voice is softer, stripped of its usual edge. "It looks like the stress of the lawsuit is getting to you."

I pause, caught off guard by the genuine note in his tone. For a moment, I see past the ruthless attorney to the man beneath. I want to brush it off, to offer some trite remark, but the words won't come. Instead, I nod curtly and continue walking.

I tell Lauren what Morgan said, and she shakes her head. "I almost wish I'd never filed this lawsuit. I hate how long it's taking. I hate, I can't work while it is pending. I'm sure that even if we win, I will regret the toll it has taken on me."

I can't bring myself to say, I told you so. Instead, I say, "Let's win the case and make Benton pay you the full amount you deserve."

The next day, I receive a Motion for Summary Judgment from Morgan. If nothing else, this is Morgan's attempt to delay the trial and run up more expenses on our side. Morgan argues Benton had the right to terminate Lauren's golf course design contract at any time and take over the design of the Lake Tierra Golf Course. He further alleges there are no "net profits" on the Lake Tierra Hill Country Development project, meaning his company is not obligated to pay Lauren any bonus.

I file a reply to the motion, contending that it's simply another tactic to delay the trial. I argue that there are many factual disputes, including the design of the award-winning golf course, protecting girls' and women's sports under the Constitutional right of free speech, and the legality of Mr. Benton denying Miss West's bonus by artificially increasing expenses through his firm's charging of unreasonable management fees.

Judge Hawkins sets a date to hear the motion, and sadly for us, delays the opening date of the trial. As expected, Lauren is upset. I try to console her, but each day that goes by upsets her.

When I was a young lawyer, a friend once told me, "Litigation is a rich man's sport." Robert Benton is a living example. He's a rich man, and litigation is a sport for him. Benton knows Lauren has run out of money to fund the case. Benton knows it, and he's taking advantage of his wealth to delay the trial and make it as expensive as possible.

After a long day, I head for home. The sun is setting, so I pull down my visor. My mind drifts from my driving to the events of the day. I think of ways I could have, should have, put more fear in Robert Benton. He probably thinks he got the best of me.

I'm brought back to reality when my phone buzzes. The screen lights up with his mother's name. I'm not sure what she wants. She knows I've been in a deposition all day. I press the hands-free button. "Hey, Mom. What's up?"

"Luke," my mom's voice cracked, barely above a whisper. "You need to get home. Right now."

"Why, Mom? What's going on?"

"There are people." My mom's voice is trembling; her words are coming out in a rush. "Protestors. They're in your yard. The girls are so scared. I've tried to text you for the last hour."

I can hear muffled sounds in the background: angry voices, chants, and the faint sound of a bullhorn. I step on the gas and remind myself to stay calm.

I turned my phone off during Benton's deposition and only turned it back on when I got in my car.

"I'm on my way," I tell her, trying to picture the scene at my home. I end the call and press down even further on the accelerator. Thankfully, I'm on a county road with virtually no traffic.

As I turn onto my street, I see the sidewalk is swarming with protestors, their faces obscured by masks. They hold signs that read "Trans Rights are Human Rights," "Bigots Not Welcome," and "Stop the Hate, Luke Hartley!" The bullhorns blare, amplifying their chants.

I turn into by driveway and find it blocked. I get out. The throng of protestors opens a gauntlet lane for me to walk through. I catch snippets of their shouts.

"How can you defend hate?"

"This is just the beginning, Hartley!"

Ignoring them, I make my way to the front door, where my mother stands, and her face pale and strained. “Mom, where are Megan and Abby?”

“They’re in Abby’s bedroom,” she says, her voice barely audible over the din. “They’re scared.”

I quickly nod and hurry down the hallway, feeling concerned for Abby. As I enter Abby’s bedroom, I find her huddled on the bed, rocking back and forth; her eyes filled with terror. She’s clutching a stuffed animal, her knuckles white. Megan is beside her, gently rubbing her back, whispering soothing words.

“It's okay, Abby,” Megan says softly, her voice calm and steady. “Dad’s here now. The police are coming, and they’ll make the protestors go away.”

Abby looks up at me; her face pale and tense. “Dad, why are they here? Why are they so loud?” she asks, her voice barely audible.

I kneel in front of her, taking her hands in mine. “They’re upset about something, but the police are handling it. You’re safe inside, I promise.”

Abby's breathing is shallow and rapid, a sign of her growing anxiety. “I don't like the noise, Dad. It's too loud. It hurts.”

“I know, sweetheart,” I say, my heart breaking at the sight of her distress. “We'll make it stop soon. Try to focus on something else for now.”

Megan continues to console Abby, her own face showing signs of strain but determination. “Let's work on your puzzle book, Abby. You always feel better when we do that, remember?”

Abby nods slowly, her breathing starting to steady. “Okay, Megan,” she whispers, clutching the stuffed animal tighter.

The doorbell rings, and I turn and go back to the front door. Tommy Todd is standing there. “Luke, what’s going on? We’ve never had a protest in Corona County. Why are these out-of-town protestors in front of your house?”

“They’re here to intimidate me by scaring my mother and daughters and get me to abandon Lauren.”

I’ve never abandoned a client before a trial. But I’ve never had protestors in my front yard.

Chapter 19

Lauren

After several weeks, Luke calls and tells me Judge Hawkins denied Benton's Motion for Summary Judgment. "The judge saw right through their tactics," he says with a hint of satisfaction in his voice.

He reads from notes on what he told one media reporter. "Harvey Morgan, on Robert Benton's behalf, filed this Motion for Summary Judgment, not because he believed Judge Hawkins would grant the motion, but rather to delay the trial and run up Miss West's expenses. It was a frivolous motion Mr. Morgan could have filed months ago. Robert Benton is using his wealth to delay the inevitable loss in court. Lauren and I now trust that Judge Hawkins will schedule a trial as soon as possible."

As I listen, I'm relieved. But I know this battle is far from over. "Thank you, Luke. I appreciate everything you're doing," I say. "Benton keeps delaying the trial."

"Hang in there, Lauren. We're making progress, but Benton and Morgan aren't done playing their games," he replies.

Later that day, I'm relaxing in my living room, the news playing softly in the background. As I almost doze off, my phone buzzes with a notification. It's a news alert about my case. The headline reads: "Judge Denies Summary Judgment in West vs. Benton Case."

The reporter's voice fills the room. "In a significant development today, Judge Hawkins denied the Motion for Summary Judgment filed by Robert Benton's legal team. This decision paves the way for the case to go to trial. We reached out to Lauren West's attorney, Luke Hartley, for comment."

The screen switches to a clip of Luke speaking to reporters outside the courthouse. "Harvey Morgan filed this motion not to seek justice but to weaponize the judicial process against my client, Lauren West. This is an attempt by Robert Benton to use his vast resources to delay the trial and financially drain my client. But we remain steadfast. Judge Hawkins' ruling today is a step towards holding Mr. Benton accountable."

I feel a mix of emotions—relief that Judge Hawkins denied Benton's motion, but also a growing frustration at Benton's relentless tactics.

That evening, Luke calls again. His voice is tense. "Lauren, I just received another document from Morgan's team. They've filed a motion to compel discovery on several trivial matters. They previously asked for an exhaustive list of all your communications related to your golf course designs and your statements and comments about transgender athletes. Their request included personal emails and texts, including any communications with the LPGA. I told Morgan, we had provided all the documents he requested. They moved to compel the discovery of documents I've already provided them."

I slump in my chair, exhaustion creeping in. "Is this just another delay tactic?"

"Absolutely," Luke replies. "They're filing motions to bury us in paperwork and legal fees. It's their way of wearing you down, hoping you'll drop the case."

I take a deep breath, summoning my resolve. "What do we need to do next?"

"We'll respond promptly, of course, but I want to bring this up to Judge Hawkins. We must show the court that Benton is abusing the legal process."

A week later, I'm sitting in the courthouse hallway, my foot tapping anxiously against the floor. The steady hum of activity around me only heightens my nerves. Judge Hawkins scheduled the hearing for 1:00, and Luke is late. I glance at my watch and feeling uneasy. He was supposed to meet me here fifteen minutes before the hearing, and we're scheduled to meet with Judge Hawkins in five minutes.

I pull out my phone and shoot him a quick text: "Where are you? The hearing is in five minutes."

I wait, staring at the screen, willing it to light up with a reply. Nothing. My heart pounds in my chest as I imagine the worst-case scenarios. Is he okay? Did something happen on the way here? Or is it something else—something related to those memory lapses I've noticed more and more lately?

Unable to sit still any longer, I decide to call him. The phone rings twice before he picks up.

"Luke, where are you?" I ask, trying to keep the edge of panic out of my voice.

"Lauren, I'm on my way," he says, but his voice sounds flustered. "I had the wrong time on my phone. I'm sorry. I'll be there in five minutes."

I close my eyes, taking a deep breath to steady myself. "Okay, just hurry."

Hanging up, I slip my phone back into my bag and glance at the door to Judge Hawkins's chambers. Benton and Morgan have already arrived and are chatting quietly, their confident postures only adding to my anxiety. They've noticed Luke's absence, too, and it's clear they're enjoying it.

Finally, Luke appears in the hallway, slightly out of breath, and his expression is apologetic. "I'm sorry, Lauren," he says quietly as he joins me. "Let's go."

We walk into Judge Hawkins's chambers together. The judge is already seated, and his gaze sharpens as he looks at Luke.

"Mr. Hartley," Judge Hawkins says, his tone stern. "You're fifteen minutes late."

"Yes, Your Honor, I apologize," Luke replies, his voice is steady but strained. "There was a mix-up with the time on my phone."

Judge Hawkins narrows his eyes, clearly unimpressed. "Mr. Hartley, this is a hearing, not a casual appointment. In all the years you've practiced in my court, you've never been late."

"Yes, Your Honor," Luke says, a hint of tension creeping into his voice. I can feel his discomfort, and it only makes me more anxious about how this will affect our case.

Benton and Morgan exchange a glance, and I catch the slight smirk on Benton's face. They know exactly how much this little slip-up could work in their favor, and it makes me sick to my stomach.

We take our seats, and Judge Hawkins turns his attention to the documents in front of him. "Now, let's get to the matter at hand. Mr. Morgan, it seems your client is intent on filing motions to delay these proceedings. Mr. Hartley claims he's provided you with all the documents you requested."

As the judge speaks, I can't help but glance at Luke. He's focused, but I can see the strain in his eyes. I know he's under a lot of pressure, but I can't shake the worry that something more is going on. If Benton and Morgan sense any weakness, they'll pounce, and we can't afford that. Not now.

Morgan's smile is thin. "Your Honor, we have reason to believe that is not true. We believe there are damaging documents they have not provided."

Luke speaks. His voice is calm but firm. "Your Honor, this is a clear abuse of the discovery process. We've provided all the documents requested. The defendant's motions are meant to harass and financially drain Miss West."

Judge Hawkins nods thoughtfully. "I agree, Mr. Hartley. Mr. Morgan, you and your client are trying to delay this trial. I'm denying your motion to compel discovery on these matters. The court's resources are not to be wasted on such petty delays. This case will proceed to trial without further obstruction."

When we get up to leave, I see Luke's cell phone on his chair. I pick it up and look at the screen. It's his calendar for that day. He shows a hearing with Judge Hawkins at 1:00. How did he miss the time?

As we leave the courthouse, I'm still troubled by Luke not remembering the time of the hearing. Reporters swarm us, and I'm quickly on to something else. Luke gives a brief statement, echoing what he told me earlier. "This latest motion is another example of Benton using his wealth to weaponize the judicial system against Lauren. But we're not backing down. We're moving forward to trial and seeking justice."

I'm determined more than ever as I face the cameras. "Robert Benton can try all he wants to intimidate me and delay this case, but I won't him silence me. I stand for what's right, and I believe justice will be served."

Later that night, as I try to relax at home, my phone buzzes incessantly with notifications. Social media is ablaze with comments and posts about me. Many are supportive, but others are vicious, accusing me of all sorts of falsehoods and attacking my character.

I get a call from my friend, Courtney Barr. "Lauren, have you seen what's happening online? They're saying horrible things about you!"

"Yes, I've seen it," I reply, trying to keep my voice steady. "It's all part of Benton's plan to break me."

The following day, we meet at 8:00 AM at Luke's office. He's brought a nonfat vanilla latte for me, and he's sitting at his desk with an almost empty coffee cup.

I smile. "Thank you for thinking of me," I say as I pick up the latte.

"Harvey Morgan called me with an offer to settle your case," Luke says. Before I can ask, Luke says, "I almost didn't pass Benton's offer to you because it wasn't a legitimate offer. I was certain you'd reject receiving no money and taking away credit for your Lake Tierra golf course design."

I frown. "There's no way in hell I'll settle with Benton for no bonus. I'm spending my life savings, and I've had no work for over a year. Benton knows that's not really a serious offer. He knows that I'm bored out of my mind and running out of money to finance my lawsuit against him. But, there's no amount of money I would accept to give up credit for designing the Lake Tierra Golf course."

I take another sip of my latte, wanting to change the subject. "Do you remember I told you I had a plan for us to defeat Benton in court?"

"Sure," Luke says. "But you wouldn't tell me your plan."

I pause for effect. "Would you like to hear it now?"

"Yeah," Luke says.

I sit up in my chair, "I've spent the last few days contacting Lake Tierra owners. Several who I contacted have agreed to testify that they bought into the Lake Tierra Hill Country Development because Robert Benton represented that I had designed the golf course. They will testify that Benton misled them when they bought their property and paid initiation for the country club."

"That will be helpful," Luke says. "Give me their names so I can talk to them before the trial."

I pull out a list of each Lake Tierra homeowner's names, addresses, and telephone numbers willing to testify on my behalf.

"Don't you think with the homeowners' testimony; there's no way Benton can claim my interview caused a loss in sales."

"He can bring in others who could testify they decided not to buy property because they believe you are transphobic."

I finish my latte and change the subject.

"I want to stop talking about our case. I've been thinking."

"I need you to stay focused on winning our case. We have work to do to get you ready to testify."

"We have time to prepare me later. I'm sorry, I need a break. I've got to do something else, or I'll go stir-crazy. I'd like to teach Abby to play golf if that would be okay with you. After Abby asked me about learning to play golf, I've been looking into golf programs for autistic teens that I might start at Lake Tierra. Did you know that Ernie Els, the professional golfer, created a program called #GameON Autistic Golf Program?"

Luke shakes his head and I show him the program description, which I printed from the website.

I read to Luke, "The #GameON Autism Golf Program is aimed at developing life skills, encouraging social interaction, and promoting healthy living through golf for individuals on the autism spectrum. Each session is designed to help build self-esteem and confidence in a fun, welcoming, and supportive environment, encouraging participants to learn golf skills while practicing specific autism learning concepts."

Luke nods, but I can tell he's still a little uneasy. "We have work left to do. Can you wait until the trial is over and work with Abby then?"

"I need a break. Let's get me ready for the trial next week," I say. "I want to get outside and spend time with Abby."

Luke grumbles about me not spending the time we have left getting ready for the trial. Finally, he gives up.

"Before you go, give me the list of Lake Tierra Golf Club members you say will testify they bought their property, built their homes, and joined the Lake Tierra Country Club because they were told you were the golf course designer."

I pull out the list of names and hand it to Luke.

Luke looks over the list. "You once told me that Benton had built his empire on two principles. He had never lost a single battle, whether in the boardroom or the courtroom. He pays the adversary to go away whenever he thinks he might lose, and then he spins it like he won to the press. After he learns the homeowners at Lake Tierra got together and agreed to testify against him, Benton will probably sweeten his offer to you."

Luke walks me to the door of his office. We'll finish the trial in a couple of weeks. After the trial, I'll be back in Dallas, and we may not see each other again. I want to continue seeing him, and I want to teach Abby how to play golf.

Luke holds the door open, and as I step out, I find myself lingering, not ready to say goodbye just yet. "Luke," I say, "after the trial, if you'd like, I'd still love to teach Abby more about golf."

His eyes meet mine, and there's a flicker of something in them—hope, maybe, or understanding. "I think she'd like that," he says warmly.

I nod, forcing a smile. "Good. I'd like that too."

As I walk away, the weight of the trial feels different now. It's not just about winning or losing; it's about what comes next and the choices I'll have to make. For the first time, I'm not sure what I want. I will have to plan my future, and that scares me more than anything.

I start towards my car when my phone buzzes. I pull it out, expecting a message from Luke or maybe Abby. But it's not. The text is from an unknown number.

"You think you can just walk away? This isn't over, Lauren."

Who left that message?

I glance back at Luke's office door, wondering if I should tell him about the message. But I hesitate, uncertainty gnawing at me. My fingers hover over the screen, torn between deleting the message and saving it as evidence. What if this is just the beginning of something darker or something I'm not prepared to face?

I slip my phone back into my pocket, my heart racing. The trial might be ending soon, but it's clear that this fight is far from over. And as I leave, a sense of dread grips me. Whatever happens next, I know I can't let my guard down.

Chapter 20

Lauren

The next day, I spend the morning with Luke, preparing for our trial. At noon, I say I've had enough.

"Abby and I are going to the golf course. What kind of clubs do you have?"

Luke hesitates, a slight furrow forming between his brows. He opens his mouth to respond but then closes it, shaking his head in frustration. "I can't believe I can't remember the brand of clubs I own," he mutters, more to himself than to me.

It's not the first time I've seen this lately. Luke told me he has short-term memory losses from being on a ventilator for five days. I've noticed those memory lapses. Short-term memory loss and brain fog are hitting him harder as he stresses about the trial. And now it's creeping into the little things, like remembering his golf clubs.

I worry about what this could mean when we're in court. I'm sure before having COVID and being put on a ventilator, Luke was always sharp, the kind of lawyer who never missed a detail. But if his mind's not firing on all cylinders, that's a problem we can't ignore. Still, I decide to let it go, for now.

"I'll take care of it," I say, steadying my tone.

I find the Callaway golf clubs in the garage and load them into my car. As Abby and I head to the range, the concern gnaws at me. We arrive, I take her to the practice putting green, and we spend the next hour working on putting. Abby's initial putting strokes hit some putts short and others zipping by the hole. After an hour, she's improving her speed. Her putts either drop in or are slightly short or slightly long.

Later, I place tees in the green from where she is putting to a point close to the hole. I tell Abby her goal is to keep the ball between the tees. She starts out hitting tees along the line of the putt, and after a few putts, she's getting frustrated. When I consider quitting, she putts straight into the hole from the tees. She jumps up from her crouch, rushes over, and hugs me. We spend two hours on the putting green, moving back from three feet out to six feet out and then nine feet out.

When I have her nine feet away from the hole, I watch Abby line up her putt. She takes a deep breath, draws the putter back, and taps the ball. It rolls slowly across the green and drops into the hole. Abby jumps up and down, clapping her hands in excitement. She looks at me, her eyes shining with joy.

"That was awesome," she says.

I smile at her. "You're a natural," I say. I see she is good at repetitive tasks and enjoys doing them. I can see that her autism suits her well for something repetitive like a putting stroke. Abby finds great joy at making a putt from whatever the distance.

"Can I come back with you tomorrow?" Abby's hopeful eyes catch mine.

"Of course," I reply, but a movement at the edge of the parking lot pulls my attention away. My heart skips a beat when I see the white Dodge Charger parked there, the same car that has been following me. The man inside is watching us intently.

I keep my voice steady. "Abby, why don't you take a little break and get a drink of water? I'll be right there."

As Abby runs off to the clubhouse, I pull out my phone and snap a quick photo of the Charger. I send it to Luke with a brief message: "He's here. The white Charger. Watching us at the golf course."

Luke's reply comes almost immediately: “Stay calm. I'm on my way. Don't let Abby know.”

As I slip the phone back into my pocket, my pulse is racing. I force a smile as Abby returns, her face flushed with excitement.

“Ready to putt some more?” she asks.

“Sure,” I say, trying to keep my voice light. “Let's see if you can make another one from nine feet.”

As Abby lines up her putt, I glance back at the Charger. The man is still there, watching. A shiver runs down my spine, but I push it aside. I have to stay strong for Abby.

When Luke arrives, he parks his car near the Charger and gets out, making sure the man sees him. The man in the Charger glances at Luke, then back at me, and finally drives away.

Luke walks over to us. He’s far more calm than I am. “Everything okay here?” he asks.

I nod, though my heart is still pounding. “Thanks for coming.”

Abby looks up at Luke, smiling. “Dad, look, I made another putt from nine feet!”

Luke smiles back, his eyes softening. "That's great, Abby. Keep up the good work."

As we continue practicing, I'm reminded that Benton and his team will stop at nothing to intimidate us. But seeing Abby's joy and determination gives me a reason to be out there with her.

Working with Abby teaches me patience in a way I've never experienced before. She draws me out of my own head, away from the relentless thoughts of the lawsuit. As I step onto the golf course, I feel a sense of familiarity, but it's Abby's presence that truly makes me feel at home. The air is crisp, carrying the faint scent of freshly cut grass, and the warmth of the sun and the breeze on my face remind me of why I love being out here. But today, it's not just the game that soothes me; it's being here with Abby.

There's something about the way she approaches things—with her unique perspective and determination. She gets excited over the simplest things, like making a good putt or feeling the grass beneath her feet. Working with Abby is a reminder that there's more to life than the lawsuit, more than the endless drive for perfection. It's about being present, sharing a moment, and finding joy in the small victories.

As I guide her through her swings and we laugh together at her triumphs, I realize that these are the moments I've been missing. Abby brings out a softer side of me, one that I didn't even know existed. I enjoy getting outside and teaching her, not just because it's something I'm good at but because it's a chance to connect in a way that feels real and meaningful. In her company, I'm not just a golf teacher; I'm a mentor, a friend, and maybe even something like family.

"May I ask you one more question?" Abby asks, taking me out of my thoughts.

"Sure," I respond.

"Do you like my dad?"

"Yes, your dad is my lawyer. He's also a nice person and a great dad."

"I mean, do you like him like a boyfriend?"

My heart skips a beat, and I struggle to find the right words. "Abby, your dad is a fine lawyer who cares about his clients, and I appreciate him."

She fidgets with her hands, avoiding my eyes. "It's just... little things. Like how your father talks about you at home, always making sure we know how amazing you are. And he smiles more when you're around. He hasn't smiled like that since Mom died."

I'm still gathering my thoughts when Abby continues. "And the way he looks at you. He hasn't looked at anyone that way since Mom."

Touched and a bit flustered, I try to respond carefully. "Abby, your dad is a wonderful person and a fine lawyer. He cares deeply about his clients, and I appreciate everything he's doing for me."

Abby nods, but her eyes remain thoughtful. "I just wanted you to know. We like you, Lauren. And if you ever became Dad's girlfriend, we'd be okay with that."

I smile, touched by her sincerity. "Thank you, Abby. That means a lot to me. You and Megan are amazing, and your dad is lucky to have such wonderful daughters."

Abby beams at the compliment, and the moment feels lighter, more connected. Yet, the unspoken feelings hang in the air, adding another layer to the complexities of our situation.

When we arrive back at Luke's, his mom and my mom are preparing dinner for all of us. It's become a weekly event since my mom and I've been staying in Corona. I know Laura cared deeply for Allison, but as we clean up, she tells me that Luke's been lonely and is still grieving the loss of his wife and son, but he's perked up while spending time with me. I understand her point, and I sense our mothers are playing matchmaker, but I know Luke's getting ready for the upcoming battle, and my presence has little influence on it.

"Laura, I don't know how Luke does it. How does he find time for his work, time for Abby and Megan, and his hobbies?"

Laura smiles and looks over at my mother. "I taught Luke early on that he'd never find time for his family and hobbies. He'd have to make time. He makes time for his family outside of his work."

"I recommend you make time for important things besides your work," my mother adds.

My mom is right. It explains why I have few friends and no relationships other than with her. My father instilled in me a single-focused mindset. It made me a better golfer, but it denied me having meaningful relationships. Suddenly, I feel sad, a hollow ache settling in my chest.

As I sit there, it really hits me how much I've sacrificed for golf. I think back to all the moments I could have spent with friends, the relationships I never pursued, the family I never built. My whole life has been about chasing perfection on the golf course, driven by my father's relentless belief that I could be the best in the world. And I was, for a while. But at what cost?

I glance at Luke and his girls, the easy way they laugh together and the warmth they share without even thinking about it. It's something I've never really known, something I never allowed myself to know. All those years, I believed that the trophies, prize money, and accolades would fill the void, but now I'm starting to see that they didn't. They couldn't.

Laura must have picked up on my feelings. She says gently, "You know, Lauren, it's not too late to recalibrate and make time for more than your work."

I let her words sink in. "Recalibrate," I repeat softly. It's a word that feels foreign to me but also like something I desperately need. "I've been so focused on winning, on being the best, that I never really thought about what I was missing."

"Balance is important," Laura continues. "You've achieved incredible things, but you deserve to have a full life, not just a successful one."

I nod. The sadness is still there but now mixed with a flicker of desire to discover if there's more to life than just golf. I've spent so long with my head down, pushing forward, that I never looked up to see what else was out there.

"I've never been good at balance," I admit. "My dad taught me that anything less than complete focus was a distraction. But maybe... maybe I've been too focused."

Laura smiles, a look of understanding in her eyes. "It's never too late to find balance, Lauren. You've still got time to build those relationships, to find what makes you happy outside of work. You deserve that."

As we sit there, I'm thinking that maybe I can start to find a different path. One where I don't have to sacrifice everything else to be successful. One where I can find joy in more than just winning. My only problem is I have no idea what that path might be.

Later that night, I receive a call from Maggie Parks, who says she's a California-based newspaper reporter. When she asks for my comment on Robert Benton's statement about me, I know she's one of Benton's media connections.

That set the tone for the interview. "Which time?" I ask.

"This morning," the reporter says. "Harvey Morgan and Robert Benton say you are selfish, self-centered and have never been a team player, and that you are too assertive and emotional. He says his team frequently referred to you as a bitch, and that's the reason you remain single."

"Isn't that what most men who are bullies say about confident and ambitious women? Tell me what men, like Morgan and Benton, find wrong with a woman who sets career goals and works to achieve them."

I tell Parks that Morgan and Benton are using her to divert attention from why we are in court.

The reporter doesn't mention that Benton has called me transphobic and that he claims he terminated my golf design contract because of it. I realize what Morgan and Benton are doing. They know most potential Corona County jurors feel strongly that men who claim to be women should not compete in women's sports or expose themselves to women in the locker room. So, they're disparaging me in the press, hoping it will turn the local jurors against me. It reminds me once again that I've focused entirely on my career goals and never even created personal or relationship goals. I'm comfortable with that choice, and I won't let Morgan and Benton get to me. I am confident in my identity and principles. No amount of media manipulation can change that. I pour myself another glass of wine as the reporter continues.

"Benton says you bungled several holes at Lake Tierra, and he fixed your mistakes before the construction of the golf course started. Do you have a comment?"

"Yes, did Benton tell you specifically what holes he claims he fixed?"

"No, I didn't ask."

"Well, Miss Parks, how can I comment on what he claimed when you have no idea what holes he claims to have redesigned.? I'd recommend you ask him to provide you with the drawings I created and then I'd recommend you go visit the golf course."

Parks doesn't respond. Instead, she says. "Mr. Morgan and Mr. Benton made one more accusation against you."

"What's that?" I ask.

"Mr. Morgan and Mr. Benton claim you slept your way into golf course design, including with several of his married clients. He read to me several emails you sent and received. Morgan and Benton also claim you are having intimate relations with your lawyer and say they have photos and videos to prove it. Do you have a comment?"

WTF! What emails is she referring to, and how did Morgan and Benton get my emails? It's one more reason I want to get to trial and be done with it. I want to move forward in life without the concern of Robert Benton or his lawyer.

My mind races, trying to figure out how I can explain this away when Morgan and Benton are, at best, bending what emails I exchanged and what I wrote in my journal and, at worst, telling lies about me. I've worked tirelessly to earn a master's degree in landscape architecture, and I've studied golf courses from around the world. What's more, I am designing unique golf courses designed for families. I feel anxiety rearing its ugly head like I had felt when my father died. I take a deep breath and try to compose myself. With a calm and collected voice, I respond to the reporter.

"There are no photos or videos of me having intimate relations with anyone. Have you seen any of the photos and videos?"

"No, I haven't asked to see them, and I haven't looked for them online. Do you have any further comments, Miss West?"

"Yes. Instead of addressing the issues in my lawsuit against him, Benton continues to make vicious, deeply personal, and untrue attacks on my character and my support of women's sports. Based on what you've told me, Benton not only stole my golf course design and took credit for it but also copied what was on my laptop computer, including my emails and journal."

"So, Miss West, you acknowledge that Mr. Benton has correctly described emails and a journal that were on your computer."

"Miss Parks, as a female reporter, you must understand this isn't just about me. It's about how ultra-rich men in power, like Robert Benton, use their influence to try to destroy the reputations of women who dare to stand up to them. They dig into our personal lives, twist our words, and use every dirty trick in the book to discredit our achievements. It's exhausting, demoralizing, and unfair, but I won't let Robert Benton and his attack dog lawyer get away with it. I've worked too hard to let them take that away from me. This is bigger than just one lawsuit—it's about sending a message that women won't be intimidated into silence."

Parks pauses, seemingly unsure of how to proceed. Eventually, she asks, "Are you aware there are videos of you on the internet spewing hate towards transgender people?"

"What?"

"You heard my question. Do you have a response?"

"I have never spewed hatred of any kind towards anyone, including people who identify as a different gender than their birth. I have spoken out supporting transgender individuals' right to live the life they have chosen without fear of harassment. I've spoken out against anyone who has harassed or threatened transgender individuals. Whatever video that is on the internet is fake, created by someone trying to bring shame or harm to me."

"One final question: can you comment on the teenage high school girl who was beaten in the girls' bathroom solely because she identified as a girl who wanted to be on her high school girl's basketball team?"

Her question caught me off guard. "I'm not aware of that happening, and my only comment is, if that happened, I condemn those who ganged up on the teenager."

"You mean teenage girl," she replies and then hangs up before I answer. I worry if what she has told me is true. Benton and Morgan will find a way to link the beating to me.

I call Courtney and tell her the story of my day, starting with Luke not remembering his golf club's brand, followed by Benton's private investigator harassing me at the golf course, and concluding with my unpleasant call from Maggie Parks.

"Are you sure Luke Hartley will be mentally ready to try your case against Benton?" she asks.

"That's just it. I won't know until the trial," I reply.

Courtney pauses, and when she speaks again, her tone is more serious. "Lauren, I don't want to worry you more than you already are, but I'm sure you are aware that Benton and his lawyer, Morgan, are known for exploiting any sign of weakness in their opponents. If they suspect that Luke isn't at the top of his game, they won't hesitate to use it against you. They might push harder, drag out the proceedings, or throw more legal curveballs, hoping to catch him off guard."

I've had that same thought. "So, you think they know he's recovering from being on a ventilator?"

"It's possible," Courtney says softly. "You know how they operate. They're ruthless, and they'll exploit anything they can to win. If Luke's struggling with memory lapses and brain fog, it could be a real issue, especially under the pressure of a high-stakes trial."

I feel a knot tightening in my stomach. "He's been more forgetful lately, and that worries me. But what choice do I have? He's my lawyer, and he's the best I can get."

Courtney's voice is gentle but firm. "Lauren, just be prepared. You need to stay sharp, too. Maybe have a backup plan or at least someone else in the courtroom who can step in if needed. This is your life and your career on the line. You can't afford any missteps. I heard he's been having trouble keeping track of even simple things like schedules lately."

A small alarm bell goes off in my head. How would Courtney know about Luke having trouble with schedules? I haven't mentioned that to anyone.

I take a deep breath, trying to steady my nerves. "You're right. I'll have to stay vigilant and make sure everything is airtight. No room for errors."

"Exactly," Courtney agrees. "And remember, I'm here for you. Whatever happens, you're not alone in this."

"Thanks, Courtney," I say, feeling both grateful and more anxious. As I hang up, the weight of the situation settles on my shoulders even more heavily. Benton and Morgan will stop at nothing to win, and now I'm not just worried about the trial—I'm worried about Luke, too.

Chapter 21

Luke

I file a motion demanding that Robert Benton return Lauren's journal and anything else he uncovered from her computer. Judge Hawkins schedules a hearing on my motion. After the hearing, Judge Hawkins orders Benton to turn over all documents from Lauren's computer by Friday of next week. He adds, "I will not permit the defendant to use any information from Miss West's computer during the trial." Judge Hawkins refused to rule that Benton had stolen documents from Lauren's computer or that Benton had committed a crime by possessing her personal documents.

Sadly, Judge Hawkins refuses to issue the gag order I requested. I tell Lauren she should expect Morgan and Benton to make a viral smear campaign before the trial to throw me off, divert her and my attention, and destroy her in front of potential jurors. Lauren is usually calm, cool, and collected, but I can see she's mad and stressed out. She tells me that she can't fall asleep. Even though Judge Hawkins ordered Benton not to use personal information from her computer during the trial, the lack of a gag order means he can use it to criticize her in the press. Worse yet, we have no idea how to find out who is posting the artificial intelligence-created fake videos of Lauren.

I find and hire a media forensic company that specializes in detecting deepfake videos. Over the next two days, using Deepware Scanner and Reverse Image Search, they review videos of Lauren naked, having sex, and saying hateful things about transgender athletes. The program uses artificial intelligence to analyze videos and identify deepfakes by recognizing patterns and inconsistencies in facial expressions, movements, and lighting. After looking at the videos of Lauren, they report that someone has manipulated Lauren's voice using a voice-cloning process. Additionally, they report that the videos of her are fake. Through the use of the Reverse Image Search, they can identify the actual videos of Lauren from which someone made the deepfake videos.

While we can now show the videos and images of Lauren are deepfake, getting them taken down is a whole different story. I contact an online reputation company to mitigate the impact on Lauren. At their suggestion, I publish the media forensic company's report and conclusions as broadly as possible.

In the meantime, while dealing with that distraction, I get back to trial preparation.

I call the first Lake Tierra resident on Lauren’s list.

“Hello?” A tentative voice answered from the other end, the uncertainty palpable.

“Hi, this is Luke Hartley, Lauren West's attorney. I was hoping you could help us by providing testimony on Lauren's positive impact on the Lake Tierra development.”

“Of course, Mr. Hartley. Lauren has been nothing but professional and dedicated. She doesn't deserve the lies some unknown person is spreading about her.”

“Thank you,” I say, feeling a surge of hope. With each call, I find more Lake Tierra residents who agree to testify that they bought their Lake Tierra property primarily because Lauren designed the golf course.

That’s all good until I speak to the fifth resident on Lauren’s list. He says he will not voluntarily testify, and if I subpoena him, I’ll be sorry. I ask, “Why?” He hems and haws, then finally says it will be for me to figure out. He ends by saying he doubts other residents I called will testify now.

Damn, Benton has gotten to them.

As I sit in my office, drowning in paperwork, my cell phone buzzes, and I see it's Sue Baker, my mother-in-law. "Luke, we need to talk," she says, her tone more serious than usual.

"About what?" I ask, though I have a sinking feeling I already know.

"I've heard some things about you and that golfer you're representing. Lauren West."

"What things and who did you hear it from?" I try to keep my voice calm.

"I'm not one to gossip. I'm not saying who talked to me." Her words are carefully chosen, but I can almost see her pointed look through the phone. Abby must have said something after Lauren took her for the golf lesson yesterday.

"Sue, there's nothing going on between Lauren and me. She's a client. That's it. I'm representing her in a very tough trial that's coming up soon."

"I'm sure that's what you believe, but Luke, you're lonely. And I know the girls are still hurting over Allison and Tom."

"I know, Sue. I'm still grieving, too. It's not just the girls who miss them every day."

There's a pause before she speaks again, her voice softer this time. "I understand that, Luke. I really do. But I'm worried. I don't want you getting too close to someone just because you're feeling vulnerable."

"I get it. But trust me, Sue, Lauren doesn't need any more pressure right now. We're both focused on this trial. I'm her lawyer. That's all there is to it."

"I want to talk with Miss West and let her know how I feel."

"Please don't talk to her. We're getting ready for a very tough trial against a bully. Lauren needs no more pressure."

"I'll take you at your word for now," she tells me. I want to address her "for now" comment, but I let it pass.

I sigh as I hang up the phone. My mother wants Lauren and me to get together for the girls' sake, while Sue wants us to stay apart for the same reason. I need both of them to chill so I can win Lauren's case.

Later that morning, I see the Dallas, Fort Worth, and Austin newspapers preview of the trial. This news gets disseminated nationwide by the national media, highlighted on both liberal and conservative cable news channels. Regardless of their spin, it is either Dallas' own LPGA celebrity versus Silicon Valley mogul or transphobic former LPGA golfer versus California billionaire in a battle for women's sports fairness. Other than my quote, none of the headlines or opening lines of the broadcast media hone in on what the trial will be about. Instead of writing or broadcasting about Benton stealing Lauren's design of the Lake Tierra golf course, the writers and newscasters focus on Lauren's denouncement of transgender athletes competing in women's sports. Each writer or broadcaster asserts it's a matter of fundamental fairness. The only difference is who they believe should receive fair treatment.

I read the first paragraph of Robin Howell's Dallas article.

In a trial scheduled to start next week in the historic Corona County courtroom, Dallas native and former LPGA star seeks to prove she designed the award-winning Lake Tierra Golf Course, seeks to recover bonuses Silicon Valley entrepreneur and real estate developer Robert Benton refused to pay her, and seeks damages for his defaming her. Robert Benton is expected to mount a cut-throat defense asserting he terminated West's golf course development contract when he discovered she was disparaging and taunting high school, college, and professional transgender athletes. In a deposition, Benton declared that he, not Miss West, designed the award-winning Lake Tierra Golf Course. Miss West, who has become the voice of girls' and women's sports, denies disparaging anyone and asserts she is only advocating for fairness and safety for girls and women.

Each newspaper has photos of Lauren, Benton, and Benton's Lake Tierra Hill Country Development. The writer's reference statements made by Lauren and Benton.

Benton's strategy is to lie about designing the Lake Tierra Golf Course every chance he gets. One writer actually focuses on what the case is all about. He's interviewed several Lake Tierra homeowners who say they bought a lot and built a home at Lake Tierra Hill Country Development because they believed Lauren West had designed the Lake Tierra Golf Course. They say when they bought the real estate, sales staff pitched the community as a luxury family-oriented community with a golf course for all ages and levels designed by Lauren West.

I say, "Hallelujah," which prompts my girls to ask what I'm saying hallelujah about. I say that I just read some good news, hoping they won't ask what the good news is that I read. When they don't ask, I call Lauren and tell her the residents must have spoken to the reporter before Benton threatened them.

For several weeks before the trial date, I worked out every morning and again in the evening, trying to recover as much energy as possible. When I started, it was more difficult than I had ever imagined. I didn't feel well, and I was fatigued. Each day, I've added more to build my stamina. I've also taken IV therapy to energize my body with electrolytes, minerals, and vitamins.

I've meticulously prepared for the trial. I've created organized and detailed notes, summaries, and outlines that I've stored in an iPad to assist with recall during proceedings. I've spent hours with Lauren and other witnesses. Lauren and I have gone over what I will ask her and what I say Morgan will ask on cross-examination. I think she's as ready as she'll ever be. I'm just not sure I'm ready.

I tell Lauren that Court TV plans to broadcast her war with Benton. Each day, other lawyers on Court TV will comment on my performance, and when she testifies, they'll comment on her performance. Their commentary will have little to do with the merits of Amy's case and more to do with her performance and mine. I suggest Lauren watch an hour or two of Court TV to get a first-hand idea of what I am telling her. Given her public position on not permitting transgender athletes to compete against girls and women, I'm confident that her detractors will take to social media to disparage her.

The day before the trial starts, Court TV sends a reporter to Corona County, and she takes the audience outside and through the courthouse. I watch and feel like I'm watching a tour, not a preliminary report of the upcoming trial. The reporter tells viewers that Texas has more historic courthouses than any other state. Eighty-six are on the National Register, and seventy-eight are Texas Historic Landmarks. The Corona County Courthouse is one of the historic landmarks. Builders constructed it in 1893 and renovated it one hundred years later. It is the signature landmark of Corona County, and the outside has served as the courthouse for several movies, with its battlements, turrets and spires and its working clock tower.

She steps through the heavy oak door adorned with intricate wrought-iron details, and viewers hear the door creak loudly. She tells viewers that the interior of the courthouse is a blend of elegance and history, with polished marble floors not found in any California courthouse. She points out the mahogany panels and brass chandeliers in the entranceway. As the reporter walked further in, viewers hear the faint echo of her heels on the marble floors.

I haven't slept well in over a week. I'm not mentally ready to do combat with a courtroom bully. I'm afraid I might lose, and how devastating that would be for Lauren. My mother says Abby has been talking about Lauren and learning to play golf all week, and she wants to watch the trial. I plead with her to stay away and not bring Abby. She understands and agrees to watch the trial on television.

The night before the trial starts is worse. I'm hallucinating like I did after getting off the ventilator. I have the weirdest nightmare that keeps me awake. I'm trying a case. I see the judge, and I know my opposing counsel. I even know my client. My nightmare is I haven't prepared sufficiently for the trial, and I don't have Lauren prepared for the onslaught I expect to come from Morgan. I think about the endless hours and days I've prepared for the war that will start tomorrow. I feel like I'm walking to the plate with two outs in the ninth, and it's up to me to pull out the win. When I wake up in the morning, I see on my watch that I've only slept a couple of hours.

On the first morning of the trial, I arrive with Lauren. I park my car in a lot a block from the town square. We walk to the antiquated Corona County Courthouse. When we near the front of the building, I first see hundreds of protestors with commercially made signs disparaging Lauren. It is clearly an organized rally. I'm certain that Robert Benton has paid those hostile demonstrators to disrupt our walk to the courthouse and have at least a dozen reporters and cameramen on the front lawn of the courthouse, film them screaming obscenities. Two of the protestors unfurl a banner with thick black letters on white fabric declaring, Stop Trans Hate

Now, and hold the banner in front of us so we can't move forward. The reporters and their camera operators swarm like flies, wanting to catch any physical confrontation that might take place.

Lauren and I stand there frozen. I grab Lauren's hand. It's shaking either out of fear, anger, or both. Finally, two policemen come forward and guide us around the banner.

The press wouldn't be here if this was just a simple case of Lauren seeking to get credit for the golf course she designed. The state and national press have taken an interest in our case because of Lauren's support of girls' and women's sports or, alternatively, her wrongfully being accused of wanting to ban transgender athletes from sports and to report on Benton protestors calling her names. When we finally navigate around the banner, the reporters pepper Lauren with questions. Some are so biased that I'm convinced Robert Benton has paid those reporters. I follow closely behind Lauren, making our way through the swarm of reporters as they shout out their questions. I sense Lauren wants to speak, but she's following my advice to not engage.

I sense the tension in the air, the excitement and anticipation of a high-profile case. But as we step through the oak doors, the noise fades away, and we're enveloped by the quiet of the courthouse. Lauren remains silent, her face set with determination as she walks through the marble hallway towards the courtroom.

We head to the small conference room where I'll meet with Lauren before and during the trial. I pour us both a cup of coffee, and I take a long sip of my coffee. I can tell Lauren's nervous, but she's doing her best to hide it.

"Hey, how are you doing?" I ask.

"Nervous," Lauren replies with a weak smile. "I know Morgan will throw everything he can at me."

I nod in understanding. "I understand why you are nervous. The important thing to remember is we have a strong case. We're fighting for something that's right. Benton stole your golf course design, took credit for it, and refused to pay you the bonus as required by your contract." I don't tell Lauren that I'm likely more nervous than she is.

Lauren nods and takes a sip of her own coffee. "I just hope the jury sees it that way."

"Juries in Corona County don't like bullies. I promise you that the jury will not like Morgan or Benton."

I stop by the men's room. I once read that lawyers on their way to the courtroom all stop by the restroom one last time. I'm living proof that is true.

We enter Judge Hawkins' packed courtroom with cameras in each rear corner. Several LPGA golfers and several teenage girl golfers are in the first two rows behind our table. This will be the first trial in Corona County to be on national TV and make the national news networks. Judge Hawkins has summonsed over two hundred potential jurors, as he knows he will excuse most of them and that Morgan and I will challenge many who remain.

When the potential jurors are assembled, Judge Hawkins asks questions while first focusing on whether there's any reason they feel being on the jury will present a problem that makes them feel the need to be excused from the jury. None respond, so he asks if any of them know him or members of the courthouse staff. A few respond affirmatively, and Judge Hawkins excuses them.

When the judge asks if any of the prospective jurors know me, over half of them indicate that they do. In contrast, no one responds when asked if they're familiar with Harvey Morgan. A few individuals acknowledge knowing Lauren, leading Judge Hawkins to excuse them as well. None of them, however, recognize Robert Benton.

The judge then questions the group about whether they have watched Lauren during her time on the LPGA tour. Those who have are also dismissed. By the time he's finished, only a couple of dozen people remain in the room.

When asked if there is anything about the case that may make it difficult for them to be a fair and impartial juror, several in the jury pool raise their hands. Judge Hawkins asks why they feel it will be difficult for them to be fair and impartial, and each person responds it is because Robert Benton had taken the most scenic land in the county and developed it for wealthy people from far away to have multimillion-dollar second homes.

Judge Hawkins continues questioning the panel for the next thirty minutes. Once the assembled group is ready, he begins by asking if anyone feels that serving on the jury would present a personal issue requiring their excusal. No one responds, so he moves on, inquiring whether any of them know him or members of the courthouse staff. A few raise their hands, and Judge Hawkins excuses them.

I look over and see Robert Benton elbowing his lawyer. Morgan gets up and asks the judge if we could have a conference in his chambers. Lauren and I, Morgan and Benton, follow the court reporter back to the judge's chambers. As soon as the court reporter sits, Morgan begins.

"Your Honor, there is no way that Mr. Benton can get a fair trial in Corona County."

"What makes you believe your client cannot get a fair trial in my court, Mr. Morgan?"

"For starters, even the jurors who don't know Mr. Hartley know of him and like him. That puts Mr. Benton at an unfair disadvantage before we even start."

"Just because some of you are acquainted with Mr. Hartley doesn't necessarily mean you have a bias or that you can't be fair in this trial," Judge Hawkins comments.

"Judge, you need to transfer this case to Austin, where the jurors won't be predisposed against my client," Morgan argues.

I laugh. Travis County, where Austin is located, is as liberal an enclave as California. Corona County, on the other hand, is as conservative as any county in Texas. Morgan knows that.

"Not one potential juror has said anything that would cause me to believe they are biased against Mr. Benton. Your client chose to build his exclusive development in Corona County. I believe people in this county are entitled to serve on a jury involving your client's development. Your motion to transfer the location of this trial to Travis County is denied. Is there anything else you want to take up away from the public and the television cameras?"

"Judge, you've already proven Mr. Benton can't get a fair trial here. Your ruling proves you cannot give my client a fair trial. I urge you to recuse yourself now before your bias becomes obvious."

"Mr. Morgan, if you don't like the results at the end of this trial, your client can appeal."

"Miss West can count on an appeal when we don't like the result. We will ultimately win on appeal based partly on your bias against my client."

Morgan is baiting Judge Hawkins to enhance Benton's chances on appeal.

Judge Hawkins shakes his head and waves the back of his hand to make clear he's had enough of Harvey Morgan.

I look back at Benton. His gaze is cold and calculating, never blinking or wavering. He clenches his fists in his lap and glares at Judge Hawkins. On the way out of the chambers, Benton reaches

Morgan's arm and pulls Morgan toward him. I can't make out what Benton is saying. I only know he's not happy.

Lauren writes on the legal pad I gave her.

When we are out in the hall, I see Harvey Morgan talking to the press.

He says. "Mr. Benton cannot get a fair trial here. That's become obvious to us. We will fight Miss West here and then appeal if we don't like the local, biased jury's decision. Many potential jurors fought against the Lake Tierra Hill Country Development. Many are friends with Mr. Hartley, Judge Hawkins, or both of them. I've asked Judge Hawkins for a change in venue and to recuse himself. His bias in this case is obvious. He's refused both motions. That, among other things, will be grounds for an appeal, which we will win, and then we can try this case in another Texas county."

Benton adds, "When I informed Miss West that her contract was terminated, she practically pleaded with me to settle. I made it clear to her that I don't throw money at problems, especially when I'm in the right. I had the right to terminate her contract when her crude comments and conduct embarrassed me and deterred potential clients from buying property at Lake Tierra." He enjoys the attention and flashes a smug grin at the media cameras.

Morgan leans forward, his tone sharp. “We've received information suggesting that Miss West's attorney is engaging in an inappropriate relationship with her. That is unethical. Lawyers in California face disbarment for having intimate relations with clients. Texas has no ethical rules on intimacy with clients, and Texas lawyers can get away with whatever they want to do with clients.”

As Morgan’s words hang in the air, a cold dread settles over me. It’s not just the potential damage to Lauren’s case that worries me, but the inevitable fallout with Sue. She’s never hidden her belief that I should devote my entire life to raising the girls and that there’s no place for another woman in our lives. To her, this isn’t about ethics or professionalism; it’s about whether I’m shirking the sacred duty of being both father and mother to her grandchildren.

The idea that I might be involved with a client would only confirm her worst fears—that I’m somehow neglecting the responsibility she believes is all that should matter to me now. I can already hear the disappointment in her voice, the thinly veiled disapproval that I might be looking for solace in someone else when I should be solely focused on the girls. I picture Sue confronting Lauren, not out of anger but out of a desperate need to protect what’s left of her family. She’s lost her only child, and the last thing I want is for her to think that I'm betraying the promise I made to her daughter to always put our children first.

Chapter 22

Luke

When we file back into the courtroom, I notice that Morgan has brought along Carlotta Hampton, the celebrated Los Angeles trial consultant. Seeing her in person for the first time, it's easy to believe the hype. Carlotta Hampton is a vision of style and sophistication, her long blond hair cascading down her back. She's wearing a navy power suit with angular lines and sharp edges that seem to cut through the air with authority. Her high heels click against the wooden floor with a rhythm that commands attention. As she strides forward, every head in the courtroom turns to watch, drawn to her rock-star-like presence. Potential jurors seem to sit up straighter under her gaze as if sensing the weight of her influence. I can feel the tension tighten around Lauren and me, an unspoken understanding that Hampton's presence could shift the entire tone of the trial. She isn't just any consultant. Hampton is a woman who boasts on her website that she wins over ninety percent of the cases.

We, of course, have no jury consultant. It wasn't until the trial began that I discovered Carlotta Hampton had flown in from Los

Angeles to assist Benton and Morgan with jury selection. Court TV commentators have been buzzing about her presence, hailing her as the top jury consultant in the country. She wrote the book on the subject, and she's a regular on the network as an expert analyst. Her reputation precedes her, and I can see why. She's known for her uncanny ability to handpick jurors who will sway a case decisively in her client's favor.

But while Carlotta's skills are impressive, I feel a quiet confidence in my own approach. She may have years of experience, but her expertise is honed in the sprawling, diverse courtrooms of California, where jurors come from all walks of life and every corner of the world. This isn't Los Angeles. We're in Corona County, deep in the heart of the Hill Country, where people value straightforwardness, common sense, and an honest day's work.

I've lived here, worked here, and I know these people. I understand what makes them tick, what they respect, and what they'll see right through. Carlotta may have all the data, the psychological profiles, and the polished strategies, but I've got something she doesn't: a lifetime of knowing these jurors, their values, and the quiet dignity they carry. In a place like this, intuition and local knowledge can outweigh all the research in the world.

So let Carlotta Hampton bring her best. I'm ready. This jury won't be swayed by flashy credentials or out-of-town tactics. They'll see through the glitz and find the truth, and that's where I'll win this case.

I watch as Hampton slyly nods her head toward specific individuals, who I assume are part of Benton's entourage. I can see the calculation in her eyes as she mentally assesses each person. Morgan leans over to her and whispers something, causing her to nod in agreement. Hampton's confident demeanor and commanding presence catch my attention and the attention of everyone in the courtroom.

Morgan asks many questions of each potential juror and challenges many for cause, stringing out the jury selection for as long as possible. If Judge Hawkins denies his motion, Morgan states his objection for the record and the television audience watching the trial. After two hours and having seated six jurors, we break for lunch. During the break, Morgan and Benton once again speak on camera, complaining that Judge Hawkins is biased against them and that there is no way they can get a fair trial in Corona County.

One reporter asks Morgan if he's always as bombastic and abrasive when discussing a judge about to preside over his client's trial. Morgan sneers. "Only when the judge's bias is so blatant that it's impossible for my client to get a fair trial," he replies. "Judge Hawkins has made it clear from the start that he's not impartial. He's been pandering to the cameras, and it's a disgrace. But let me be very clear: I'm not about to let him railroad my client. Not on my watch."

Benton chimes in. "I understand that Judge Hawkins and Mr. Hartley are in the same Rotary Club, drink coffee together, and are on the same bowling team."

A reporter asks Benton what evidence he has showing the cozy relationship between Judge Hawkins and Hartley.

"I don't need to provide you with any evidence. His and Hartley's relationship is simply one more reason Judge Hawkins should recuse himself and transfer the case to another county."

I turn around and shoot a look at Benton. I don't bowl. I don't belong to the Rotary Club, and I don't meet Judge Hawkins for coffee. I suspect that Judge Hawkins will be terribly offended when he finds out what Benton and Morgan are saying about him. Their scorched earth, verbal abuse, and lying strategy tell me they're not planning on a favorable result from a Corona County jury. They are trying the case in the national media so that they can claim the judge and jury were biased if they lose, and can prolong the day of reckoning on appeal.

As the hours tick by, the jury pool dwindles down to a final panel of twelve. I sense Carlotta Hampton has played a crucial role in the selection process, and I can see Morgan's confidence in his eyes as he looks over at her. We finally have a jury of seven men and six women who will decide whether Lauren gets credit for designing the Lake Tierra Golf Course and whether she's entitled to a bonus. Three additional people will serve as alternated jurors. Two of them are men and one woman. None of the jurors or alternates play golf, none of them watched Lauren play on the LPGA tour, and none of them protested against the Lake Tierra Development.

Judge Hawkins adjourns the trial for the day. I watch as all eyes are on Carlotta Hampton as she exits the courtroom. I'm confident she'll be the subject of the Court TV reporters.

As we pack up to leave the courtroom, two of Lauren's LPGA friends approach us. Each one introduces herself to me. I recognize one of their names. Courtney Barr grabs my hand, leans in close, and whispers, "Thank you for representing Lauren. She needs a warrior like you to take care of her." Barr pulls back, but not before giving me what I perceive to be prolonged eye contact with a wide, almost teasing smile. Her fingers linger just a bit longer than necessary on my hand, a light touch that feels deliberate. The intensity of her gaze and the playful curve of her lips make me uncomfortable, and the way her eyes seem to scan my face feels more personal than friendly. She must sense my unease because she quickly shifts her eyes away and releases my hand, though her fingers trail off as if reluctant to let go. When Courtney turns to leave, she tosses a quick glance over her shoulder, her expression carrying a hint of something. I shake off the feeling, dismissing it as courtroom tension, but the moment lingers in the back of my mind.

Later, as we step outside, we're immediately met by a gauntlet of reporters, their voices rising in a chaotic chorus as they shout questions at Lauren. I stay close to her, guiding her through the crowd with a steady hand, keeping my focus on the task at hand.

As we push forward, I catch sight of Carlotta Hampton just a few steps away, holding court with a group of reporters. Even from a distance, it's clear she has them in the palm of her hand, their attention riveted on her every word. I can't make out what she's saying, but it doesn't matter. Let her work her magic—her reputation is built on dazzling people with her expertise and charm.

I'm not impressed. I've seen it all before, and I know that in the end, it's not about who can captivate an audience of reporters. It's about who can connect with a jury who can tell a story that resonates on a deeper level. Carlotta may have her captivated audience now, but the real work happens in the quiet moments, in the minds of the jurors as they weigh what they've seen and heard.

I keep moving, my confidence unshaken, knowing that when it comes down to it, I trust my instincts and my connection to this place more than any outsider's polished presentation.

On my way home, I receive a call from my mom. After greeting me, she asks, "Are you a hunk and heartthrob or a good ol' boy, or maybe both?"

"What? Why are you asking that question?"

"Because, when I watched the trial today, one commentator said her heart was palpitating when she saw you on the screen. She referred to you as a hunk and later as a heartthrob. Later, a commentator said you and Judge Hawkins are good ol' boys from a hick town in Texas."

"I told you not to watch the trial on television."

After we hang up, I see a call from Lauren coming in on my cell phone. She tells me that a liberal cable news network is interviewing both Hampton and a well-known Los Angeles lawyer. Hampton tells the audience that she believes she has picked the most liberal jurors in Corona County. The Los Angeles lawyer says watching in court today reminded him of the hit song: "Try That in a Small Town." He says Harvey Morgan and Robert Benton should have taken the lyrics of that song to heart when they decided to defend Lauren West's claim and file a counterclaim in what he describes as a small town in Texas. He further remarks that while Hampton may have helped pick the most liberal jurors in all of Corona County, he doubts they'll be liberal enough to give Robert Benton a fair trial, featured during the local news report. The Court TV reporters question whether a successful businessman from California who supports the rights of the LGBTQ community can get a fair trial in Texas.

She also reports that one of the Austin news networks interviewed Morgan and Benton. They applauded the work done by Carlotta Hampton while the station played a video of her leaving the courthouse with them. They say they are defending the rights of transgender athletes against the hate espoused by Lauren West. Morgan and Benton must have paid bloggers and X, formally known as Twitter influencers, to spread the word that Lauren hates transgender girls and women and that her hateful comments about them are putting them in danger throughout the country. Bloggers also repeat that Morgan was the only developer willing to give Lauren a chance to design golf courses. Morgan tells bloggers and social media that as time went on, he realized that Lauren's designs were mediocre at best, and he had to fix each one of them.

As Lauren continues, I hear the frustration in her voice. "Everywhere I turn, Morgan is there, disparaging me," she says. "He's on television, and he has social media influencers spreading hateful remarks about me with my photo. One of them, a transgender blogger named Gloria Moore, posted a video of her confronting me outside the courthouse. She's also posting the names of Lake Tierra witnesses, along with their phone numbers and addresses. Her posts have gone viral, spreading like wildfire, reposted by as many as a thousand social media accounts."

I listen carefully, knowing what Lauren is facing, but I keep my voice calm and measured. "Lauren, I'm sure you feel overwhelmed by this, but don't let Benton rattle you. The truth will come out in court, where it matters. Trials are marathons, not sprints. We've prepared a winning strategy. Let's keep our strategy steady and not get rattled by Hampton's immediate impact or what Morgan and Benton are doing. Let them try their case in the media. We'll win your case in the courtroom. I'll talk to our team about the social media issue and see what we can do to protect our witnesses. I'll handle this one step at a time."

As I hang up, I force myself to take a moment, trying to push away the fatigue that's creeping in. I know that Benton's and Morgan's media blitz and social media attacks are designed to throw us off balance. But despite the confidence I projected to Lauren, doubt lingers. Normally, I could handle anything they throw at me, but the exhaustion that's settled into my bones is a relentless reminder of the damage done by long COVID-19 and the long-term effects of being on the ventilator.

Benton and Morgan must know about my condition, and that's one reason they will make the road ahead as treacherous as they can. I'm exhausted at the end of each day, but I have to win this. I'll find the strength to push through, to fight them. I know one thing for certain: we're far from finished, and the hardest battles are yet to come.

Chapter 23

Lauren

I get up early to go out and run, to breathe the fresh air before I'm stuck back in the courtroom all day. The early morning air is crisp against my skin, but it does little to make me calm. The silence outside is broken only by the distant sound of tires on wet pavement and the rhythmic thud of my feet against the ground. Sleep is a distant memory, my mind replaying the day's events like a broken record.

Morgan's smug face flashes before my eyes, his words cutting deeper than I let on to Luke. He's everywhere, his voice echoing in the background of every news broadcast, his poison spreading across social media like wildfire. He and Benton are trying to break me and turn me into a pariah by telling lies about me.

My phone vibrates, and I reach for it. The screen lights up with yet another notification. I don't need to look to know what it is. The hateful messages poured in all night, one after another. I press my palms against my eyes, trying to block out the images, but they're seared into my memory. I see strangers calling me every vile name under the sun, intending to harass and intimate me and make me sorry for ever standing up for girls' and women's sports.

I take a deep breath, but my chest feels tight, the air barely filling my lungs. I've faced pressure before. I've stared down opponents on the golf course, my heart pounding as I lined up the winning shot, but this is different. In golf, I have control. I have no control over this, and it isn't a game. This lawsuit has become my life and my reputation. Everything I've worked for, Morgan and Benton are trying to tear it apart. No matter how hard I try, no matter what I do, they and their minions are always one step ahead, ready to twist the knife just a little deeper.

Gloria Moore's smug face looms large in my mind, the memory of our confrontation outside the courthouse replaying like a nightmare. I kept my composure then, but now, in the quiet of my kitchen, the fear is creeping in. Moore's followers are relentless, their harassment growing bolder with every post. I know I can't afford to show any sign of weakness, but it's becoming harder to keep up the façade, harder to pretend that I'm not crumbling under the weight of it all.

I had expected Morgan and Benton to do whatever was necessary to deny me justice, but I underestimated the extent to which they would go. I'm sure Benton has someone paying the bloggers, the social media influencers, deepfake media manipulators, and the protestors who shout obscenities at us at the courthouse each morning.

Last night, Luke's mother texted me with a simple message: stay strong, and don't let Benton and Morgan rattle you. I replied, thanking her and promising that I wouldn't back down, no matter how tough they make it. What I didn't mention is how much I've been worrying about my testimony and how the fear of not getting it just right has kept me up the past few nights.

I finish running, shower, and get ready for another day. Luke picks me up, and after walking through the protestors, we're back in the courtroom.

After our short hearing with Judge Hawkins, he summons the jury. Judge Hawkins tells the jurors not to read anything about the trial in newspapers, blogs, or social media sites. He points to the cameras in the courtroom and tells the jurors not to record the Court TV broadcast to watch when they get home. Finally, he tells them not to listen to anyone discussing the trial. They shake their heads, expressing that they understand.

Judge Hawkins looks over at Luke. "Mr. Hartley, you may make your opening statement to the jury."

I watch as Luke rises slowly, his presence filling the room despite the rasp in his voice. "Ladies and Gentlemen of the Jury, my name is Luke Hartley, and I have the honor of representing Miss Lauren West." His voice carries a weight that commands attention, even though I can hear the strain in it. He gestures toward me, and I feel every eye in the room turn my way.

"I believe the best way to introduce you to Lauren is to show you a brief video," Luke says, his tone firm. We had discussed this; his voice isn't as strong as it used to be, but the determination in his eyes hasn't wavered.

Morgan's already fidgeting, and I can see the scowl forming on his face. The moment the video begins, he leaps to his feet. "Your Honor, I object! Mr. Hartley should not be allowed to deliver an opening statement through a video. A slickly edited video is both highly prejudicial and irrelevant to the matters of this case."

Luke turns toward the judge, unflinching. "Your Honor, this video is crucial in understanding who Lauren West is and why she is here today. It's not just her life story. It's the foundation of her work, her dedication, and what's at stake."

Judge Hawkins seems to ponder this for a moment, then nods. "I've never seen this before, but I'll allow it," he turns to the jury.

"The jury will be reminded that opening statements are not evidence."

Morgan isn't satisfied. He scoffs, his voice dripping with condescension as if the cameras are rolling just for him. "Your Honor, this is nothing short of a mockery. Mr. Hartley's video is designed to tug at the jury's heartstrings, not to present facts."

But Judge Hawkins is firm. "Mr. Morgan, I've ruled. Sit down."

The video resumes, and I see myself as a child, barely four years old, gripping a golf club with more determination than most adults. Morgan shifts uncomfortably in his seat. I'm waiting for him to stand and object again.

The narrator's voice fills the courtroom. "Lauren West, born in Dallas, Texas, picked up her first golf club before she could barely walk. By the age of sixteen, she had won the Texas State Amateur, setting the stage for an illustrious career."

Morgan can't take it any longer. He jumps up, practically sputtering. "Objection, Your Honor! This video is nothing more than a highlight reel. You must not allow it!"

Judge Hawkins dismisses him with a wave. "Overruled. But I remind the jury that this is not evidence."

The video continues, showcasing my college victories, my time on the LPGA tour, and those unforgettable moments in the Solheim Cup. I see my younger self teaching a group of minority children, passing on my love of the game to the next generation, and I feel a lump in my throat. Luke's video has captured who I am. I couldn't have presented my story as well as he did.

When the video ends, Morgan is on his feet again, his face red with anger. "Your Honor, this is absurd! These are cherry-picked moments meant to create an emotional response. This is not how we conduct a trial!"

Judge Hawkins leans forward, his tone sharp. "Mr. Morgan, your objections have been noted. Now sit down."

Luke steps forward again, calm and collected, though I can see the effort he's making to stay composed. "Ladies and Gentlemen, you've now met Lauren West. The evidence we will present will support every moment you just saw in the video."

He pauses, letting the room absorb his words. "This case is not complicated. It's about a woman who poured her heart and soul into designing world-class golf courses, only to have her work stolen and her reputation tarnished by Robert Benton."

Luke gestures toward Benton, who's glaring back at him. "Lauren West designed the Lake Tierra Golf Course right here in Corona County. We will prove the Lake Tierra development is the crown jewel of Benton Land Company's empire. But instead of paying Lauren a bonus of ten percent of the net profits that she had rightfully earned, Robert Benton chose to wrongfully terminate her contract."

I can see Luke's struggle; his voice falters slightly, but the power of his words does not. "Mr. Morgan, sitting over there, will argue Lauren's public support for women's and girls' sports gave his client cause to sever her contract. But when you hear all the evidence, you'll see his argument is nothing more than a pretext. It was his way of robbing her of her hard-earned rewards."

Luke pauses again, catching his breath, and he worries me. But he doesn't falter. "At the end of this trial, when you've heard all the evidence, and Judge Hawkins has instructed you on the law, we will ask you to find that Lauren West is entitled to the one million dollars Benton owes her and to ensure she receives what she is due from future profits."

Luke finally returns to our table, his face flushed and his breathing labored. I reach out, squeezing his hand, trying to convey how much it means to me that he's fought so hard for me, even now. But I'm still worried. Luke is strong, but I know this trial will test him in ways he's never faced before.

Judge Hawkins's voice is firm. "Mr. Morgan, you may make your opening statement to the jury."

"Yes, Your Honor," Morgan says, straightening his tie with a flourish that reminds me of an actor preparing for his close-up. He buttons his suit coat as he rises, the movement deliberate, as if he's about to step onto a stage. His air of confidence borders on arrogance, and I can already sense the performance beginning. I've seen this kind of showmanship before, the kind audiences would expect in a Hollywood courtroom drama. Morgan's playing to the jury like they're his audience and he's the star of the show.

"Ladies and Gentlemen, my name is Harvey Morgan. I represent Robert Benton and Benton Land Company. Mr. Benton builds developments with golf courses for families to enjoy. He also builds golf courses for children who live in poverty to learn life skills through learning how to play golf."

Morgan pauses, letting the words hang in the air like a well-rehearsed sermon. The screen lights up with images of black and brown children holding golf clubs, their faces innocent and hopeful. It's a calculated move, and I know it.

As Morgan continues, his voice drips with self-assuredness. “What seems like many years ago, I taught High School Sunday School at the church my wife and I attended. I remember telling parents how wonderful their high school kids were when I taught. Many parents told me I should see their high school students during the week. Mr. Hartley showed you during his opening statement what Miss West is like on Sundays. He didn’t bother to show you any video of what she is like during the week.”

My stomach tightens. I know what’s coming. Morgan’s laying the groundwork to paint me as something I’m not. I glance over at Carlotta Hampton, her smile smug as if she’s already congratulating Morgan on his performance. I doubt Morgan ever set foot in a Sunday School classroom. His Sunday School analogy reeks of Hampton’s handiwork.

Morgan continues, “In this instance, Miss West over here is a know-it-all and thinks she knows more about transgender athletes playing sports than our United States Department of Education, which has issued rules explicitly bar schools from discriminating based on sexual orientation and gender identity. She’s spewed hatred and put recipients of her hatred in danger. Miss West’s public statements have also damaged Robert Benton and Benton Land Company by loss of sales of property at Benton Land Company developments throughout the United States, including the Lake Tierra Hill Country Development here in Corona County."

Morgan is doing precisely what I've seen him do before when he defended star athletes against women who accused them of rape or sexual harassment. He's turning the tables, making me the villain in this story, just as he's done to those women in Los Angeles courtrooms. Carlotta's smile grows wider; she's seen Morgan do this before. He has the jury's attention, and he's using every trick in the book to make me look like the bad person here.

"Ladies and Gentlemen, we live in a changing world. One change you may not have seen here in Corona County is children and adults who are transgender, meaning their gender identity does not match their assigned gender at birth. Many of those children want to be able to play sports like other children and adults. You may not think transgender athletes should be allowed to play girls' and women's sports. That's your right, just as it is Miss West's right to think so as well."

I hold my breath, waiting for the inevitable twist.

"But Miss West made it a public campaign and a talking point for the hard right news media. I'm sure you know sports like golf are not the most important thing in life. Miss West made public statements, mostly on far-right-wing television stations and news media. What she said not only goes against the principles of inclusivity and equal opportunities that made our country great but more importantly, what she has said puts transgender girls' lives at risk. Miss West has alienated about half of the country, meaning half of the potential purchasers of homes and land in Benton Land Company developments won't want to build or buy a home with a golf course she designed."

Each word cuts deeper, twisting the narrative to suit his purpose. I feel a knot forming in my throat as he continues, my hands clenching into fists under the table. He's turning my beliefs and my words into something ugly, something I never intended.

Morgan concludes with the same infuriating confidence, "The evidence will show Mr. Benton could have terminated Miss West's golf design contract for any reason, but he terminated Miss West's golf design contract for cause because her public statements were hateful and something she should have kept to herself. For that reason, she is not entitled to receive ten percent of the profits from the sale of Lake Tierra homes and golf memberships. We are confident when you hear all the evidence, you'll agree Mr. Benton had the right to terminate Miss West's contract for cause."

Judge Hawkins announces a fifteen-minute break, and I feel the air rush out of me. Luke leans over, giving me a reassuring smile and a brief squeeze of my hand as he tells me I'll do well on the witness stand. But even with his calm assurance, the knot of anxiety in my chest remains. The thought of facing Benton, Morgan, and everyone else, with all eyes on me, brings a nervousness that only grows as the moments pass.

When we return to the courtroom and the jury is seated, Judge Hawkins's voice cuts through my swirling thoughts. "Mr. Hartley, you may call your first witness."

I can feel my heart pounding as I realize the moment has arrived. I'm about to testify in a trial for the first time, and the pressure is nothing like the final round of the US Amateur. The room seems to close in, the faces of the jury blurring into a mass of expectation and judgment.

Luke stands, his voice steady as he says the words I've been dreading. "The plaintiff calls Lauren West to the stand."

I feel the ground shifting beneath me as I rise from my seat. My legs are heavy, almost numb, as I take those first few steps toward the witness stand. The courtroom is deathly quiet, the air thick with tension, and I can feel every eye in the room fixed on me. The stakes are higher than I've ever faced. It's not just money, but my life's work, my reputation, everything I've built.

I take a deep breath, but it feels shallow. My throat tightens as I swear to tell the truth, the words coming out more like a croak than a confident promise. This is it. There's no turning back now. My ordeal as a witness is about to begin, and my reputation and future depend on how I come across to the jury in the next few hours.

Chapter 24

Luke

The press and spectators in the gallery fall silent as Lauren rises. Every eye is on her. Standing tall, she starts towards the witness chair. She's wearing a soft gray blazer and a navy-blue pencil skirt tailored perfectly to fit her, with a conservative white blouse and two-inch heels. She exudes a commanding presence, with the poise and confidence of someone who knows how to hold a room's attention.

Lauren raises her right hand, and the court clerk administers the oath to tell the truth. After being sworn in, I ask Lauren to state her name and occupation for the record.

"Lauren West," she states in a clear and strong voice, as I had instructed her. She spent less time with me preparing than I would have liked, so I hope she paid as much attention to my other instructions. "My current occupation is designing golf courses the entire family can enjoy playing. Previously, I was a professional golfer on the LPGA tour."

I begin by guiding Lauren through our rehearsed direct examination, starting with the familiar territory of her life story. This will help her feel more at ease and create a connection with the jurors. As she begins, I can see the nerves in her eyes, but she steadies herself, drawing on the preparation we've done.

She recounts her first memory of her father, Ben West, placing a golf club in her tiny hands. I can see the jurors listening intently, their attention captured as her voice softens with nostalgia. At that moment, I bring up a photo of Ben and Lauren on the screen for the jury to see, a tender moment captured in time. It's a powerful image that I hope will humanize Lauren in the jurors' eyes, making her more than just a plaintiff in a lawsuit but a person they can relate to.

After introducing the tender memory of her father, I guide Lauren through the highlights of her early golf career. She recounts her junior golf successes with quiet pride, detailing how she won the Texas Amateur, then the NCAA tournament, and later, the U.S. Amateur, each victory propelling her closer to the professional stage. As she talks about her rise to stardom on the LPGA tour, winning sixteen tournaments, the jurors seem captivated by her story.

The mood shifts as Lauren speaks of her father's battle with cancer and his eventual passing, a loss that took much of the joy out of playing on the LPGA tour. Before she can continue, Morgan jumps to his feet. "Objection, Your Honor. This testimony is irrelevant and intended solely to prejudice the jury."

I try to keep my expression neutral, but I can't help thinking, "That's exactly what I'm trying to do."

Judge Hawkins nods slightly. "Overruled. Miss West, you may proceed."

She explains how, after several months of caring for her mother, she returned to the tour, hoping to find solace in the game she once loved. Despite having one of the top caddies by her side, it wasn't the same without her father's presence. Each week became a struggle, the emptiness following her to every tournament. Eventually, the physical strain caught up with her, leading to a back injury that forced her off the tour for good. The jurors listen closely, seeing not just an accomplished athlete but a devoted daughter who faced immense personal challenges while trying to maintain her career.

It was during this difficult time that she decided to return to school, earning her master's degree in landscape architecture. As she speaks, her voice remains steady, though it's clear these memories are not easy for her to revisit.

I move on, asking her to describe her undergraduate and graduate studies in landscape architecture. This is where her expertise truly shines, but I keep my questions simple and straightforward, knowing that only some in the room are familiar with the intricacies of course design.

"How did your studies relate to the steps involved in designing a golf course?" I ask, giving her the space to explain in her own words.

Lauren responds with confidence, outlining how her education provided the foundation for her work. She talks about the principles of balance, aesthetics, and environmental considerations, topics that could easily become technical, but she keeps them accessible. She describes how each design begins with a deep understanding of the land and how the contours, natural features, and even the local climate all play a role in shaping the course.

As she speaks, I watch her closely, noting how she glances at the jurors, making eye contact and drawing them into her world. I see some of them nodding along, engaged, and I feel a sense of relief. She's connecting, just as we planned.

I keep guiding her, asking questions that flow naturally and keep her in control and comfortable with every response. Each answer adds depth to the narrative, highlighting not just her expertise but also her passion for designing golf courses that offer more than just a challenge. Lauren's courses are thoughtfully crafted spaces where families can enjoy time together, with each member finding joy in the game.

I introduce into evidence a publication by the American Society of Golf Course Architects (ASGCA), a respected authority in the field, and I ask Lauren to tell the jury about the document.

"This publication," she begins.

Before she gets any further, Morgan stands abruptly, his tone sharp and dismissive. "Objection, Your Honor. This document is irrelevant. It has no direct connection to the design of the Lake Tierra Golf Course and serves only to confuse the jury with unnecessary information."

I glance at Lauren, who remains composed, but I can sense her unease. Judge Hawkins takes a moment before responding, then, with a firm voice, denies the objection. "Overruled, Mr. Morgan. The jury will decide what is relevant."

Morgan sits down heavily, a scowl on his face, clearly displeased with the ruling. His attempt to undermine the significance of the ASGCA publication has failed, but the tension he brings into the room lingers.

Lauren begins again. "This document highlights the standards and principles that guide the design of golf courses worldwide. The ASGCA is not just a professional organization; it's the benchmark for excellence in our industry."

I turn back to Lauren and give her a reassuring nod. "Lauren, can you walk us through the key parts of this publication and explain how these principles guided your work on the Lake Tierra project?"

She begins to explain, her voice steady as she outlines each section of the publication. She talks about the importance of sustainable design and how the ASGCA emphasizes integrating natural landscapes with thoughtful and innovative course layouts. As she speaks, she draws connections between these principles and her approach to golf course design, making it clear that her work on Lake Tierra was informed by the highest standards in the industry.

Her detailed explanation takes us right up to lunch. My voice is raspy, and I can feel the exhaustion creeping in, an unwelcome reminder of the ventilator's lingering effects. The break is a welcome relief, allowing me a moment to catch my breath and gather my strength for the rest of the day.

As we leave the courthouse, I spot Morgan and Benton surrounded by a swarm of reporters. Video cameras, perched on shoulders or held aloft, capture every movement, their red recording lights blinking steadily. Microphones are jostled forward, almost colliding as reporters vie for the best position. Their hands grip the mic handles tightly, eager to catch every word. Benton, ever the seasoned media pro, speaks with a calm demeanor, his words measured and smooth. He knows exactly how to play to the cameras.

Morgan, on the other hand, is more direct, and his disdain for the local setting is clear. "Ladies and gentlemen," he begins, his voice carrying over the crowd, "you've seen it with your own eyes. Judge Hawkins denies every objection I make. There's no way he will give Mr. Benton a fair trial in small-town USA."

A reporter from a West Coast news outlet, her tone slightly condescending, interjects, "Mr. Morgan, are you suggesting that the local court is biased simply because of its location?"

Morgan doesn't miss a beat. "Absolutely," he replies, his expression hardening. "This is Hill Country Corona County, where everyone knows everyone and the old boys' network runs deep. Odds are Judge Hawkins played a round of golf with Mr. Hartley just this past weekend, giving Hartley the perfect opportunity to poison my client before the trial even started."

Another reporter, clearly angling for a more sensational story, pushes further. "Are you saying the entire judicial process here is compromised, Mr. Morgan?"

Morgan gives a tight-lipped smile dripping with sarcasm. "Let's just say I'm not holding my breath for impartiality in Corona. We've had no chance of getting a fair trial from the start."

The reporters nod, their expressions almost eager as they take in Morgan's words, sensing a headline that will play well with their audience. It's clear they're more interested in the narrative of a city lawyer battling small-town bias than in the facts of the case itself.

As I watch, I'm getting more angry each moment. Morgan isn't just trying to sway public opinion. Instead, he's attempting to undermine the very foundation of the trial. He's playing to the cameras, but the real audience is the jury. If they catch wind of this, it could taint everything.

After leaving the courthouse, Lauren and I walk a few blocks to Rosie's Diner, a local spot that's been around for decades. The familiar neon sign buzzes overhead as we step inside. Rosie herself, a fixture in this town, greets us with a warm smile. Her hair is pinned up in the same style she's worn for years, and she hands Lauren a menu, knowing what l will order.

"Good to see you, Luke. And you must be Lauren," Rosie says, her voice carrying the warmth of someone who's seen it all. "Take your time, hun. I'll be back to check on you."

As we take our seats in a booth by the window, Lauren's concern surfaces. "They're trying the case to the media. How am I doing with the jurors in the courtroom?"

I keep my expression calm, not letting on how much Morgan's tactics have irritated me. "You're doing a great job explaining something complicated to the jurors," I say, keeping my tone steady and reassuring. "You're coming across as a true expert on golf course design."

"Are you sure?" she asks, her voice wavering slightly. "I'm not convinced the jury really understands. What could I do better?"

"Lauren, you're doing fine," I respond, leaning in a bit to emphasize my point. "Don't overthink it. Just keep being yourself."

She nods, still unsure, but I can see she's taking my words to heart. When Rosie returns, Lauren glances at the menu and then hands it back to her with a small smile. "I'll go with something light. How about a garden salad with grilled salmon and a lemon vinaigrette on the side?"

I order my usual, grilled chicken breast with a side of steamed vegetables and a whole wheat roll. I expect that it's the kind of meal that will keep my energy up for the afternoon session.

Rosie nods approvingly. "You got it."

While waiting for our meals, I focus on keeping the mood light, making sure Lauren feels supported without realizing how much Morgan's stunt has rattled me. We talk about the afternoon ahead, and I do my best to keep the conversation away from the courtroom drama, letting her relax and recharge before we head back.

Lunch wraps up quietly, and the tension from the courtroom temporarily lifted as we finish our meals. Lauren seems more at ease, her nerves calmed, at least for the moment. I catch Rosie's eye and signal for the check.

Rosie brings the bill over with a smile. "Don't worry about it, Luke," she says, but I insist, sliding a few bills into her hand.

"Thanks, Rosie," I say while standing up. "We'll need to get back."

"Good luck this afternoon," she says warmly, her sincerity making this place feel like home.

Lauren and I leave the diner and step into the harsh afternoon sun. The courthouse is just a few blocks away, but as we walk, I notice a small crowd of reporters gathered near the entrance, their eyes already locked on us. The moment they spot us, they close in like a pack, their cameras and microphones thrust forward, voices rising in a barrage of questions.

"Mr. Hartley, do you believe that Judge Hawkins is biased against Mr. Benton?"

"Miss West, how do you respond to the media's portrayal of the case?"

I raise my hand to shield Lauren and keep the reporters at bay. "No time for questions now," I say, my voice firm, guiding her toward the courthouse steps. We push through the crowd, but I can feel their relentless gaze, every step under scrutiny.

As we approach the courthouse doors, a lone reporter, standing slightly apart from the others, calls out a question that stops us both in our tracks. "Mr. Hartley, can you comment on the new evidence that just came to light?"

My heart skips a beat as I glance at Lauren. Her eyes meet mine, a flicker of uncertainty there. What new evidence? Could this be real new evidence or be something that Morgan has fed the media to interfere with Lauren's testimony? The question hangs in the air, unanswered, as we push through the doors and into the courthouse, the weight of it pressing down on us both.

Chapter 25

Luke

As we return from lunch, Lauren retakes her seat on the witness stand. I watch as she settles in, still carrying some of the nervous energy from our earlier conversation. Once she's ready, I ask her to walk the jury through the steps she took in designing the Lake Tierra Golf Course.

"Lauren, let's dive into the specifics," I say, my voice sounding better. "Can you explain to the jury the process you followed, step by step, and how you applied it to the Lake Tierra project?"

She nods her eyes focused as she begins recounting her work's details. "The first step is to find the land," she says. "That was my first step for the Lake Tierra Golf Course. I chose the land because of the views of heavily wooded hills, the potential elevation changes, and a creek that runs through the land. One of the most important aspects of a golf course design is working the unique land features into the design and preserving the environment. For example, when I come across a stand of trees, I design the golf hole so that the trees are a feature rather than an obstacle to be removed."

I can see the jurors leaning in again, their interest piqued as she describes the careful consideration she gave to every element of the course, from the layout to the environmental impact. She's like a professor teaching a class. This is where Lauren shines, and I make sure to highlight that, guiding her with questions that allow her expertise to take center stage.

I ask, "What sets Lauren West's golf courses apart from those designed by others?"

Lauren sits up a little straighter, the nerves from earlier now giving way to quiet confidence. "What makes my courses unique is my focus on ensuring the entire family can enjoy playing together. Golf can be intimidating, especially for beginners or younger players, so I design every course with them in mind right from the start."

She pauses, looking at the jurors, most of whom probably have never set foot on a golf course. I can see her thinking about how to connect with them.

"For example," she continues, "I design the tee boxes with different skill levels in mind," Lauren explains as I display photos of golf holes with tees on courses for the jury. She points to one of the images. "For the forward tees, I position them so that beginners or younger players can avoid intimidating obstacles like water, brush, or ravines. My goal is to ensure they can have a positive experience on the course, building their confidence without feeling overwhelmed by the challenges more experienced players might enjoy. For better golfers, I make the holes challenging but fair, so there are plenty of opportunities for all players to succeed. I also consider the flow of the course, making sure it's not too strenuous, so families can enjoy walking together, even if they're at different levels of play."

She glances at me, and I nod, encouraging her to continue.

"Beyond the technical aspects," she adds, "I incorporate elements that appeal to everyone, not just the golfers. There are scenic views, areas where kids can explore safely if they need a break, and even spots designed for family gatherings. It's about creating an experience where everyone feels welcome and has fun, not just the seasoned golfer."

I can see the jurors nodding, some of them smiling, as they begin to grasp her vision. Lauren's words are reaching them, painting a picture of a golf course that's more than just a game, but a place where families can bond and enjoy time together.

Lauren's eyes sparkle with enthusiasm as she explains that many male golf course architects design golf courses for men. Many times, the forward tee box is downhill or where trees get in the way of a good tee shot. Finally, it's far less fun if golfers playing the forward tees are forced to use woods or hybrid clubs on every approach shot to the green.

I hear a noise and glance over in Benton's direction. He's shaking his head from left to right, muttering "no" under his breath. His expression is one of barely concealed disdain, and I can tell his goal is either to distract me or, more likely, to intimidate Lauren. His arrogance is showing, as if he believes the courtroom rules don't apply to him.

Judge Hawkins strikes his desk with his gavel, the sharp sound cutting through the tension. "Mr. Benton, you are not to make any gestures or comments while Miss West is testifying. Do you understand?"

Benton doesn't flinch. Instead, he leans back in his chair, crossing his arms with a smirk. "Judge, I was simply expressing that I believe her testimony is, at the very least, an exaggeration and, more likely, a lie."

The room goes silent, the tension thick in the air. Judge Hawkins's eyes sharpen, silently waiting. His patience is clearly wearing thin. “Mr. Morgan, would you kindly instruct your client to refrain from making noise or gestures while Miss West testifies?”

“Yes, Your Honor.” Morgan quickly places a firm hand on Benton’s shoulder, leaning in to whisper something I can’t quite make out. Benton’s smirk fades slightly, but the contempt in his eyes remains. It’s clear he’s not used to being told what to do, especially not in a place like this.

As Morgan pulls back, Benton doesn't speak, but his glare speaks volumes, locking onto Lauren with quiet contempt. I glance at Lauren, noticing how she straightens in her seat, refusing to be cowed by Benton’s attempts at intimidation. It’s a small victory but an important one.

I ask Lauren about the Lake Tierra contract. She shares with the jury how her other Benton Land Company development golf course designs won praise from golf publications and the media, including praise from Mr. Benton. She says she had received other far more generous offers to design golf courses for well-known developers. Benton begged her to stay, and that’s when she negotiated a ten percent profit bonus in her contract. In return, Benton demanded that she agree to a non-compete provision keeping her from designing golf courses for another developer for two years.

In excruciating detail, Lauren goes over each and every step she took to design the award-winning Lake Tierra Golf Course. I worry she's providing so much detail that she's losing the jury. But, if anything, it shows the jury all the work and effort she put into the project. Morgan frequently objects, and Judge Hawkins never rules in his favor. He's objecting to throw us off course for a moment.

I turn to Lauren with a smile, knowing this topic truly reflects her passion. "Lauren, can you tell us about your efforts to promote golf for girls?"

Before she can answer, Morgan jumps to his feet again. "Objection, Your Honor. Miss West's involvement in promoting golf for girls is irrelevant to this case."

Judge Hawkins studies me closely, waiting for my response.Judge

"Your Honor," I say, keeping my tone measured, "Lauren's efforts to involve girls in golf are directly relevant. They speak to her deep commitment to girls' and women's sports, which played a significant role in Mr. Benton's decision to terminate her golf course design contract."

Judge Hawkins considers this for a moment, then nods. "Objection overruled. Miss West, you may answer the question."

Lauren sits up straighter, her eyes bright with enthusiasm. She begins, addressing the jury with genuine warmth. "Promoting golf for girls has been one of the most fulfilling parts of my career. I felt honored to contribute to the development of the LPGA Foundation, which has brought golf opportunities to communities where girls previously had little chance to play."

She pauses, her voice strong and clear as she continues. "The first golf course I designed in South Dallas was part of that effort. I wasn't just designing a place to play golf. I was creating a space where girls from all backgrounds could learn and grow. In many of these communities, the girls not only needed a golf course, but they also needed help acquiring golf clubs and equipment. We worked hard to ensure they had everything they needed to succeed."

Lauren's voice takes on a more personal note as she looks directly at the jurors. "But golf is only part of what we're accomplishing. These programs are about more than just a game. They're teaching girls life skills, such as discipline, perseverance, and confidence, that will help them beyond the golf course. Today, the fastest-growing group playing golf are girls under eighteen, and because of these efforts, the number of non-white girls playing the sport has increased dramatically."

Her words hang in the air, and I can see the jurors nodding. That's a good sign. Lauren's genuine passion and the impact of her work resonate in the room, leaving no doubt about the positive influence she has had on the lives of so many young girls.

Now. I turn more directly to the heart of the issue. "Lauren," I say, my voice steady, "can you explain your stance on the issue of biological men competing in girls' and women's sports?"

Lauren draws a breath, clearly aware of the gravity of her words. "While I strongly believe that biological boys and men should be allowed to live the life they have chosen," she begins, "I just as strongly believe that it should not extend to biological boys and men competing against girls and women. My efforts to raise money, build golf courses, and increase the number of girls with opportunities to compete would be undermined if biological boys and men could compete and take those spots. Studies have shown that in almost every sport, a biological boy or man has a physical advantage over —"

Before she can finish, Morgan is on his feet, his voice laced with anger. "Your Honor, unless Miss West can present the studies, her statement should be stricken from the record, and the jury informed to disregard it."

The room falls into a tense silence. Judge Hawkins looks from Morgan to me. I can't read his expression. "Mr. Hartley," he says, his tone measured, "what is your response to the objection?"

I stand firm, knowing this is a crucial moment. "Your Honor, I have two studies that I'd like to offer in evidence to support Miss West's statement." I reach into my briefcase and hand copies of the studies to Morgan, who snatches them up with a scowl.

Judge Hawkins takes the studies from me, his eyes narrowing as he begins to read. The room is so quiet I can hear the rustling of the paper as he turns each page, carefully reviewing the contents. Every eye in the courtroom is fixed on the judge as he deliberates. Lauren sits in the witness chair, her hands folded tightly in her lap, her calm exterior belying the anxiety I know she's feeling.

Finally, Judge Hawkins looks up, his gaze moving slowly from the studies to Lauren and then to Morgan. "After reviewing these studies, I find them relevant to the testimony. The objection is overruled. Miss West may continue."

A breath I didn't realize I was holding releases as I nod to Lauren to proceed. She resumes her testimony, her voice steady and sure, but the tension remains thick in the air. The jury's attention is laser-focused, and I can tell that this moment, this testimony, could very well determine the outcome of the case.

I have Lauren summarize the conclusions of the studies, her voice steady and confident as she testifies. "The scientists concluded in both studies that transgender girls and women have inherent physical advantages over biological girls and women."

She pauses, glancing at the jurors, then continues, "You may be aware that when the top women golfers in the world have competed in PGA events, they've never finished in the top half at the end of two days. The reason is simple: they are physically at a disadvantage because men, on average, hit the golf ball farther."

I lean forward slightly, prompting her to elaborate. "Can you further explain what you mean by that?"

"Sure," she says, with a hint of resolve in her voice. "This whole idea that a biological boy or man can simply say he identifies as a girl or woman and then competes in girls' or women's sports is, frankly, absurd. Imagine if a twenty-five-year-old male golfer claimed he identified as an older man and then demanded to compete on the men's senior tour. It would be preposterous, and no one would take it seriously."

I notice a ripple of laughter among the jurors. It's the kind of laughter that carries a sense of agreement as if they're reacting to the clear-cut logic of her comparison. But I can't help but wonder if they're laughing because they find the notion of a birth male identifying as a different gender to compete equally baffling or if the absurdity of the age comparison struck a chord.

"Are there other reasons for your stance?" I ask, guiding her to delve deeper.

Lauren nods, her expression more serious. 'In some sports, it's not just about fairness. It's about safety." I'm aware of a teenage volleyball player who suffered severe injuries after a biological male spiked a ball so forcefully that it struck her face, causing long-term concussion symptoms, including vision problems. And just recently, in the 2024 Olympics that concluded in Paris, a female boxer who had dedicated years to training had to concede in a match because the transgender boxer she faced hit harder than anyone she had ever encountered."

Before Lauren can continue, Morgan stands abruptly. "Objection, Your Honor," he says, his tone sharp. "What happened in Olympic boxing is not relevant to Miss West's lawsuit." Before

Lauren can continue, Morgan stands abruptly and says in a sharp tone, "Objection, Your Honor. Miss West's lawsuit has no relevance to what happened in Olympic boxing. We request that you strike her testimony on that subject from the record and instruct the jury to disregard it."

The room goes silent as Judge Hawkins considers the objection. He squints his eyes a bit. Then, after a brief pause, he agrees. "Sustained. I will strike the testimony regarding Olympic boxing from the record. The jury is instructed to disregard Miss West's comments on that matter."

I glance at the jurors, gauging their reactions. Despite the judge's ruling, I can see the impact of Lauren's words lingering. I believe most of the jurors likely watched the Olympics and will not easily disregard what they've just heard. The point has been made, and I can tell it's resonated with them.

"Have you spoken out about any other issues?"

"I have publicly expressed my disapproval of biological males accessing women's showers and locker rooms. It's terrible for girls or women to witness a biological man exposing himself in their locker room. When I played golf in high school and college, I never dreamed there would come a day when high school girls and college female athletes would share showers and locker rooms with naked men."

"Has that actually happened?"

"Yes," Lauren replies.

While Morgan stands to object, I hand news articles to him, then turn to Lauren. "Lauren, can you identify these articles and testify about what you've read regarding incidents in high school girls' locker rooms, college women's locker rooms, and even in locker rooms at spas in Los Angeles?"

Lauren takes a moment to review the articles before looking up at the jury. "These articles detail instances where girls and women have reported feeling uncomfortable or even unsafe when sharing locker rooms with transgender individuals. It's not just limited to high school or college environments; there have been similar reports from women's locker rooms at spas in Los Angeles. In some cases, women have expressed concerns about privacy and security, which have sparked significant debates and legal challenges."

I trust that Lauren's testimony has made an impact on the jurors, and I decide to shift my focus.

“Why do you believe Robert Benton terminated your Lake Tierra Golf Course Design Contract?”

Morgan jumps to his feet again. “Your Honor, this calls for pure speculation. Mr. Benton is the only person who can testify why he terminated the witness’ contract.”

“I’m going to allow her to answer,” Judge Hawkins says. “You can address your point in cross-examination and in your final argument.”

“You’re what?” Morgan asks.

“I said I’m going to allow her to answer. You may sit down and listen to what she says.”

After all this, I repeat the question for Lauren.

“Mr. Benton habitually refuses to pay his contractors what he owes them. He terminated my contract when he discovered he’d owe me as much as one million dollars as a bonus. It was his way of cheating me out of what I had earned. The only thing worse was when he claimed credit for designing the Lake Tierra Golf Course.”

With that answer, I say, “I have no further questions, Your Honor.”

Judge Hawkins glances at the clock and nods. "Mr. Morgan, you may begin your cross-examination in the morning."

The gavel strikes, signaling the end of the day's proceedings, but the weight of what's coming next worries me. I can see the anxiety etched on Lauren's face, and I know she'll get little sleep tonight, dreading what Morgan will throw at her tomorrow.

She once confided in me that she battled performance anxiety during her golf career, so severe that she had to hire a sports psychologist just to keep competing. I'm no psychologist, and I'm not sure I can provide the support she needs to overcome the fear gnawing at her now.

But it's not just her anxiety that concerns me. It's mine. I keep telling myself to stay detached, to focus on the case and not the woman sitting beside me. But the line is blurring, and with each passing day, it's becoming harder to separate the two. Tomorrow, Morgan will be relentless, and I'm not sure how Lauren will hold up under the pressure.

As I watch Lauren gather her things, I look over at her. Tomorrow could be the turning point, and the outcome will hinge not just on the facts but on how well she withstands the assault that's coming. We've spent hours and days getting her ready to face Morgan. All I can do now is hope that when the time comes tomorrow, she'll be ready.

Chapter 26

Lauren

The next morning, as we walk from Luke's car to the courthouse, we see that the protestors are already there, more aggressive than the day before. Word must have spread that today is the day I'll face Morgan's cross-examination. They swarm around us, their faces twisted with anger as if they can already sense my vulnerability. The shouts are louder, more vicious. "Racist!" "Sexist!" "Transphobic!" The words hit like a barrage of stones, each one aimed to cut deep. Reporters and camera operators jockey for position, capturing every moment of our approach, their lenses trained on me, ready to broadcast any sign of weakness. I try to keep my head down, but the vitriol and the relentless scrutiny are impossible to ignore.

As we near the courthouse steps, a few protestors push forward, spitting in my direction. I feel the wetness on my arm and cheek, the insult stinging more than the spit itself. My stomach churns with a mix of disgust and humiliation. I'm used to pressure, but this is something else entirely. The thought of being spit on makes me want to recoil, to escape somewhere safe and clean.

"Stay close," Luke says firmly, moving shield me. But the crowd is relentless, and three protestors link arms, blocking our path. One of them steps closer, eyes wild, and shouts, "You're putting lives at risk, you bigot!" Another lunges forward as if to attack, but before he can reach me, uniformed policemen and women push through the crowd, finally creating a barrier between us and the mob.

"Keep moving," one of the officers says as they lead us through the courthouse doors. Inside, the noise from outside fades, but the tension doesn't.

"I need a moment," I tell Luke, my voice shaky. "I need to clean up."

He nods. "I'll wait for you."

I make my way to the ladies' room, the cold and sterile tiles a stark contrast to the chaos outside. At the sink, I scrub my face and arms, the water washing away the physical remnants of the protest but doing little to soothe the emotional toll. As I stand there, trying to steady my breath, the door swings open, and I tense, expecting another confrontation.

Instead, Carlotta Hampton strides in, her presence commanding as always. She catches my eye in the mirror, but instead of the sharpness I expected, her gaze has a softness. “Tough morning, Miss West?” she asks, her voice carrying a note of genuine concern.

I swallow the sharp retort that springs to mind, taken aback by the unexpected softness in her tone. “Nothing I can’t handle,” I reply, my voice still firm, but less guarded.

Carlotta steps closer, adjusting her immaculate blonde hair in the mirror beside me. “You know,” she says gently, “this case isn’t just about you. A lot of people are watching, and it’s a tough position to be in.” Her gaze meets mine in the mirror, and for a moment, I see understanding in her eyes.

With that, she offers a small reassuring nod before turning to leave. I take a deep breath, steadying myself, but I’m still nervous like never before. I’ve faced pressure before, but today feels different, heavier. The uncertainty of what lies ahead lingers despite the brief moment of empathy.

When I walk towards the courtroom, Luke stands just outside the door, his eyes scanning my face. I nod, and together, we enter and walk to our counsel table and sit.

A few minutes later, Judge Hawkins enters as everyone in the courtroom rises. Once he takes his seat, he nods to the bailiff. "Please summon the jury."

As I walk to the witness chair and take my seat, my eyes catch the Court TV camera fixed directly on me, its lens unblinking, ready to capture my every move. I also spot reporters scattered among the gallery, prepared to document any slip-up I make. I feel greater pressure now, knowing they will scrutinize my every word and every gesture. I do my best to steady myself as Judge Hawkins surveys the courtroom, then turns his attention to Morgan. "Mr. Morgan, you may begin your cross-examination."

I can feel the eyes of the courtroom on me, the pressure building with each passing second. In the back of my mind, I hear my father's voice, just as I did all those years ago before the final round of the U.S. Open. After a double bogey on the fifteenth hole, my lead had dwindled to a two-shot lead, with three holes to play. I feared I was going to blow it. He looked me in the eye, his voice steady and sure. "Stay calm, Lauren. Focus on each shot, one at a time. You've got this. You prepared your whole life for this moment."

I close my eyes for a brief second, visualizing him standing beside me now, just as he did then, his presence as solid as ever.

The courtroom fades away, replaced by the memory of his reassuring smile and the way he made everything seem possible. I take a deep breath, grounding myself in his words, knowing that, just like before, I must stay focused and answer Morgan's questions one at a time.

"Good morning, Miss West," Morgan says.

I don't respond.

"Did you hear me, Miss West? I said good morning."

"I heard you, Mr. Morgan. I didn't respond because you didn't ask a question."

I hear a couple of jurors laughing. Luke had advised me not to make any flippant answers, and out of the gate, I was not following his advice. I'm determined not to let Morgan get the best of me.

Morgan catches on. "Then, I should ask, is it a good morning, Miss West?"

"I'd say no," I answer. "I'd far rather be on a golf course with girls."

"You mean biological girls, don't you?"

"No, I said girls."

"Your public image is important to you, isn't it?"

"Yes, like most people, I care about being seen in a positive light," I reply.

"And you know that your public image was important to Mr. Benton. Isn't that true?"

"I don't know. We never talked about it."

"You know that your image as a former LPGA golfer and champion was important to Benton Land Company selling land and homes in its golf course communities, right?" Morgan's voice is smooth, almost too casual as if he's setting a trap.

"I suppose so," I reply, keeping my tone steady. "But my expertise in designing extraordinary golf courses for a whole family to enjoy was more important."

I fidget slightly in the witness chair, sensing the shift in the air. This semi-friendly back-and-forth is about to take a darker turn. I can feel it. Morgan's eyes narrow as he leans on the podium, his voice dropping slightly.

"Miss West, tell the jury about your professional interactions with the married Benton Land Company clients."

My stomach tightens as I realize what he's insinuating. He's trying to paint me as someone who slept with these clients. I pause to gather my composure before responding.

"If by 'professional interactions,' you mean playing a round of golf with clients who purchased properties in our developments, then yes, I've played golf with each of them. But if you're suggesting anything improper, that's absolutely false."

Morgan smiles, but it doesn't reach his eyes. He leans over the podium, savoring the moment, pausing just long enough to let the tension build. "You only played golf with them, you say. So, you're telling this jury that there's never been an occasion when you've personally interacted with them outside of a golf course?"

"Several clients have invited me to their homes for dinner, and I've gone out for lunch or dinner with several clients," I answer, trying to keep my voice calm, though my heart is starting to race.

"Interesting," Morgan murmurs. He leans over the podium again and turns toward the jury as if sharing a secret. "And these professional interactions always occurred in public settings or in their homes. Were private meetings away from their homes ever necessary?"

I swallow hard while trying to maintain composure. "I'm sorry, Mr. Morgan. I don't understand what you mean by private meetings. Are you asking if I met privately with any clients to persuade them to buy property in the development? If that is your question, then yes, private sales meetings were necessary. I spent countless hours talking to clients about how the Benton Land Company development would bring joy to their entire family."

Morgan's smile widens, but there's nothing kind in it. His eyes gleam with something darker.

"Did you ever have, let us say, extracurricular intimate relations in one of these private meetings?" Morgan's words piss me off. If we weren't in court, I'd tell him where he should go. The jury's eyes are on me, and I have to keep calm and not blurt out what I'm thinking.

Luke is on his feet immediately. "Your Honor, Mr. Morgan is badgering Miss West, and his question is both inappropriate and irrelevant."

Judge Hawkins looks over at me. "I'll allow her to answer."

I take a steady breath to calm myself. Turning to the jury, my voice is firm and laced with offense. "Never. I have always conducted myself with the highest level of professionalism. The mere suggestion that I would use anything other than my golf course design skills and expertise to gain a client's trust is not only insulting, but it's also a baseless attack on my character."

I make sure to meet the eyes of the women on the jury, letting them see my reaction, knowing they'll understand the insult beneath Morgan's question.

"Of course," Morgan responds, his grip on the podium tightening as he leans forward, his voice slow and deliberate. "But surely you can understand how one might interpret your private consultations with male clients as something more intimate?"

"Mr. Morgan," I say, my voice steady despite the anger bubbling beneath the surface, "I can understand why someone like you might interpret my meetings with clients that way, but anyone who knows me understands that those meetings were purely professional. I met with Lake Tierra clients with the sole purpose of showcasing my golf course design and persuading them to become homeowners—nothing more."

Morgan's eyes narrow slightly, but he presses on. "Miss West, would you say your personal charm played a significant role in persuading clients to invest in Benton Land Company's golf developments?"

I take a slow, steadying breath, refusing to let him rattle me. "Mr. Morgan," I respond calmly, "the clients were drawn to the developments because of the exceptional golf courses I designed, not because of any so-called charm. The courses spoke for themselves, not whatever influence you're insinuating I had."

Morgan's expression remains unchanged as he plows ahead, ignoring my response or, more likely, dismissing it entirely. "But surely," he presses, his tone thick with suggestion, "a woman in your position, dealing with wealthy, powerful men, might be tempted to use her... assets... to close a deal."

Morgan's words carry a clear bias against professional women, and I can see the jury processing it, their eyes shifting between us. They may be judging me, but I refuse to let Morgan rattle me.

"Isn't it true you've been involved in a sexual relationship with your lawyer, Mr. Hartley?" Morgan places a photo on the screen, accusingly showing Luke and me in a close embrace. A murmur ripples through the courtroom as the jurors absorb the image.

Luke immediately stands, objecting, but before Judge Hawkins can rule, I can't hold back. "I've never had sex with my lawyer," I state firmly, my voice cutting through the whispers.

"This photo shows Luke hugging me after I told him that Mr. Benton's protestors had harassed me and my mother."

Judge Hawkins raises his hand to stop me. "Miss West, when your attorney objects to a question by Mr. Morgan, I ask that you not answer before I rule on the objection."

I swallow, nodding. "Yes, sir. I'm sorry I jumped the gun. I just couldn't let Mr. Morgan get away with besmirching my character."

Judge Hawkins' gaze softens, and he nods before turning to Morgan, who stands silently, watching me with a slight smirk. The room is tense, the jury's eyes shifting between us, trying to decipher the truth from the innuendo.

"Miss West, isn't it true that while you were in college, you received financial deals with sponsors violating NCAA rules?"

How does that bastard know about that?

"Well. Mr. Morgan, as you know, the Supreme Court ruled that it is illegal for the NCAA to ban athletes from receiving Name, Image, Likeness, known as NIL funds. I was ahead of my time."

"In violation of NCAA rules. You thought those rules didn't apply to you?"

"As I said, the Supreme Court ruled that the NCAA rules were illegal."

"Miss West," Morgan begins, his tone laced with accusation, "isn't it true that more than once the LPGA tour fined you for dressing inappropriately during tournaments?"

I keep getting angry, but I force my voice to remain steady and controlled. "Yes, I was fined by the LPGA, but I wasn't the only one. I'm tall, and I have long legs, which made it difficult to find skirts, skorts, or shorts that met the strict LPGA dress code. Other tall golfers faced the same issues. After I retired, the LPGA relaxed those rules. If you watch any LPGA tournaments today, you'll see the golfers wearing shorts far shorter than I ever did."

Morgan's smirk widens, his eyes riveting on me. "And like the NCAA rules, you believed the LPGA rules didn't apply to you?"

"I believed the LPGA rules were outdated by about forty years when they were first published," I reply, keeping my tone even.

Morgan presses on, his voice dripping with skepticism. "What about the other incidents? Didn't you flaunt the rules to get more attention and endorsements?"

I take a breath, resisting the urge to say more than necessary. "There were times when I wore what the manufacturer provided, only to find out it violated the dress code. But it was never intentional or done for attention-seeking purposes. I even met with the manufacturer afterward and told them I wouldn't wear their clothes again if they put me in an embarrassing situation. As I have already testified, after I retired, the LPGA relaxed their standards, acknowledging that the young women joining the tour grew up in a different era."

Morgan turns to the jury with an exaggerated look of disbelief, clearly signaling that he doesn't buy my explanation. I feel the urge to add more, to defend myself further, but I remember Luke's advice: keep my answers short and on point.

"But isn't it true," Morgan continues, his voice now almost mocking, "that your fight with the LPGA landed you modeling contracts?"

I meet his gaze, refusing to let him rattle me. "I can't say that my disagreements with the LPGA led to my modeling contracts. I don't believe the two are connected."

Morgan pauses, letting the implication linger, giving the jury time to piece together the conclusion he's aiming for. He's baiting me for a reaction, but I remain steady, confident that I've fully answered his question.

"Since you are one not to follow the rules, I bet you thought it was okay when you cheated while playing a golf tournament. Isn't that true?"

"No, Mr. Morgan, golf rules are sacred."

"Isn't it true one of your competitors once accused you of cheating?"

Morgan puts a news article on the screen with the headline, LPGA Golfer Lauren West Accused of Cheating. Your competitor accused you of lying about where your errant drive crossed the water hazard. Isn't that true?

"That was a misunderstanding. The televised replay of where my drive crossed the hazard later proved my competitor was wrong."

Morgan plays the television video with the announcers pointing on the screen where Lauren's drive crossed the hazard and where Lauren took a drop. The jury hears them show there was a difference of about ten yards.

"You didn't drop where your ball crossed the hazard. It was ten yards closer to the hole. So, you lied about it, didn't you?"

"Mr. Morgan, you're dead wrong. I didn't lie and would never knowingly break a rule of golf. I didn't have access to the television coverage. I dropped the ball where I thought it crossed the hazard, and it was a lot closer to the actual spot than where my competitor claimed I should have dropped."

"If it wasn't an out-and-out lie," Morgan sneers, "at the very least, you chose a spot to drop that was more favorable for you. Isn't that true?"

I can feel the weight of the accusation settling over the courtroom, and I'm acutely aware that many jurors likely don't understand the intricacies of golf rules. Morgan is trying to paint me as someone who will cheat to win, whether in a tournament or this trial.

I take a breath, keeping my voice steady. "Mr. Morgan, in professional golf, a difference of ten yards when hitting a second shot on a par five hole doesn't make much of a difference. If you had continued showing the television footage, you would have seen that I hit my second shot onto the fairway about one hundred yards from the hole. If I had played the shot from ten yards farther back, I would have used a different club and still placed the ball in roughly the same spot."

I pause, letting the truth of my words hang in the air. I resist the urge to look at the jury, unsure if they understand the significance of what I've just said—or if Morgan's insinuations have already planted seeds of doubt. I'm angry and tense, but I know I've spoken the truth, and that's all I can do.

"And Miss West. You claim that Mr. Benton breached Benton Land Company's contract with you, but the truth is, you breached your contract with Benton Land Company."

"No, that's not true."

"Your contract with Benton Land Company provided that you could not design a golf course for anyone but Benton Land Company, right?"

"No sir, you're wrong. I've agreed in the contract to not design a golf course for a competitor, which means another developer."

"Whatever the language, you designed golf courses for others. Isn't that true?"

"I designed two public golf courses in lower-income communities, and those golf courses in no way compete with those I designed for Benton Land Company."

"Miss West, if you were so certain you were not breaching your contract with Mr. Benton, why did you choose to keep that work a secret from him?"

"Because it was none of his business."

"Wouldn't you agree that if someone does a Google search of your name, they'll likely find more photographs of you in skimpy bikinis than in golf attire?"

Before I can answer, Luke stands. "Your Honor, Objection relevance."

"Mr. Morgan, I agree with Mr. Hartley. His objection is sustained. Please move on."

I suspect jurors might make a Google search of their own.

"You'd do anything to make more money, wouldn't you?"

"No, Mr. Morgan, I'm not like Mr. Benton."

Judge Hawkins instructs jurors to disregard my reference to Mr. Benton.

"Do you agree that Mr. Benton told you those photos might offend some clients?" Morgan asks.

I know where Morgan is going with this, and it's not a place I want to go. But I have to stay composed. I can't let him see that he's rattling me.

"Actually," I say, forcing my voice to stay calm, "he conveyed the opposite. Mr. Benton would often flaunt those photos to his male clients, using them to stir up interest in my golf course designs. He once admitted to me that he was marketing our developments by exploiting my so-called sex appeal. I thought it was the most ridiculous thing I'd ever heard, but that's exactly what he said."

Morgan's eyes gleam with satisfaction, sensing he's touched a raw nerve. I notice a shift in the jurors' expressions; some seem to be processing what I've said, while others appear unsettled. I can only hope they recognize the truth in my words.

Judge Hawkins glances at the jury, then at the clock. Just as Morgan leans forward, ready to push further, the judge cuts him off. "Let's take a fifteen-minute break," he declares. I catch a few jurors exchanging relieved looks, clearly needing the pause as much as I do.

As I step down from the stand, my heart pounds. Morgan is relentless, and I can feel him closing in, determined to twist every word I say. This battle is far from over, and after the break, Morgan's cross-examination could be the most brutal yet.

Chapter 27

Lauren

During the break, I can see from his frown that Luke is frustrated as he asks the question I knew was coming.

"Lauren, why didn't you tell me that you were designing municipal golf courses while under contract with Benton Land Company?" His tone carries the weight of his exasperation.

I feel defensive but try to stay calm. "Because I didn't think it mattered. Those municipal courses weren't in competition with Benton's developments. They serve entirely different communities."

Luke runs a hand through his hair, clearly struggling to keep his composure. "It's not about competition. It's about transparency. I asked for no surprises, remember? If you had told me, we could have handled it upfront instead of letting Morgan use it against you."

I clench my fists, trying to keep my frustration in check. "I wasn't hiding anything, Luke. Those inner-city courses weren't a secret. I didn't even get paid to design them. I thought they would reflect positively on Benton, not become ammunition for Morgan."

He exhales sharply, the tension between us palpable. "Lauren, are there any more surprises waiting for me in this case?"

I can see how frustrated he is, and it hits me that he's only trying to protect me. I decide to let it go. "No more surprises, Luke," I say softly, hoping to diffuse the tension.

Minutes later, we return to the courtroom. After the jury enters and I nervously retake my seat on the witness stand, Judge Hawkins says, "You may continue your cross-examination now, Mr. Morgan."

"Yes, Your Honor," Morgan says, staring at me with that smug look. "Isn't it true, Miss West, that when you first approached Mr. Benton to design golf courses for his developments, you attempted to seduce him?"

I pause, making sure the television camera catches the devilish grin spreading across my face. Then, I laugh loud enough for everyone to hear.

"Mr. Morgan, Mr. Benton is not my type. He's too old, too fat, and definitely not attractive. I'd never try to seduce him."

"Your Honor, please instruct the witness again to answer yes or no questions with a yes or no answer," Morgan snaps.

"Judge, Miss West is entitled to explain her answer," Luke interjects calmly.

"Your Honor, by explaining her answer," Morgan continues, pointing at me like I'm on trial, "Miss West is implying that she would have seduced Mr. Benton if he were younger, slimmer, and more attractive."

I turn to Judge Hawkins, who meets my gaze. "Miss West, while you could have simply responded with a 'no,' you chose to insult Mr. Benton instead. Let's refrain from that by moving forward."

I smile inwardly, knowing I got my point across. Morgan presses on, visibly rattled. Score one point for me.

"Miss West, you had no golf course design business clients when you pitched your luxury golf course community idea to Mr. Benton, right?"

"Yes, you're right. I shared my idea with your client before speaking to anyone else. I'm the one who put the idea in your client's head."

Morgan leans on the podium again and stares at me. “And you needed Mr. Benton’s money to finance the developments where your golf courses were to be built?”

I exhale slowly, gathering my thoughts. I can sense the jury’s eyes on me. I wonder if any jurors have bought into Morgan’s salacious accusations. I turn and speak to them.

“I didn’t need Mr. Benton’s money. There are plenty of other developers out there. They call me all the time, asking me to work with them. I chose to work with Mr. Benton because we’d already talked about my ideas during a charity pro-am event a few years ago. He was enthusiastic and asked me then if he could have the first shot at bringing them to life.. You can throw around all the accusations you want, but I’ll keep setting the record straight.”

“That was a nice speech, Miss West. Let’s talk about the harm you’ve caused transgender athletes. You must hate transgender people.”

“Mr. Morgan, is there an actual question in there, or just another one of your false accusations? I’ve supported—”

Morgan cuts me off sharply. “Miss West, I’m asking for yes or no answers, not long-winded speeches.”

I can see I'm getting under his skin, and I decide to push back. "Mr. Morgan, you're not asking questions. You're making baseless accusations. I believe I have the right to defend myself. If anyone is putting athletes at risk, it's people like you who condemn those of us standing up for girls' and women's sports."

"Your Honor, please instruct Miss West to answer my questions directly and stop grandstanding for the cameras."

Judge Hawkins looks over at me before addressing Morgan. "Mr. Morgan, I have to agree with Miss West. You're making accusations, and she has the right to respond to them."

Morgan shakes his head, clearly irritated. "Your Honor, no judge should allow a witness to make speeches like this."

"Mr. Morgan, I suggest you move on," Judge Hawkins says.

Morgan asks permission to show me a document. Judge Hawkins grants permission.

"Miss West, I've shown you an email you sent to a news reporter. In the email, you referred to transgender athletes as 'a joke' and said they were 'just guys in dresses trying to steal medals from high school girls and college women.' Do those characterizations fairly represent your views of transgender athletes?"

I look over at Luke. He's clearly unhappy. "No, Mr. Morgan. It was hyperbolic. I was commenting about male athletes who suddenly claim to be girls or women to compete in state tournaments or in NCAA college sports. I was upset when I learned of two high school track athletes who could not compete in their state track championships because a transgender athlete who competed as a boy had competed against girls and beat them."

Morgan shows me another email I sent. "Miss West, isn't it true that this is another email you sent to the same news organization?"

"I believe that is true."

"In the email. You say, 'We can't let them redefine what a girl or a woman is just so they can compete in girls' and women's sports."

"Yes, Mr. Morgan, I said that. Girls and women fought for years to have fair opportunities to compete in sports. Title IX opened doors and removed barriers for girls and women. Since Title IX, high school girls' participation in sports has increased by over 1000 percent. College participation has increased by over 600 percent. I simply stated we can't lose what Title IX has granted to girls and women."

“Miss West, do you recall Mr. Benton directing you to keep your political views to yourself?”

“No, I don’t recall.”

Morgan pulls up a copy of an email from Benton and displays it on the screen. “Please read it aloud.”

I read, “Lauren, I know your political views are far to the right of mine. You are a MAGA supporter. Please keep those views private because more than half of our clients disagree with you. We don’t want to alienate any potential clients.”

I look up at Morgan, trying to keep my voice steady. “I’ve never been a MAGA Republican or anything of the sort. I believe Americans should feel proud of our country, but I’ve never aligned myself with that political movement. This email feels like a fabrication, an attempt to discredit me. I’ve always kept my focus on my work, not on politics.”

“Miss West, you responded to Mr. Benton’s email. Do you remember your response?”

“No,” I reply, my voice firm.

Morgan displays an email on the screen, supposedly from me, and instructs me to read it aloud. “Good point, Robert. I agree it’s important not to offend our potential clients.”

I stare at the screen, my heart pounding. That doesn’t sound like something I would say. I look back at Morgan, determination in my voice. “I’ve never seen this email before, and I certainly never sent that response. This feels like a setup, an attempt to fabricate evidence against me. I’ve never received any such email from Mr. Benton, and I would never respond in that way.”

Morgan changes the subject but keeps attacking me. “Miss West, you misgendered trans athletes, didn’t you?”

“I don’t think so.”

“You refused to call them by their preferred gender. Instead, you referred to them as biological boys and men. That’s called misgendering them.”

“Mr. Morgan, are you telling me or asking a question? If you are asking a question, I said people who are males when they are born should compete against boys and men or in a category with other biological boys and men who now consider themselves to be girls and women. I don’t consider that misgendering.”

"Miss West, what you just said is the very definition of misgendering. You are telling trans people they don't deserve to compete in sports based on their chosen gender."

"Mr. Morgan, I respectfully disagree with your definition of misgendering. Are you saying that when I was winning tournaments on the LPGA tour, I could choose to be twelve-years-old and compete against other twelve-year-old girls in junior tournaments, and if someone said that was out of line, they'd be misjudging me?"

"Miss West, I'm here to ask the questions, not to answer yours," Morgan replies.

I look over at the jurors. Some are shaking their heads. They get my point.

"Can you understand why Mr. Benton would want to make sure you didn't express your hateful views and put transgender athletes in danger?"

"What I said in support of girls' and women's sports was not hateful and didn't endanger anyone. What Mr. Benton has done has put my mother and me in danger. His band of protesters have threatened to rape me and my mother. They've blocked…"

"Judge," Morgan interrupts. "I ask you once more to instruct Miss West to answer my questions and not give speeches."

"Miss West, you're entitled to explain your answer, but you are not entitled to go off on another unrelated subject."

"Your Honor, Mr. Morgan asked me if I thought what I said put trans athletes in danger. I answered no. Then, I explained that what I had said about trans athletes had put my mother and me in danger. I wanted to add that I've been forced to call the police several times to break up the crowd tormenting me and my mother."

"Miss West, please just answer Mr. Morgan's questions. Your lawyer can ask you to describe what you've experienced when he asks you questions on redirect. Go ahead, Mr. Morgan," Judge Hawkins says. "Ask your next question."

"Miss West, that may be what you believe, but you didn't answer my question. I'll ask again. Can you understand why Mr. Benton would want you not to make public comments that put transgender athletes in danger?"

"Mr. Morgan, I don't believe Robert Benton cares about transgender athletes. He was looking for a reason to deny me the bonus I had earned and used my response to an interview question.

If I had not responded to the question, Robert Benton would have come up with another reason."

"There you go again, giving a speech. Please answer my yes or no question."

"Yes, I do understand. Other than the people who have threatened to rape me and my mother and those who camp out at our house and won't let me enter the front door, I don't know of anyone who wants to put people in danger as a result of what they or anyone else says."

"Your Honor, I ask that you instruct the jury to disregard Miss West's answer."

"Mr. Morgan, I'm letting the jury consider Miss West's answer."

"Miss West, you condemn all transgender people because they are different, don't you?"

"Mr. Morgan, you're wrong, and you're deliberately misleading the jury," I begin, my tone deliberate. "I have always supported inclusivity, and I wholeheartedly believe in the dignity and rights of transgender individuals."

"Your idea of inclusivity doesn't include inclusivity in sports, correct?"

"I thought we'd gone over this. My stance on fair competition is equally clear. I advocate for policies that preserve the integrity of women's sports, ensuring fair and equitable competition for biological girls and women. Fairness trumps inclusivity. I also believe that transgender athletes identifying as girls and women should be able to compete either in male sports or in a transgender competition."

Morgan leans back and folds his arms. "I'll change the subject. Miss West, didn't you think at the time you attacked transgender athletes that you materially breached your contract?"

Luke objects on the grounds it calls for a legal conclusion.

"Your Honor, you will instruct the jury on the law of material breach of contract. Then, it is up to them to decide. I'm asking Miss West whether, at the time she attacked transgender athletes, she believed she was materially breaching her contract."

"I'll let the witness answer what she believed at the time."

"No, I did not. I never thought my support for girls' and women's sports had anything to do with a contract to design a golf course."

"But you agree you've been called a transphobic bigot on social media. Isn't that true?"

"I don't pay attention to social media, so I don't know."

"Wouldn't you agree that being labeled a transphobic bigot could hurt property sales in Benton Land Company Golf Communities, where you designed the golf course?"

Morgan glances at the jurors, making sure they're following his line of questioning.

Luke and I had prepared for this question, knowing it was coming. I answer confidently, "Actually, my support of girls' and women's sports has boosted property sales at the Lake Tierra Hill Country Development. What you've conveniently left out is that the vast majority of people in the United States agree with my stance. I can provide you with polls to back that up if you'd like."

"That will not be necessary. Those polls do not specifically cover states like California or New York, or Oregon, or Washington state where the laws require public schools to allow transgender students to access bathrooms and sports teams by their gender identity?"

I'd been hoping Morgan would make that claim. "Since you mention California, Mr. Morgan, you must not be aware of the

Public Policy Institute of California Poll on Transgender Athletes. I have it right here. It reflects that about half of those polls oppose transgender athletes competing in girls' and women's sports. I don't think there are polls in the other states that you mentioned."

Morgan shows me an article that reflects what he's alleged is slightly true in those states.

"Many clients who have considered buying property at the Lake Tierra Hill Country resort are from California, New York, Oregon, and Washington. Isn't that true?"

"I know many from those states and many from other states which don't permit transgender athletes to compete in girls' and women's sports."

"And isn't the main point of your golf course design contract to generate property sales in the development? Why else would Mr. Benton hire you?"

"My designs are the primary reason the Benton Land Company developments, including Lake Tierra, have been so profitable. Without the golf courses I've designed, they would be just high-end housing developments and not generate interest throughout the United States."

"I have just a few more questions, Miss West. Isn't it possible that transgender golfers are playing on the LPGA tour, and you never noticed?"

That question takes me by surprise.

"No, that's not possible," I respond.

"You have no way of knowing for sure, do you?"

"I would have known if a trans golfer played on the LPGA tour. If nothing else, the media would have made a big deal about it."

"Are you aware that the LPGA tour has a gender policy?"

I'm aware, but I didn't know that Morgan was aware. "Yes, Mr. Morgan, I don't believe…"

Morgan shows Luke a document and hands it to me. "Please read the first sentence to the Jury, Miss West."

I read, "LPGA maintains this Gender Policy ("Policy") to provide transgender athletes an avenue to membership and opportunity to participate in events, to assure fair competition for all members and participants."

"So, even your LPGA Tour rules permit transgender golfers."

I quickly scan the rest of the document.

"Is that a question?"

"Yes, Miss West, it's a question."

"Only in limited circumstances," I say.

"You're a MAGA supporter, aren't you?"

"If you define MAGA as making America great again, I wholeheartedly support that. If you are using the acronym to ask if I support the candidate who coined the acronym, I don't support him."

Morgan puts a video on the screen. Before the video starts, Luke quickly stands. "Your Honor, before Mr. Morgan can play this video, he must prove that it's authentic and not a deepfake."

Morgan counters, telling Judge Hawkins that over twenty thousand people have already viewed the video and arguing that we must prove it's a fake before he excludes it.

Judge Hawkins considers the argument, then rules, "This is the first time I've been asked to rule on the authenticity of a video. After giving it thought, I'll leave it to the jury to decide if the video is authentic. In the meantime, Miss West can answer Mr. Morgan's questions and explain her side."

The video begins, showing me supposedly speaking at a conservative forum. In the video, I say, "Transgender people are mentally unstable and should be kept away from our children. They're a threat to real women, and we should never allow them to invade our spaces or our values."

The video ends with the audience applauding loudly.

"Miss West," Morgan asks, his voice dripping with accusation, "your words in this video express your true feelings about transgender people, don't they?"

"No," I respond firmly. "I never said those words. That is not me."

"Look again, Miss West. You're telling the jurors that you are not the person spouting hate in this video?"

"I'm telling the jurors that someone created a fake video of me and put my voice in it. If you look closely, my lips moved out of sync with the voice, which proves someone created a deepfake video for the sole purpose of making me look hateful."

I look at the jurors. From their looks, they believe I am the person in the video. Before I can explain any further, Judge Hawkins calls for a recess for fifteen minutes.

"Miss West, I have an audio recording of you…"

Luke stands and objects again.

Judge Hawkins denies the objection, and Morgan plays the audio.

In the audio recording, I supposedly said, "Allowing transgender students and adults to use the same bathrooms and locker rooms as girls and women is a danger to our children. We need to protect our children from this perversion."

Morgan asks, "Isn't that what you believe and have said, Miss West?"

I have to think for a moment. "I don't believe biological males should be allowed to use the restrooms and locker rooms of girls and women, but that recording is not me."

Judge Hawkins stops Morgan before he asks the next question. "Mr. Morgan, I think you have made your point. Miss West claims that it is not her on the video and not her on the audio. Let's move on."

"Yes, Your Honor. Miss West. Isn't it true that the LPGA investigated you for gambling?"

I sit for a moment, stunned. This never became public. How could Morgan know? Damn, I look at Courtney Barr. She won't look back at me. Why would Courtney betray our trust?

"Please read this email to the jury."

Morgan hands me a printed document.

"Go ahead, Miss West, read what I've given you."

"What you have given me is an encrypted message from the Ladies Professional Golf Association. Please read it to the jury."

I begin reading, "Subject: Urgent: Allegations of Gambling.

Dear Miss Lauren West,

> *We regret to inform you that we have received credible information regarding your potential sports gambling. Our investigators have uncovered suspicious betting activity, including bets placed on Ryder Cup matches.*
>
> *As a professional athlete representing the integrity of the sport, these allegations deeply concern us. We take matters of fair competition and sportsmanship very seriously and will be launching a thorough investigation into these allegations.*

At this time, we ask that you refrain from making any public statements regarding this matter until the investigation is complete. We understand the gravity of these accusations and assure you that we will handle this situation with the utmost discretion and fairness.

Please be advised that the consequences of any wrongdoing, if proven, could have severe repercussions on your career and reputation within the golfing community.

We urge you to cooperate fully with our investigation and provide any information or evidence that may help to clarify the situation. Your prompt attention to this matter is appreciated.

Sincerely,
LPGA Tour Rules Committee"

"So, Miss West, the answer to my question is yes—the LPGA investigated you for gambling, including betting on golf tournaments you played. Right?"

I glance at the gallery, where reporters are already glued to their phones and iPads. What are they going to say about me?

"Mr. Morgan, I believe someone gave you this encrypted message." My voice wavers slightly as I look over at the jurors. "But you should also know there's an encrypted message exonerating me from this baseless allegation. You should ask that I read that email to the jury."

I glance over at Courtney, but she still won't meet my eyes. A chill runs down my spine as the realization hits me.

"Miss West," Morgan presses on, "you've broken many rules in your career, and you spoke out condemning transgender athletes after Mr. Benton told you to keep your political thoughts to yourself. Now, you expect the jurors to believe you designed the Lake Tierra Golf Course without issue?" Before I can answer, Morgan returns to his seat, smug satisfaction on his face.

As Morgan finishes his questioning, I take a deep breath and stand, trying to steady myself. On my way back to the defense table, I glance at Courtney. She still refuses to meet my eyes, a cold knot forming in my stomach. How could she betray me like this?

Judge Hawkins looks up at the clock and then at the room. "It's getting late. We'll adjourn for the day and reconvene tomorrow morning at 9:00 AM. The court is dismissed."

The sound of the gavel echoes in the courtroom, and the tension in the air begins to dissipate as everyone starts to pack up and leave. Luke and I exchange a brief look, but before we can talk, I know there's something I need to do.

As we walk out of the courtroom, I see Courtney standing near the exit. I can't ignore the sinking feeling that has been gnawing at me since I realized she betrayed me. As we approach, I stop and turn to her, my voice low but firm.

"We need to talk," I say, staring directly at her, willing her to explain herself. "I need to know why you did it."

Courtney avoids my gaze, her face pale. She doesn't say a word, just looks away as if she can't bear to face me.

My heart sinks even further, but I can't deal with this right now. I turn back to Luke, who's watching the exchange with a concerned look. We continue walking out of the courthouse, leaving the confrontation with Courtney hanging in the air. Why would she do this to me?

When Luke and I are alone, he turns to me, his expression hard. "I thought you told me there's nothing Morgan could bring up that would embarrass you. Why didn't you mention the gambling accusation?"

"Because the messages were encrypted. I never expected Morgan to get his hands on them." My voice tightens. "Courtney Barr is the only one I told about the investigation. She helped me prepare my response. And after the LPGA rules committee finished their investigation, they cleared me. I did nothing wrong."

Luke's eyes narrow. "I thought you said there wouldn't be any more surprises."

"Damn it, Luke. No, I didn't expect this."

"Were you gambling on tournaments?"

I freeze, sensing the gravity of his question. "Why do you ask?"

"Because how I handle this on redirect—if at all—depends on your answer."

I take a deep breath, feeling the weight of the moment pressing down on me. "The LPGA dropped the investigation. That's all I want to say about it."

Luke looks like he wants to push further, but exhaustion is etched into every line of his face. I can see how much today has drained him. His doctor warned him to avoid stress, yet here he is, battling Harvey Morgan in a high-stakes trial that has been nothing but stress. And I know that, despite his efforts to stay strong, I've added to that pressure.

"Are you okay?" I ask, trying to keep the worry out of my voice, though it's impossible to hide.

Luke snaps out of his daze, forcing a smile that doesn't reach his eyes. "Just sorting through the accusations Morgan made and trying to gauge how the jury might have reacted."

But his eyes betray him. They're filled with doubt, and that doubt seeps into me, making my heart sink. I realize with a cold, hard certainty that he thinks I may have blown it during cross-examination. The betrayal by Courtney still tears at my heart, but I shove it aside. Right now, I need to focus on the trial—on survival.

"I think I blew it with the jury," I admit, the knot of dread in my stomach twisting tighter with each word.

Luke gives a slight nod, seemingly in agreement, but his words, "We'll be okay," lack the confidence I desperately need.

I don't believe him. How can I? Morgan has shredded my image with a blend of truths and lies, and Luke isn't at his best—not when it matters most. His timing couldn't be worse. Tomorrow, he's supposed to question me on redirect, to clear my name, to convince the jury that I never made a hateful speech about transgender people. But as we leave the courthouse, the walls closing in around us, I can't shake the feeling that my alleged comments and the gambling accusation will dominate the evening news, casting a long and dark shadow over everything we've worked for.

As we step outside, the scorching heat hits us like a wall. It's 105 degrees with no breeze, and the sun beats down relentlessly, amplifying the weight of everything we're carrying. The air feels suffocating as if the world is closing in on us. I glance at Luke, desperately seeking some reassurance, but his tired eyes only confirm my worst fears. We're running out of time, and I'm not sure we have enough left in us to turn this around. But deep down, I can't shake the gnawing fear that it might already be too late.

Chapter 28

Luke

Morgan ended his cross-examination of Lauren by focusing the jury's attention on the LPGA investigation into her alleged gambling. Even though she was eventually exonerated, I can't shake the feeling that the jury didn't like what they heard, and Morgan let them dwell on it all night. The fact that Lauren never told me about the gambling investigation or the LPGA's rule allowing transgender golfers to compete doesn't sit well with me. Morgan will undoubtedly use that rule to paint Lauren as being out of step with the LPGA membership. And then there's the deepfake video. It was Morgan's ace in the hole to make her look bad in the eyes of the jurors. Thankfully, I have an expert witness lined up to disprove the video, but the damage might already be done.

It's bizarre. I never imagined I'd be dealing with cognitive issues in the middle of a trial. I shouldn't have agreed to represent Lauren, not like this. I know how important it is to get a good night's sleep, but I haven't slept well in months. If I wasn't the lawyer trying Lauren's case against Benton, I'd be taking naps to keep my head clear. The brain fog is relentless, and I don't know when or if it will lift.

I finish my morning routine, but the brain fog lingers at the edges. Before I can dwell on it, it's time to head to the courthouse. As Lauren and I approach the building, the protestors are already there, even more aggressive than before. They block our path, their signs thrust forward like weapons, and their shouts are deafening. "Bigot!" "Transphobe!" "Fascist!" "TERF!"!

I don't know what TERF means. The words sting, and I can see Lauren tense beside me, but we keep moving, focusing on the courtroom door just ahead.

The crowd closes in, forcing us to push through the wall of anger and hostility. I firmly grip Lauren's arm, guiding her through the chaos. Cameras flash, and reporters shout questions, but we don't stop. Finally, we reach the courthouse steps, and a couple of security guards step in, clearing a path for us to enter.

Inside, the noise from outside fades, but the tension doesn't. We make our way to the courtroom, the weight of the morning's events still heavy on our shoulders. Lauren resumes her seat in the witness chair, and I take my place at the counsel table.

When the session begins, I ask each redirect question I had written while Morgan cross-examined her. Lauren gives detailed responses, carefully explaining her points to the jury. I then ask her to explain why the video Morgan showed of her giving a hate speech is fake. She does her best to describe how someone created a deepfake video of her, but I can sense the uncertainty in the room. Morgan insists the videos are real, and I'm not sure the jurors believe they're fake. That uncertainty gnaws at me.

I then turn to what I read and ask, "Lauren, are you aware that many are calling for the LPGA to change its rules back to requiring that LPGA golfers be female at birth?"

"Yes, I know there are many different opinions on this subject. But, even former trans professional golfers have recognized the problem, and along with many current LPGA golfers and former LPGA golfers, have spoken out about the inherent physiological advantages trams athletes gain being a male when born. They point to scientific studies showing birth males have advantages that hormonal therapy cannot reverse."

"Lauren, Mr. Morgan brought up an investigation by the LPGA regarding alleged gambling. Can you clarify for the jury what the outcome of that investigation was?"

Lauren takes a deep breath, steadying herself. "The LPGA conducted a thorough investigation and found no wrongdoing. They dropped the case because there was no evidence that I had gambled, and no action was taken against me."

I nod, keeping my tone even and reassuring. "So, to be clear, you were exonerated by the LPGA rules committee, correct?"

"Yes, that's correct."

"Lauren, let's clarify a few things for the jury. Yesterday, Mr. Morgan suggested that you're willing to say or do anything to advance your career. Would you agree with that characterization?"

She shakes her head firmly. "No, absolutely not. I've always believed in earning everything on my own merit."

I nod, appreciating her strength in this moment. "Let's talk about your achievements. You've had a successful career on the LPGA Tour, correct?"

"Yes, I did well and won several tournaments," she replies, her voice steady but tinged with the weariness of the day.

"And in that time," I continue, "have you ever felt the need to manipulate or deceive anyone to win a tournament?"

"No, never," Lauren responds without hesitation. "That's not who I am."

I pause, allowing her words to resonate with the jury. "Mr. Morgan brought up an email that he suggested had some political undertones, specifically referencing MAGA. Do you recall that?"

"Yes, I do," Lauren says, a slight edge in her voice, but she remains composed.

I look over at the jurors, making sure they're with me. "Can you tell the jury your stance on that email and how it reflects your actual beliefs?"

Lauren takes a deep breath, her eyes meeting mine briefly before she looks out at the jury. "The email was twisted to make me look like someone I'm not. I believe Americans should feel proud of our country, but I've never aligned myself with any political agenda like MAGA. My focus has always been on my work, not on politics."

I see the jurors taking in her words, and I soften my tone as I ask the next question. "Lauren, when you spoke out about transgender athletes competing in girls' and women's sports, what was your intent?"

"My intent," she begins, her voice strong but measured, "was to protect the integrity of girls' and women's sports. I wasn't trying to hurt anyone or push any agenda. I was standing up for something I believe in because I've lived it, and I know what it takes to compete at the highest levels."

I let her words hang in the air for a moment before continuing. "Did you ever expect that speaking out would lead to Mr. Benton terminating your contract and refusing to pay the bonus you earned?"

"No, not at all," she says, the shock still evident in her voice. "I was shocked when it happened."

I turn slightly, making sure the jury can see me. "Now, Mr. Morgan suggested that your support of girls' and women's sports might have a negative impact on property sales for Benton Land Company. Can you explain what the actual impact has been on property sales at the Lake Tierra Hill Country Development?"

Lauren meets my eyes, finding confidence in his steady presence. "The support I've shown for girls and women's sports has actually increased property sales at the Lake Tierra Hill Country Development. The vast majority of people in this country support the stance I've taken."

"And when you found out that Robert Benton was refusing to pay you what you earned, how did you feel?"

Lauren's voice softens, and I see the vulnerability she rarely shows. "I felt betrayed. I'd put everything into that project, and the Lake Tierra golf course I created won awards. When Robert Benton terminated my contract and refused to pay me the bonus I earned, I felt he had done it as a way to avoid paying me what he owed me."

I take a moment, letting the weight of her words settle with the jury. "Finally, Lauren, why are you fighting this case?"

Lauren straightens in her seat, her resolve clear. "Because it's not just about me. It's about standing up to someone who thinks they can bully and silence anyone who disagrees with them. I won't let that happen to me or anyone else."

I nod with satisfaction, knowing she's spoken from the heart. "Thank you, Lauren. No further questions."

As I step back, I feel the shift in the room, the jury now seeing the real Lauren. She's strong, principled, and determined to stand up for what she thinks is right.

I make a slight turn, ensuring the jury's view of me. "Now, Mr. Morgan suggested that your support of girls' and women's sports might have a negative impact on property sales for Benton Land Company. Can you explain what the actual impact has been on property sales at the Lake Tierra Hill Country Development?"

Lauren meets my eyes, finding confidence in his steady presence. "The support I've shown for girls and women's sports has actually increased property sales at the Lake Tierra Hill Country Development. The vast majority of people in this country support the stance I've taken."

I give a slight nod, acknowledging her statement. "Mr. Morgan also played a video in which you were allegedly seen making derogatory remarks about transgender individuals. Can you tell the jury your thoughts on that video?"

Lauren's voice is firm as she responds. "That video is a fabrication. I never made those statements, and I have always believed in treating everyone with respect. The words in that video do not reflect my views or my character."

I allow the jury to absorb her words before continuing. "Finally, Mr. Morgan implied that you have broken many rules throughout your career. How do you respond to that accusation?"

Lauren straightens, her gaze steady. "I've always conducted myself with integrity, both on and off the golf course. Any allegations suggesting otherwise are false."

I pause, then take a step back. "Thank you, Lauren. No further questions, Your Honor."

Morgan asks one question: "Miss West, the LPGA has not changed its rule permitting transgender golfers to compete on the tour, has it?"

Lauren replies, "The LPGA has not changed their rule, but they are considering changing it."

After Lauren resumes her seat, Judge Hawkins says, "Mr. Hartley, call your next witness?"

Your Honor, we call "Dr Jonathan Mitchell."

As I anticipated, Morgan springs to his feet and objects. "Your Honor, Jonathan Mitchell is not on the plaintiff's witness list."

Judge Hawkins shuffles papers. "Mr. Hartley, I don't see Dr. Mitchell on your witness list."

"Your Honor, we only decided to call Dr. Mitchell after Mr. Morgan presented what we believe are deepfake video and audio of Miss West."

"In that case, I'm going to allow Dr. Mitchell to testify."

Lauren and I didn't have money to pay Dr. Mitchell, so his analysis wasn't as thorough as it would have been had he spent more time.

Mitchell begins to state his qualifications. After Mitchell tells the jury that he holds a PhD in Computer Science from MIT and is currently the lead researcher on deepfake technology, Morgan stands and stipulates he's an expert.

I ask Dr. Mitchell to explain to the jury what a deepfake is.

"Sure," Mitchell replies, turning to the jury as I had instructed him. "A deepfake is a type of synthetic media where someone takes a person in an existing image or video and replaces their likeness with someone else's using artificial intelligence and machine learning. This technology can create highly realistic, but completely fake, visual and audio content."

I look at the jury, and they seem interested but need clarification. I continue. "Please tell the jury how to determine if a video or audio recording is a deepfake."

"There are several forensic techniques we use to detect deepfakes for the video. We analyze the inconsistencies in the video's lighting and shadows, facial movements, and expressions. We use advanced software to identify pixel-level anomalies."

The jury looks completely lost, but I continue to ask if he analyzed videos of Lauren West allegedly speaking out about transgender people.

"My analysis revealed multiple examples of manipulation. The lighting and shadows are inconsistent with the setting. Miss West's facial movements do not align with her speech patterns, and there are pixel-level discrepancies typical of AI-generated videos. Whoever created the video knew what they were doing, but it still is a deepfake video."

I take Mitchell through the same steps on the audio recording of Lauren, and then it is Morgan's turn to cross-examine.

"Mr. Mitchell,…"

I rise, "Your Honor, it's not Mr. Mitchell. It's Dr. Mitchell."

Before Judge Hawkins rules, Morgan continues. "Okay, Dr. Mitchell, you mentioned inconsistencies in lighting and facial movements as indicators of deepfakes. Are these always conclusive proof of manipulation?"

“Not always. While these indicators strongly suggest manipulation, they are part of a broader analysis and not conclusive on their own.”

Morgan must sense he’s on a roll. He pauses for a moment, looks over at the jury, and then asks, “Isn’t it true, Dr. Mitchell, that these inconsistencies can be present in authentic videos due to technical issues or poor video quality?”

“It’s possible, but the combination of multiple indicators I mentioned before supports my conclusion that the video of Miss West is a deepfake.”

“Dr. Mitchell, isn’t it true that the software you rely on can and has given false positives?”

If the jurors weren’t confused before, they’re sure to be confused now. That’s obviously what Harvey Morgan has in mind as he cross-examines.

Mitchell admits that no software is infallible, but the software he used has a very high accuracy rate.

I glance at the jury, trying to read their faces, but they’re inscrutable, giving nothing away. My gut twists with unease. Has Mitchell done enough to plant doubt in their minds, or has Morgan managed to undermine him just enough? The room feels heavy with tension as Judge Hawkins shifts in his seat.

“Dr. Mitchell,” Morgan says, his voice smooth, almost too casual, “you’re not here as an expert on Miss West’s speaking patterns, are you?”

“No,” Mitchell replies, his tone steady, but I can sense the slight crack in his confidence.

I debate whether to ask any redirect questions. But before I can decide, Judge Hawkins steps in.

“Ladies and gentlemen,” he says, his gaze sweeping across the courtroom, “let’s take a break for lunch.”

I watch the jury file out, their faces unreadable, leaving their thoughts a mystery. . Morgan catches my eye, a smirk curling at the corner of his lips. He raises an eyebrow as if to say, 'Did you really think you could win this?' He turns and struts out of the courtroom, Benton following closely behind, both of them exuding confidence.

I gather my notes, but the nagging doubt in the pit of my stomach grows stronger. Morgan has spent more time tearing down Lauren’s character than addressing the actual facts of the case. Has he managed to plant enough seeds of doubt in the jurors’ minds?

Do they believe the videos are fake, or has Morgan successfully convinced them that Lauren is someone who doesn't follow the rules and can't be trusted?

I glance at Lauren, who looks as uncertain as I feel. The relentless attacks have taken their toll, and I can see the worry etched in her face.

As we leave the courtroom for lunch, I can't help but wonder—what do the jurors think of Lauren now? Have they bought into Morgan's portrayal of her, or do they still see the truth?

Chapter 29

Luke

As we leave for lunch, Morgan and Benton are once again holding court with the reporters, their voices carrying over the crowd's buzz. They claim Dr. Mitchell is a fraud, insisting that he either lied or didn't properly analyze the video and audio of Lauren. They're playing to the public, repeating over and over that thousands have seen the videos and heard the audio and believe Lauren is a hateful person who despises transgender individuals.

While walking in silence, Lauren's shoulders droop as she carries the weight of the accusations. She hardly eats her food during lunch, her usual spark faded. The toll of Morgan's constant attacks is clear in her eyes, filled with doubt. She's worried that we're losing control and the jury might get swayed by Morgan's twisted version of events.

I lean in, my voice firm. "Lauren, listen. Benton and Morgan are playing their usual game, using the courts to wear down their opponents. But this time, it won't work."

Her eyes meet mine, searching for reassurance. I give her both assurance and my plan. “When he testifies, I will show the jury that Benton is a man who manipulates the system, crushes anyone in his path, and believes he can bully you into submission. Remember, the truth is on our side, and I will expose him for the fraud he is.”

I see the spark reignite in her eyes, her resolve returning. “We have laid the groundwork, and now it is time to drive it home. The jury will see Benton’s real motive: to silence you and take what is yours. I will not let him succeed. I will make sure they see him for what he really is—a manipulative bully who thinks he is above the law.”

Lauren nods, the worry lines on her face softening as determination takes hold. I offer her a reassuring smile, but it’s more than just a gesture—it’s a promise. “We are going to win this, Lauren. Benton is going to regret the day he ever tried to take you down.”

We finish our lunch in relative silence, the weight of the day pressing down on us as we mentally prepare for what comes next. Stepping outside, we are immediately hit by the brutal, suffocating heat. The temperature has climbed to 107 degrees, and it feels even worse in our suits. The air is thick and heavy, clinging to our skin, making each step feel like a challenge.

The few remaining protestors, clearly worn down by the heat, still linger near the courthouse. As soon as they spot us, the insults start again, though their voices are hoarse and less vigorous than before. Sweat beads on my forehead, but I stay focused on the courthouse, determined to keep my composure.

Lauren walks beside me, her stride purposeful despite the oppressive heat. I can see the sweat on her brow, but her posture is straighter, her resolve visibly stronger. She's pushing through, just like I am.

As we approach the entrance, Morgan and Benton are still holding court with the reporters, their smug expressions standing In stark contrast to the heat draining everyone else's energy, I overhear words like "fraud," "phony," and "hatred," each chosen to paint Lauren as the villain.But I refuse to let it get to me. I have a strategy, and soon, I'll put it into action.

We push through the courthouse doors, leaving the noise of the protestors and the media circus behind. The air inside is cooler and quieter, but the tension remains. We make our way back to the courtroom. I want to get through the rest of our witnesses quickly so I can get at Benton when Morgan calls him as his first witness.

I had put every contractor involved in the construction of the Lake Tierra Hill Country Development on our witness list. Benton had refused to pay their original contract price to each one, making up reasons he should not have to pay them. When I contacted them, I learned from one contractor, Earl Gibbs, that Benton had gone back and negotiated settlements with each one. The settlement agreement required them to keep the settlement confidential and not disclose that Benton had failed to pay their contract price before the settlement. That meant none of them could testify in our case. I had put on our witness list every contractor involved in the construction of the Lake Tierra Hill Country Development. Benton had refused to pay their original contract price to each one, making up reasons he should not have to pay them. I learned from one contractor, Earl Gibbs. Benton had gone back and negotiated settlements with each one.

Thankfully, Mr. Gibbs, whose company handled the grading work on the Lake Tierra golf course site, had heard of Mr. Benton's reputation and halted work until Benton caught up on payments. As a result, Benton had only failed to make the final payment after he accepted Gibbs' grading work. Gibbs refused to accept the terms of Benton's buyout for not testifying. He believed Benton's offer was both unethical and witness tampering. He turned down Benton's proposal and agreed to testify. I call him to testify.

During direct examination, I stick to the questions I had carefully prepared. After asking Gibbs to introduce himself and describe his grading construction business, I have him explain how he became the grading contractor for the Lake Tierra golf course. Supporting our case, Gibbs tells the jury that he was eager to work on a golf course designed by Lauren. He admits that while he didn't know Robert Benton personally, he had heard rumors about Benton mistreating his contractors.

Morgan objects on the grounds that it's hearsay. I argue that we are not introducing what he heard to prove it is true, only to show why he proceeded cautiously. Judge Hawkins overrules Morgan's objection, resulting in Morgan slamming a book down on his counsel table as he sat down. Judge Hawkins tells Morgan to stop having temper tantrums in his court. I see some jurors laughing, and others look shocked as if they never expected to see a show like Morgan was putting on for Court TV.

I introduce Gibbs' grading contract into evidence and have him read the provision his lawyer added, allowing him to abandon the work if Benton failed to pay in full. Gibbs then reiterates to the jury that he insisted on this clause because of Robert Benton's reputation for not fully paying his contractors.

Morgan objects again, and Judge Hawkins overrules his objection. This time, Morgan hisses while sitting down.

After a few more questions, I get to the heart of why I called Gibbs to testify. He tells the jury that after agreeing to testify for Lauren, Harvey Morgan contacted him with an offer to settle his claim for the final payment. Gibbs testifies that he was inclined to settle until Morgan sent him a draft of the agreement. I put the non-disclosure clause on the screen and ask Gibbs to read it aloud to the jury. I notice Morgan seething in his seat as Gibbs reads the wording.

When I inquire whether Gibbs agreed to the settlement, he firmly declines, explaining to the jury that he refused because he suspected Morgan's intention was to prevent him from telling the jury that Benton consistently fails to fully pay his contractors.

Morgan immediately jumps up, objecting to the statement and arguing that Gibbs has no basis for assuming his motives. Judge Hawkins sustains the objection and instructs the jury to disregard the comment.

But I can see in their faces that the jury has already absorbed the implication, and regardless of the judge's instruction, the seed of doubt has been planted, serving exactly the purpose I intended.

On cross-examination, Morgan tries to discredit Gibbs, starting with questions about whether he was paid to testify or if I had coached him on his responses. Gibbs answers straightforwardly, stating that I had gone over his testimony with him but only instructed him to tell the truth. He firmly denies any suggestion that he was told what to say or what to omit.

When Morgan asks if I made the first contact, Gibbs surprises him by revealing that while I did reach out, it was only after Gibbs had initially contacted me following Morgan's request for him to sign a non-disclosure agreement. Morgan clearly wasn't expecting that answer and returns to his seat, momentarily thrown off.

Despite Morgan's attempts to undermine Gibbs, it's clear the jury is impressed. Gibbs comes across as honest, articulate, and committed to doing what is right, making Morgan's attacks seem desperate and ineffective.

I feel a surge of confidence, revitalized by the impactful testimony of a credible witness. Eventually, Morgan realizes that with each question, he's only making matters worse for his client. Frustrated, he finally sits down, looking thoroughly disgusted. I had lined up a parade of at least a dozen Lake Tierra homeowners to testify they had bought their property to be part of a golf course community with an Lauren West designed golf course. Like the contractor witnesses, I had listed the homeowners on my witness list. One day later, I received several phone calls from their lawyers telling me that a California lawyer had asked their clients for an interview. Each lawyer said their client had refused to talk to the lawyer.

I call each witness to testify one at a time. On direct, each witness says they became interested in the Lake Tierra Hill Country Development when they learned that Lauren West had designed the golf course. Each witness testifies they would not have bought property in the development if they thought Robert Benton had designed the golf course.

Frank Jacobs does the best job explaining why he and his wife invested in property at Lake Tierra Hill Country Development. He says, "My wife and I are avid golfers, and our two boys are learning to play. We knew of Miss West's work. Her courses are like green sanctuaries for the entire family to enjoy. Once we learned she was behind Lake Tierra, we didn't hesitate. Her name gave us confidence in the value of our investment and the joy we'd enjoy as a family."

When asked why she bought property at the Lake Tierra Hill Country Development Ann Majors tells the jury she bought a lot on the golf course overlooking the tenth fairway, framing hills in the background. As each homeowner testifies, it becomes increasingly clear that none of the witnesses bought property at Lake Tierra because of Robert Benton. They bought it because Lauren designed the golf course. Lauren West's creative vision is the brand.

Harvey Morgan asks only a few questions on cross-examination. He asks each witness if Lauren contacted them to testify. Each witness says no. He asks if I, or someone from my office, had contacted them. Each witness testifies that I contacted them. Morgan tries to get each witness to say that I told them what we needed them to say when called as a witness. Each witness answers that I had asked them why they looked at and ultimately buy property at Lake Tierra. Morgan tries to get each homeowner to say they bought property because of the location in the Hill Country. Each mentions how beautiful the Hill Country location is, but they only considered it in the first place because they knew I designed the golf course.

Having no success with those questions, Morgan asks each Lake Tierra property owner if they knew Lauren West was a "transphobe." I object each time. Morgan rails over my objection, stating that he is entitled to find out what each witness thought of Miss West's views on transgender athletes. Judge Hawkins sustains my objection. After sustaining my objection a second time, he directs Morgan not to ask the question of any more of the witnesses.

Morgan systematically asks each witness if they know what a TERF is. I have no idea what he's getting at, and when I glance at Lauren, she shrugs, clearly just as clueless. Morgan then explains that TERF stands for "trans-exclusionary radical feminist." He follows up by asking each witness if they were aware that Lauren West was a trans-exclusionary radical feminist when they purchased their property.

Sensing the damaging insinuation, I object, pointing out that Miss West has already testified that she supports the right of transgender adults to live the life they have chosen without harassment. Judge Hawkins sustains my objection. Despite this, Morgan repeats the question with the next witness, prompting the judge to intervene again, this time directing Morgan not to ask the same question of any additional witnesses.

Morgan methodically questions each witness, asking if they are aware that Miss West has misgendered transgender athletes. I object again, but Judge Hawkins overrules based on Lauren's earlier testimony. The witnesses, visibly confused by the question, each admit that they don't know what misgendering is.

Morgan seizes the opportunity to educate them, putting a Healthline article on the screen titled, "What Does It Mean to Misgender Someone?" He instructs each witness to read aloud: "Misgendering occurs when you intentionally or unintentionally refer to a person, relate to a person, or use language to describe a person that doesn't align with their affirmed gender. For example, referring to a woman as 'he' or calling her a 'guy' is an act of misgendering."

With the definition now clear, Morgan asks if they can imagine that purposely misgendering someone could be considered harassment or bullying and even put the person in danger. I object, arguing that the question calls for speculation, but the damage is done. Morgan knows full well that it's speculative, yet he has already planted the idea in the jury's mind.

As the last resident finishes testifying, Judge Hawkins glances at the clock. "Ladies and gentlemen, I'm going to call it a day. We all appreciate your attention to the witnesses today. Remember not to discuss what you've heard with anyone, including each other. We'll reconvene tomorrow morning."

I'm relieved as the day finally comes to an end, and I hope Lauren feels the same. She asks if there is anything she can do to help me feel better in the morning. I try to smile, hoping to ease her worry. I tell her that I'll go home, exercise, and get to bed early. "I'll be better tomorrow. I promise."

"I'm counting on it," she replies.

As we leave the courthouse, the scene outside is chaotic. Benton stands with a megaphone, addressing the growing crowd of protestors. Carlotta Hampton is on one side of him, while a Hollywood starlet, whose name escapes me, stands on the other. The media is capturing every word. Benton claims that Lauren's case isn't about him, it's about his unwavering support for them. "I could have settled this case long ago, but I'm fighting for your right to be safe and free from harassment," he declares, drawing cheers from the crowd. As they spot Lauren and me, their cheers turn into chants of "bigot, bigot. Why do you hate so much?" Benton sounds like a politician, eager to be one of the lead stories on the nightly news.

When I get home, I'm greeted by my mom, Megan, and Abby, who are setting the table for dinner. My mom takes one look at me and says, "Looks like you had a tough day."

I don't want her or the girls to know how drained I really am. "It was a grind today," I reply, trying to downplay it. "The 107 degrees heat didn't make it any easier, either." After dinner, I take two sleeping pills and lie down, hoping to catch up on much-needed rest. But my mind won't stop racing, replaying the events of the trial in a haze of fatigue and worry. I finally drift off, only to be jolted awake by a call from Lauren. Her breathing is panicked, and I wait until she calms down enough to speak.

"Over a million people have seen the fake video of me spouting hatred towards transgender people," she says, her voice trembling. "I'm receiving emails, texts, and phone messages condemning me. I've been called vile, disgusting, repugnant, evil, foul… and that's just a few of the messages. It feels like the whole world believes that video is real. I'll never have peace again. Can the police do anything to stop this?"

I hesitate, knowing the truth won't bring her comfort. "The police likely can't stop them, and they can't do anything about the people who have already seen the video."

After the call, I lie back down, but sleep doesn't come easily. My mind is still racing, and the exhaustion is settling in deeper. I keep telling myself to go to sleep, hoping to will away the fatigue, but the weight of the day lingers, making my rest elusive.

As I lie on my left side, my eyes fall on the television remote. The temptation to turn on Court TV tugs at me, knowing they're likely replaying today's trial. But I know better. If I hear even a hint of critique about my performance, I'll never get back to sleep.

"Please, God, just this once, let me fall back asleep. I rarely ask for help, and I can't even remember the last time I turned to You. But tonight, I need it. Help me quiet my mind, let the exhaustion fade, and grant me the rest I need to face tomorrow with a clear head."

Chapter 30

Lauren

I sit in the corner of a quiet cafe at 7:00 AM, my heart pounding as I wait for Courtney to arrive. The dim lighting and soft hum of conversation do little to ease the tension that's been building inside me since she called and asked to meet. When she finally walks through the door, our eyes meet, and I can see she's feeling guilty in the way she avoids my gaze and the tension around her mouth. The silence between us feels awkward, heavy with unspoken words. I finally break it, unable to hold back the questions that have been burning in my mind. "Courtney, why now? Why are you coming to me with this information? You wouldn't even look at me in the courtroom or talk to me when Luke and I left."

Courtney hesitates, her eyes avoiding mine as she fidgets with her phone. Finally, she looks up. "Lauren, there's something I need to tell you. Something I should have told you a long time ago."

I feel a knot in my stomach. "What is it, Courtney?"

She takes a deep breath. "After I retired from the tour, things got terrible for me financially. My financial advisor led me into terrible investments, and then it got worse. He embezzled a significant amount of my earnings. I lost almost everything. I was drowning in debt, barely able to keep my head above water."

My heart sinks as I listen, but I stay silent, letting her continue.

"Benton found out about my situation. I don't know how he found out, but he did. Benton approached me with a deal. He said he'd get me out of financial trouble, clear my debts, and give me a fresh start. But in return, I had to give Benton information. Information about you, the trial, about everything you told me."

I feel the blood drain from my face. "You've been giving Benton information about me, things I told you in confidence?"

Courtney nods, tears welling up in her eyes. "I'm so sorry, Lauren. I didn't know what else to do. I was desperate. He promised me it would be harmless, that he just needed to know what to expect from the trial. But it wasn't harmless. He used everything I told him against you, especially during the cross-examination."

I step back, the betrayal hitting me like a punch to the gut. “You were supposed to be my friend Courtney. You were supposed to have my back.”

“I know,” she whispers, tears streaming down her face. “I know, and I hate myself for what I’ve done. But I’m here now because I can’t keep living with this. I want to make it right if that’s even possible. I’ve told you everything I know about Benton’s plans. I want to help you, Lauren, even if you never forgive me.”

I stare at Courtney, not knowing how to respond. Part of me wants to scream and tell her to get out and never come back. But another part of me remembers all the years of friendship, the times when Courtney was there for me, especially after my father died. She was my rock then, helping me through some of the darkest days of my life.

I know what it’s like to feel desperate, to feel like the ground has been ripped out from under you. When my father died, it felt as though the anchor that kept me steady had been severed. Everything I had known, the foundation of my life, suddenly felt shaky and uncertain. The man who had been my biggest supporter, my coach, and my caddie was gone, and with him went the sense of security I had always taken for granted. It was like losing a part of myself, and I wandered through the days afterwards in a haze of grief, struggling to find direction without him.

In a way, Courtney must have felt something similar when she lost everything financially. The pain of losing her stability and her sense of security is not the same as losing a loved one, but the despair it brings can be just as overwhelming and must have left Courtney feeling unmoored, searching for something solid to hold on to.

I take a deep breath, trying to steady my voice. "You've hurt me, Courtney. You've hurt me more deeply than you could ever imagine. We've shared victories, defeats, and secrets I've never told anyone else—not even my own family. But you used our friendship to betray me, to feed information to the very people who are trying to destroy me. If you really want to make this right, then you need to be all in. That means helping me win this case."

Courtney wipes her eyes, her voice trembling with sincerity. "I swear, Lauren. I'm all in. I'll do whatever it takes to help you win this." I study her for a long moment, trying to decide if I can trust her again. Finally, I give a small, approving tilt of my head. "Then, let's get to work."

I leave the cafe and walk to the courthouse. There's a hot breeze in the air as I meet Luke, and we start walking to the courthouse. Despite the early hour, it's already warm, and the forecast promises another August day over 100 degrees. Luke looks well-rested compared to when I left him last night.

We push through a thick crowd, barely able to squeeze through the narrow gaps they leave for us. The signs are more professional today, with many reading "#MAGA Lauren West." The atmosphere is charged, with tension crackling like static before a storm. A few obscenities are hurled in my direction as we walk, and with each passing trial day, the remarks and threats seem to multiply, growing louder and more hostile.

But I push those thoughts aside, focusing on the trial ahead. Courtney's confession is still fresh in my mind, giving me the resolve to face whatever Morgan throws at me next.

As we walk, I see a mother with a daughter whose age is somewhere between ten and twelve. The daughter is wearing a golf hat and golf clothes and holds a homemade sign that reads: "We love Lauren West." The sign includes a photo of me when I was playing golf.

I walk over towards the mother and daughter. I lean down, hug the girl, and say, "Thank you for coming," to the mother. The mother says, "We had to come from Dallas to support you and wish you well. When I was ten, my father took me to the LPGA tournament in Dallas. We watched you practicing on the putting green, and you put your initials on a ball and gave it to me. When you went to the first tee, I followed. I followed you for all eighteen holes. I remember you talking to me while you walked between holes. At the end of the round, you talked to my father and me and let us take this photo."

She shows me a photo of us standing together from years ago. "You inspired me," she says, her voice full of warmth. "I never became a golfer like you, but I played softball and earned a scholarship. You told me to dream big, work hard, and believe in myself. I did, and it paid off. My daughter, Peyton, wants to be a golfer like you. She's playing junior golf in Dallas at the Hickory Oaks Golf Course you designed, and she sits in front of our television, watching the instructional video you did for girls on YouTube. Peyton begged me to bring her here so she could tell you she dreams of playing golf at the University of Texas and becoming a pro, just like you did."

As I listen, I can't help but reflect on what life is really about. It's more than just winning tournaments or designing courses. It's about the ripple effect of our words and actions and how they inspire and shape the lives of others. In moments like these, I'm reminded that the legacy we leave behind isn't just in our achievements but in the dreams we help others to realize.

Feeling overwhelmed by joy, I hand my phone to Peyton's mom.. "Please add your name, phone number, and Peyton's contact details. I'd love to give Peyton a personal lesson when this trial ends and I'm back in Dallas."

Luke looks at me, a knowing expression in his eyes. "I guess that's what this lawsuit is really about, isn't it?"

As I take in the moment, I realize he's right. It's not just about contracts and money; it's about the lives we touch and the future we help shape. But my brief pause to connect with this mother and daughter has allowed the protestors to close in around us, their presence reminding me of the challenges still ahead.

"Mr. Hartley, Miss West, this way, please!" a uniformed officer calls out, cutting a path through the crowd. He and other officers hold back the tide of protestors. The officer's hand grips Luke's arm firmly, pulling him through the chaos. A female officer grabs my arm. Several other officers form a protective barrier around us.

"Keep your heads down," he says as I see a plastic water bottle hurled towards me. "Keep moving," he says.

"Lauren West, the people are watching," a young woman yells at me. Another shouts, "Lauren West, transphobic hater." For one moment, I reflect on whatever happened to civil disagreement in the United States. I've never experienced anything like this.

The officers usher us into the courthouse through the heavy wooden doors. I express my gratitude to the female officer who guides us safely through the chaotic crowd. After passing through security, we are finally seated at our table in the courtroom. I take a few deep breaths, trying to calm my nerves and compose myself. My hands tremble, but I try to regain control of my emotions.

I glance over at the group huddled around the defense table. Benton is leaning close to Morgan, murmuring something I can't make out. Meanwhile, their jury consultant, Carlotta Hampton, stares at me. As I realize I should have taken a moment to freshen up before entering the courtroom, I wonder if I look like I got into a physical altercation in the hallway.

We all rise as Judge Hawkins enters the courtroom and summons the bailiff to get the jury. We all rise again as they enter the courtroom and take their seats.

"Mr. Hartley, you may call your next witness."

"We call Jordan Lawson."

After being sworn in, Jordan Lawson, a golf course designer and course rater for two major golf publications, testifies about his qualifications, including his Master's degree from Harvard and extensive experience in designing and reviewing golf courses worldwide. He explains that Lauren West's designs are unique due to her attention to the playability from the forward tees and her ability to incorporate natural landscapes into her courses. Lawson confirms that the Lake Tierra Golf Course features these hallmarks of West's design, particularly highlighting the third hole as an exact match to her original drawing.

Morgan, on cross-examination, attempts to undermine Lawson by questioning his compensation and his bias toward designers over developers. He challenges Lawson on the differences between the photos of the Lake Tierra holes and West's drawings. Lawson begins to explain that the changes are minor, likely made to claim credit for the design, but Morgan cuts him off. When Luke allows Lawson to finish his explanation, Morgan objects, and the judge sustains the objection, instructing Luke to call his next witness.

"We call Clark Mitchell."

I give Luke credit for finding Mitchell. I've dealt with many accountants who dress poorly, look like they've always been in the back room, and are uncomfortable speaking in public. Mitchell is the exception, for sure. He could be on the cover of Esquire Magazine. He walks to be sworn in with an air of confidence. He's dressed professionally in a well-tailored charcoal gray suit with a crisp white shirt and a patterned navy blue tie.

After being sworn in, Mitchell testifies about his education and extensive experience in accounting, particularly in the real estate development industry. He explains how he thoroughly reviewed Benton Land Company's financial records related to the Lake Tierra Hill Country Development despite initial resistance from Benton's employees. His analysis reveals that Benton Land Company has earned over $10 million in profits, and according to Lauren's contract, she is owed just over $1 million in bonuses.

Morgan attempts to discredit Mitchell during cross-examination by questioning the fees he was paid to testify and the legitimacy of management fees that Benton Land Company charged Lake Tierra. Mitchell counters that the management fees were a dubious expense, clearly made to deny Lauren her rightful bonus. Though Morgan tries to argue that Lauren's contract was flawed by only allowing for a share of net profits, Mitchell's testimony highlights the manipulations Benton used to minimize those profits.

Morgan's efforts to undermine Mitchell's credibility seem to fall flat, and the jury appears to grasp the essence of the case: Benton's financial maneuvering was designed to cheat Lauren out of what she was rightfully owed. Frustrated, Morgan concludes his cross-examination with a snide remark, which Judge Hawkins quickly admonishes. Luke, satisfied that the jury understands the importance of Mitchell's testimony, rests my case.

I look towards the jury. A middle-aged woman holds my gaze for a lingering second. I want to believe her gaze reflects that she supports me.

Judge Hawkins excuses the jury.

The courtroom stirs and then turns quiet as Harvey Morgan rises from his seat, straightens his tie, and clears his throat.

"Do you have a motion, Mr. Morgan?"

"Yes, Your Honor. At this time, the defendants make a motion for a directed verdict."

Luke has told me it is customary for the defense to make that motion in civil trials, and judges routinely deny it. He said he had never seen a judge grant the motion.

Judge Hawkins nods, gesturing for Morgan to continue.

Morgan pauses momentarily, realizing that every eye in the courtroom and the Court TV camera are on him.

"Your Honor, Miss West has not proven Robert Benton and Benton Land Company wrongfully terminated her design contract for fault. She's also not proven that she alone designed the Lake Tierra Golf Course since Robert Benton corrected the errors in her final design. Finally, Miss West has not proven that the Lake Tierra Hill Country Development made any profit entitling her to a bonus."

Morgan returns to his seat and leans back in his chair, aware that the courtroom camera is focused on him.

Even though Luke assured me that Judge Hawkins would not dismiss our case, I feel anger and frustration bubbling inside me at Morgan's dismissive words. Harvey Morgan has done everything possible to delay the trial, make it more expensive, and deny me the opportunity to design golf courses. Now, after we finally had the chance to present our case, he's using a motion that he knows will be denied just to publicly disparage me.

"Mr. Hartley, do you have a response?" Judge Hawkins asks, his voice steady as the courtroom cameras swivel to Luke.

"Your Honor," Luke says confidently, "Mr. Morgan's argument is so absurd that I will only say that, at the very best, what Mr. Morgan has suggested are questions for the jury to decide after you instruct them on the law."

"I agree with Mr. Hartley," Judge Hawkins states firmly. "I will allow Mr. Morgan to present the defendant's case, and then I'll instruct the jury on the law, and the jury can decide whether Miss West has presented sufficient evidence to prove her claims. Mr. Morgan, will you be prepared to call your first witness after our lunch break?"

As the courtroom empties for lunch, Luke and I discuss the next steps. "So, what's the plan?" I ask, my voice steady but my mind racing.

"Benton," Luke replies, his eyes alight with a fire I haven't seen in days. "Morgan's got to call him to the stand. Benton has to explain why he terminated your contract and refused to pay your bonus. That's where we'll dismantle his entire case."

"What if Morgan doesn't call him?" I ask, a sliver of doubt creeping in.

Luke's smile is confident, almost predatory. "He will. Morgan has no choice. Benton's the lynchpin of their defense, and without him, their argument falls apart. Trust me, Lauren, this is where we turn the tide."

I nod, feeling the anticipation build. The stakes couldn't be higher. Benton on the stand is what we've been waiting for, the moment when we can expose him for who he really is.

As we leave the courtroom, the air between us hums with anticipation. Robert Benton is a wealthy, arrogant man who's used to bulldozing his way through opponents, rarely having to answer for himself despite his involvement in countless lawsuits. But now, Luke has the chance to confront him head-on, and I can't wait to see how he takes Benton down.

Chapter 31

Luke

"Luke, got a minute?" Morgan stops me in the hallway and asks. I ask Lauren to go ahead, and Morgan gestures me back inside the courtroom. "Look. Robert is growing tired of this fight and spending time in your hometown. He has other things he wants to do. Robert's willingness to settle with your client surprised me."

"Okay, what's his offer?"

"Robert will pay your client two hundred thousand dollars. She can claim to be the designer of the Lake Tierra Golf Course. There are three conditions."

"Here we go. And what are the three conditions?"

"First, the terms of our settlement must remain confidential. All you and your client can say is we resolved the lawsuit satisfactorily."

"I expected that condition," I say to Morgan. "And what is your client's second condition?"

"Second, she has to agree that he is the Lake Tierra Golf Course co-designer."

"And what is your client's third condition?"

"Your client must never again speak out in public against trans athletes competing in women's sports, and she must not say it's because of our settlement."

I feel sure Benton knows Lauren won't go for the settlement proposal. That's why he offered the two hundred thousand.

Before I go, I tell Morgan I expect his client to call off his followers who are doxing Lauren, protesting in front of her home, posting deepfake compromising photos of her, and most recently, making swatting calls.

Morgan claims Benton has nothing to do with any of that.

When I get outside, I suggest to Lauren that we go to my office to chat. When we enter and sit in my office, I present the settlement proposal Benton is offering her. "What about Benton being able to claim he participated in the design of the Lake Tierra Golf Course?" I ask.

"I couldn't care less about that. Anyone who knows anything about golf knows Benton's claim is total BS."

"Are you willing to stop speaking out against transgender participation in girls' and women's sports?"

"Not only no, but hell no. When the reporter first asked me what I thought of trans athletes competing in girls' and women's sports, I never thought my answer would propel me to being one of the leading advocates for girls' and women's sports. Now, I will never abandon the girls and women who now see me as one of the last lines for defense of their opportunities in sports. No frigging way am I letting them down, not for two hundred thousand, not for a million dollars."

After she settles down, unsurprisingly taking a couple of minutes, Lauren asks why Benton suddenly wants to settle her case.

"I'm not sure. Maybe Benton realizes he will lose, and the jury may award you punitive damages."

"There's something more to it," Lauren replies.

Later, she tells me about the juror who stared at her before the break and quizzes me on how the jury reacted to the deepfake videos and the LPGA message on gambling. I tell her I didn't see any reaction from jurors.

She asks who I think Morgan will call as his first witness. I say, "It almost has to be Benton."

"Did we persuade them I designed the Lake Tierra Golf Course?" she asks.

"Your work speaks for itself, but I thought Jordan Lawson nailed it for you. Morgan knows the jury will decide that you designed the golf course. He's trying to show minor changes Benton made so he can also take credit, and they both want to do everything they can to punish you for taking him to court."

"What about the profits and my bonus?" She asks. "I looked at the jurors while our guy testified, and I fear they might be confused."

"I'm sure that was Morgan's goal," I reply. "That may be why he's offering you one-fifth of what the accountant testified the bonus should be."

As we continue, Lauren once again tells me how the fallout from the case is taking a toll on her mother. I remind her that we're in the home stretch, and I'm confident we will win.

While she is sitting across from me, I call Morgan on his cell and inform him Lauren rejected his offer. Morgan says Benton is now offering five hundred thousand. I hang up and share Benton's latest offer with Lauren.

Lauren's eyes widen as if her mind is racing as she weighs Benton's latest offer. "I'm sorry," she says, her voice quivering. "Benton thinks it's about the money. It may have been at the beginning, but it's much more than that now. I tell her there's something more to his willingness to settle at this late date. I'll expose him on cross-examination."

I purposely wait until the next morning to tell Morgan that Lauren rejects Bento's second offer. After Judge Hawkins seats the jury, as expected, Morgan calls Benton as his first witness. I watch Benton shuffle to the witness chair and take some time to sit there.

As I had done with Lauren, Morgan spends the first thirty minutes reviewing Benton's rags to riches tale. Benton leans back confidently in the witness chair, his smile smug and self-assured. He claims to have started with nothing but an idea of how he could make software run more efficiently and smoothly. He says he started his company in his garage, comparing himself to Steve Jobs and how he made it one of the most successful companies in the United States.

As Benton spins his tales of grandeur, he has a way of embellishing the truth, blurring the line between reality and fiction.

I realize that the challenge I have with Benton is that he's a masterful storyteller, and he tells so many lies that I never know what is actually true. My other challenge is the jury appears to believe his story. I've been told that Benton didn't create the software that made him a billionaire. Instead, he ruthlessly stole it from a brilliant but unknown programmer, leaving him with nothing. I have no way to prove the rumor is true. So, the jury will never hear about the true genius behind Benton's success.

Morgan asks Benton about meeting Lauren. His story matches Lauren's. He met her while playing in a pro-am event while she was on the LPGA tour.

"What was your first impression of Miss West?"

"I thought she had an unrelenting ambition that had led to her success but also made her someone willing to win at all costs. Based on how she treated me that day, I also thought she was skilled in the art of manipulation."

I object to his offering his opinion of Lauren, and Judge Hawkins overrules my objection.

"Mr. Benton, when you say Miss West was skilled in the art of manipulation, what do you mean?"

Benton leans forward, his arrogance in full display.

"By that, I mean she uses her seductive powers to influence and persuade others to shape their thoughts, opinions, and actions. She tried to persuade me to go into business with her. She wanted to start a women's clothing line and wanted me to finance her endeavor."

I look at Lauren, who mouths the word "liar."

"When did you next hear from Miss West?"

"About a year after she retired from the LPGA tour, she called me and asked if she could come out to California to discuss her idea for developing luxury golf course communities. When she visited, she bragged about earning a master's degree in landscape architecture. At the time, she worked with a well-known golf designer in Dallas. She boasted that her golf course designs would change golf forever. I thought that was a rather grandiose claim, as were many other claims Miss West made that day."

Morgan, who I assume senses Benton is captivating the jury, asks Benton for more specifics of Lauren's proposal.

Benton smirks, clearly relishing the opportunity to embellish his tale even further. "According to Lauren, these communities would be a haven for the wealthy, complete with state-of-the-art facilities and breathtaking landscapes. "Her idea, at best amateurish, demonstrated a lack of understanding of the factors that drive wealthy families to build expensive second homes in luxury developments."

Benton continues his story on how he took Lauren's amateurish concept and made it the success it has become. Benton claims he is responsible for creating exclusivity and privacy, meaning a gated community with fewer homes on larger lots. Benton testifies that he made clear that the homes must be custom-built and designed by the top architects in the United States and that no two homes could be alike. He claims he added spa and wellness facilities, fine dining, concierge services to handle residents' needs, exclusive cultural and social events, and environmental sustainability.

For the next thirty minutes, Morgan has Benton tell the jury about each of his luxury golf course developments. For each one, he overstates what role he had in creating the development and designing of the golf course. He claims each development became a success because his name was the brand. Lauren writes bullshit on her legal pad.

Morgan asks why potential buyers find his ideas to be important.

Benton's expression only grows, and his eyes sparkle as he begins to experience the thrill of recounting his own grandeur. "You see," he takes a dramatic pause to ensure he has the jury's attention, "What makes my ideas so important is the essence of exclusivity. My friends and clients crave something unique that sets them apart from the rest. By insisting on custom-built homes designed by the crème de la crème of architects, I ensured that each residence would be a masterpiece in its own right and, as important, a great investment. Miss West may know golf, but she's completely out of touch with what wealthy people actually want."

I fear the jury is buying his exaggerated claims about his role in the developments. I see Lauren making fists and hear her take a deep breath while listening to Benton belittle her contribution. I can just imagine how Morgan and Benton meticulously rehearsed that answer to make the biggest impression on the jury. I'm stressing over Benton's rapport with the jury.

"Mr. Benton, describe what prompted you to terminate Miss West's golf course design contract."

"I discovered that in an interview Miss West had given to a newspaper, she had misgendered trans females and made transphobic comments that discriminated against them and put them at risk. Her interview went viral on social media platforms, and friends and potential buyers bombarded me with phone calls and emails."

"Did you confront Miss West?"

"Yes, I called her and told her she needed to retract what she had said in the interview and never comment on the subject again. Miss West didn't care about girls and women's sports. All she cared about at the time was making me pay one million dollars, which she claimed was the amount of her bonus. Miss West promised to retract what she said and not comment again when she received her bonus. I told Miss West that we had no net profits, meaning she wasn't entitled to a bonus."

"Why did you terminate Miss West's contract?"

"Because Miss West materially breached the contract by disparaging trans athletes."

I stand and object, arguing it calls for a legal conclusion. Judge Hawkins tells the jury to disregard Benton's statement and that he will instruct them on the law of material breach of a contract.

Morgan asks Benton to continue.

"I informed her, as stipulated in her contract, to withdraw her statement; failure to comply would result in contract termination. She swore at me and told me she'd see me in court, and here we are."

"Why is supporting trans athletes the right to take part in sports and not having your golf course designer attack trans athletes?"

I object on the grounds there's no evidence that Lauren has attacked trans athletes. Judge Hawkins asks Morgan to rephrase his question.

After considering, Morgan asks, "Why do you place importance on endorsing trans athletes' right to participate in sports while opposing Miss West's stance against their involvement?"

"I am certain that at least fifty percent of potential buyers support the right of every individual to participate in sports. Even the President of the United States and the Department of Education have made it clear that they oppose any outright ban on trans athletes competing in women's sports."

Benton fails to mention that the rule would give universities and K-12 schools the discretion to limit the participation of transgender students if they conclude that including transgender athletes could undermine competitive fairness or potentially lead to sports-related injuries. I take note to make this point on cross-examination.

Morgan puts on the screen an article while Benton says, "The Scientific American, a highly respected scientific journal, in an article titled "Trans Girls: Belong on Girls Sports Teams," argues there is no scientific evidence to exclude them." Morgan has Benton read pertinent points in the article while showing it to the jury. Benton adds the names of several well-known female athletes who support transgender participation in girls' and women's sports.

I'm writing copious notes, knowing I won't remember all the points I wish to make on cross-examination with my current memory fog.

Benton continues. "Most importantly, I have a niece who is a transgender athlete. Because she lives in California, she can compete on her girl's high school teams. She has not excelled in any sport yet, which defies Miss West's and other MAGA's claim that transgender athletes are dominating the girls' and women's sports. If my niece lived here in Texas, they would unfairly not allow her to compete."

Lauren passes me a note.

"No HS nephew or niece. BS."

Sensing Benton is making it up, I don't expect Morgan to put any photos of Benton's supposed niece on the screen. I study Benton's body language for telltale signs he's lying. My challenge is that Benton's telling so many lies under oath that his body language has none of those signs. I don't know where to start to discredit him. I'm thinking about how I can prove he has no high school-aged niece or nephew. I type a text under the table asking my assistant to research Benton's brothers and sisters and their families.

Morgan continues asking Benton questions until five o'clock. When he says, "That's all of my questions," Judge Hawkins reminds jurors not to discuss the case, excuses them, and adjourns court until nine o'clock tomorrow.

As Lauren and I navigate through the throng of protestors, my phone vibrates. The noise around us fades into the background as I glance down at the screen. When we reach my car, I finally check the message. It's from Courtney Barr. I read it aloud, my voice barely above a whisper, "I have some information to share with you that might help Lauren's case." I can feel Lauren's eyes on me. What could Courtney possibly know? And why now? As I slip the phone back into its holster, a million questions race through my mind. Is it something that could turn the jury even more to our side?

Chapter 32

Lauren

One hour later, Courtney sits next to me across from Luke.

Luke leans in, his interest piqued. "What do you have for us.?"

"There are several liberal funding organizations that have long supported LGBTQ+ causes. Recently, some of these groups have shifted their focus more toward transgender issues, much to the frustration of their original gay and lesbian supporters. When your interview went public, one of these organizations saw an opportunity and contacted Robert Benton. They offered to fund his fight against you both in and out of court, hoping to use this case to influence public opinion on transgender rights."

"What does that mean?" Luke asks.

"The organization isn't just funding the litigation," Courtney explains. "They're behind the media storm you and Lauren have been dealing with. They're paying for Morgan's services, Carlotta Hampton's expertise and they've even agreed to reimburse Benton for any bonus the jury might award you—up to one million dollars."

"So, Benton has nothing to lose," Luke says.

"Not exactly," Courtney replies. "The organization won't cover punitive damages. My source told me that Carlotta Hampton is worried the jury might award you several million dollars in punitive damages, especially if they believe Benton used the deepfake video to defame you. Despite all their efforts, Hampton also thinks public opinion has started to swing in your favor. The organization is getting cold feet. They've told Benton he's on his own for any punitive damages. That's why Benton is suddenly so eager to settle."

I let out a breath I didn't realize I was holding. I had been worried about how the jury might respond to Morgan's accusations against me. "Can you tell us the name of the organization funding all of this?"

"No," Courtney says, her voice tinged with regret. "My source insisted on confidentiality. He's one of the original critics who feels betrayed by the shift in focus away from gay and lesbian issues."

"His latest settlement offer only covers about half of what he owes me," I say. "Do you think the LGBTQ organization would cover all of my bonus, plus pay you your attorney's fees?"

"There's only one way to find out," Luke says, a hint of resolve in his tone. "Morgan's in a tricky spot ethically. His client is Robert Benton, but the organization is the one footing the bill."

Courtney interjects, "I'm not sure what Benton wants in the end, but the organization wants this over with. If you could make a public statement similar to the one you gave in that interview reaffirming that you believe people have the right to live the life they choose and maybe expressing hope that in the future, there could be a place for trans athletes to compete, they might be willing to end this quietly."

"I suspect I'll get a call early this evening from Harvey Morgan sweetening Benton's offer, but I think we should put the squeeze on Benton," Luke says. "Let me cross-examine him."

I'm thinking about all the times I wanted the case to be over so I could move on and get back to work. The trouble is, I realize that for the first time in my life, I can't think of anything that excites me. I don't know what I'll do after we settle the case.

"I agree, Luke. Put the squeeze on him."

Later, Luke calls. "Morgan called and sweetened their offer before I cross-examine Benton."

"What did Morgan offer?" I ask.

Luke chuckles, but there's a tension behind it. "Morgan said that if you settle this case for six hundred thousand dollars, Benton would also cover my attorney's fees, which are around three hundred thousand dollars now. He said that Benton would even agree to include your name as a co-designer on scorecards and all marketing materials."

"What did you tell him?" I ask.

"I told him I'd pass the offer along, but based on our discussions, I doubted you'd accept it."

"What was Morgan's response?"

Luke's tone darkens. "He got nasty. He said you'd regret it. He said you'd never design another golf course if he and Benton had anything to say about it."

After the unsettling call with Luke, I sit down with my mother for a quiet evening, hoping to distract her from the stress of the trial. We're in the small living area of the apartment, the TV on low as we try to relax. Suddenly, the lights flicker once, then go out entirely, plunging us into darkness.

"Lauren, what's happening?" My mother's voice trembles, a mix of fear and confusion.

"Stay calm, Mom. It's probably just a power outage," I say, trying to reassure her, even though a knot of anxiety tightens in my stomach. I fumble for my phone to use its flashlight, but before I can, there's a loud crash from the kitchen, followed by the sound of glass shattering.

My mother gasps, and I can feel her panic rising. I grab her hand, pulling her closer as we move cautiously toward the kitchen, where the sound came from. My heart pounds as I shine the light from my phone, revealing the source of the noise.

The window over the sink has been shattered, and lying on the floor amidst the broken glass is a brick, a crude message scrawled on it: "Back off or else."

My mother clutches my arm tightly, her eyes wide with fear. She bends down to clean up the glass, but her hands are trembling so much that she can barely manage it. "Lauren, we can't stay here. What if they come back? What if they try to hurt us?"

I swallow hard, trying to stay calm for her sake, even as the fear claws at me. "Mom, it's okay. We're safe right now. But I'm calling the police." As I dial 911, my resolve hardens. This fight isn't just a courtroom battle. It's that and an all-out war, both online and in the streets. It's about protecting my mother and standing up to Benton and Morgan's fear tactics. Whatever happens next, I won't let them bully me into backing down. When the police arrive, they confirm what I already knew: this was a deliberate act of intimidation. But seeing my mother's terror strengthens my resolve. Benton's goons might think they can scare me into submission, but all they've done is ignite a fire within me.

After the police finish their investigation and leave, the apartment feels different. It's no longer a safe haven but a place where fear now lingers in every corner. My mother's hand trembles as she tries to clean up the glass, but I gently stop her.

"Mom, we're not staying here tonight," I say firmly.

She looks at me, her eyes wide with worry. "Where will we go? What if they find us again?"

I take a deep breath, trying to calm my emotions. I need to think clearly, for both our sakes. I pull out my phone and call Luke, my heart pounding as I wait for him to pick up.

"Lauren, what's going on?" Luke's voice is alert, sensing the urgency in my silence.

"Someone threw a brick through our window," I explain, my voice shaking despite my best efforts to stay calm. "There was a threat written on it. The police came, but I don't feel safe here."

There's a pause on the other end, and then Luke's tone shifts, becoming more protective. "You're not staying there tonight. Pack a bag, and come to my place. I have more security, and you'll both be safe here."

I glance at my mother, who's now sitting on the couch, her hands clasped tightly in her lap. "Luke says we can stay with him," I tell her. "It's safer there."

She nods slowly, but I can see the toll this is taking on her. "Lauren, when will this be over? I just want things to go back to normal," she whispers, her voice thick with emotion.

I walk over and sit beside her, wrapping my arm around her shoulders. "I know, Mom. I want that, too. But I can't let them win. I can't back down now."

She leans into me, drawing strength from my resolve. "You're right. We can't let them scare us."

We pack a few essentials, leaving the rest behind in the apartment that now feels like a distant memory of safety. As we drive to Luke's, the weight of the situation presses down on me, but I also feel a renewed determination. They've tried to intimidate us, but all they've done is strengthen my resolve to see this through to the end.

As we pull into Luke's driveway, I see lights on in the windows, casting a warm glow into the night. Luke is standing outside, waiting for us, his face a mix of concern and relief. He helps us inside, guiding my mother to a seat in the living room while I set our bags down.

Inside, the atmosphere is quiet. Megan and Abby are still up, sitting on the couch with the TV on low. When we walk in, both girls look up, surprised to see us at this hour.

"Lauren? What are you doing here so late?" Megan asks, her curiosity piqued.

Luke steps in before I can respond, his voice calm and reassuring. "There was a problem at Lauren's apartment tonight. I thought it'd be safer if she and her mom stayed here with us for a while."

Abby, who has always been more attuned to the emotions around her, looks from Luke to me, her eyes wide with concern. "Are you okay, Lauren? Did something bad happen?" she asks, her voice filled with worry.

I walk over to the couch and sit beside Abby, giving her a comforting smile. "I'm okay, Abby. Something did happen, but being here with you and your dad makes me feel a lot safer."

Abby, still holding her stuffed animal, scoots closer to me. "You are teaching me how to golf, Lauren. Now, I want to help take care of you. You can stay in my room if you want."

Her words tug at my heart, and I wrap an arm around her shoulders. "Thank you, Abby. That means the world to me. But I think your room is perfect just for you. Your dad has a guest room for us, and we'll be just fine."

Luke glances at Megan, who is watching the exchange closely. "Megan, why don't you help Mrs. West settle in the guest room?" he suggests gently.

Megan nods, rising from the couch. She offers my mother a kind smile and then leads her down the hall. My mother follows, looking more at ease now that we're in a safe place.

As they leave, Luke turns back to me, his expression serious but warm. "Lauren, you and your mom are safe here."

I nod, grateful for his support. Abby remains close, her presence a quiet comfort. The earlier fear lingers, but it feels more manageable here, surrounded by people who care about us. As I help Abby turn off the TV and get ready for bed, I can't help but feel a renewed sense of determination. No matter what Benton and Morgan throw at us next, I'm not backing down.

Once my mother is settled in Luke's guest room, I watch Luke's concern shift into something more intense. Without a word, he walks out to the porch, phone in hand. I follow him out, curious and uneasy.

He punches in a number with a determined force, and I know he's calling Morgan. The night air is warm, but there's a tension between us that makes it feel almost stifling.

"Harvey," Luke says, his voice low but edged with fury. "I want to know if you or Benton had anything to do with what happened tonight at Lauren's apartment."

I can't hear Morgan's response, but Luke's face hardens, his jaw clenching as he listens.

"Don't play innocent with me," Luke continues, his anger simmering just beneath the surface. "Lauren and her mother could've been seriously hurt. If this was some sort of intimidation tactic, you've crossed a line."

There's a pause, and Luke's expression softens, his anger fading as he listens. He puts Morgan on speaker so I can hear what he says. He looks at me, his eyes searching mine as if trying to gauge my reaction to whatever Morgan is saying.

“Listen, Luke,” Morgan’s voice crackles faintly through the speaker, loud enough that I can catch bits of it. “I had nothing to do with this. Neither did Benton. I’m sorry this happened, but don’t drag us into something we had no part in.”

Luke’s eyes narrow as he listens, not entirely convinced. “You expect me to believe that?”

Morgan’s tone softens, something almost like empathy creeping in. “I know you think the worst of us, but this isn’t how we operate. I genuinely hope Lauren and her mom are okay. If I find out anyone connected to my client had anything to do with this, you have my word. I’ll deal with it.”

Luke doesn’t respond right away, the tension between us growing as he considers Morgan’s words. Finally, he exhales, his grip on the phone loosening slightly. “If I find out you’re lying, Harvey, I’ll make sure you and Benton regret it.”

Luke ends the call, shoving the phone back into his holster. He just stands there for a moment, staring out into the darkness. Then, he turns to me, his expression a mix of lingering anger and frustration.

“Morgan says they had nothing to do with it and claims he’ll take care of it if he finds out otherwise.”

I nod, unsure of what to say. The truth is, I want to believe Luke. But after everything Benton has done, it's hard to trust anyone on that side.

"We'll deal with it in the morning," Luke finally says, his voice calmer now, though the tension remains. "For now, let's try to get some rest. We've got a long day ahead of us."

Chapter 33

Luke

I'm not feeling well the following morning after losing hours of sleep. I'm exhausted, and that worries me. Lauren and I walk the gauntlet of protestors again as we enter the courthouse. This time, many are holding professionally made signs condemning Lauren. Their words slice through the morning air, each one a reminder of the battle we're up against.

I maintain a steady expression, projecting the confidence that I know Lauren needs to see, but the doubts are creeping inside. Last night's threats to Lauren still linger in my mind, and my body feels the strain of the long hours, the stress, and the relentless pressure to be perfect in a fight that has become more personal with each passing day.

I take on Benton today. My task is to convince the jury that they can't trust most, if not all, of what he says. But as much as I tell myself I've done this before, that I'm ready, I know my health makes this time different. What if I'm not up to it? What if my body betrays me at the worst possible moment? I can't quite shake my exhaustion, the lingering effects of my illness, and the burden of knowing someone hurled a rock through Lauren's window with a note threatening her, and her mother presses heavily on my mind.

As we enter the courtroom, I draw a deep breath, summoning the confidence I've honed over countless cross-examinations. I'm the lawyer who knows how to dismantle know-it-alls and tough guys. But beneath the surface, the effects of the ventilator gnaw at me, and I can't help but wonder how much longer I can keep them from showing.

After Judge Hawkins seats the jury, he looks at Robert Benton and says, "Mr. Benton, you may resume your seat in the witness chair. Mr. Hartley, you may cross-examine now."

Benton slowly rises, sneers at Lauren and me, and shuffles again toward the witness stand.

Judge Hawkins reminds Benton that he is still under oath. I watch as Benton settles into the witness chair, leans back, folds his arms, and sighs.

"Mr. Benton," my voice is raspy from my vocal cord issues, "you've never studied landscape architecture, and you're not a member of the American Society of Golf Course Architects, are you?"

You don't need a degree in landscape architecture or affiliation with the American Society of Golf Course Architects to design a golf course. He looks over at the jury, then back at me. I hope they notice his condescending smile.

"Mr. Hartley, as you and the jurors undoubtedly know, Arnold Palmer, Jack Nicholas, Greg Norman, Tiger Woods, and many other famous golf course designers never studied landscape architecture, and they've designed some of the most famous golf courses in the world. I have developed one of the world's most successful software companies and don't have a degree in software engineering. Your client has a degree in landscape architecture and belongs to the American Society of Golf Course Architects. Her designs were amateurish, not what I would expect from someone with her supposed reputation. I had to rework each of her designs."

Benton's dismissive tones fill the room as he continues rambling on. I look at Judge Hawkins. "Your Honor, please instruct Mr. Benton to answer the question?"

Morgan rises. "Your Honor, Mr. Benton is entitled to explain his answer."

"Mr. Morgan, your client's gone beyond explaining his answer. I'm instructing him to answer Mr. Hartley's questions and not make a speech."

When I ask Benton to acknowledge that Lauren had designed nine golf courses for him, Benton claims he had to redesign each golf course, and that's why he's taking credit for being the designer. He continues, but I talk over him.

"Mr. Benton, I'm showing you an interview you gave in Golf Business Magazine. I ask that you read the third paragraph."

Benton reads. "Lauren West, the former LPGA golf star, has created a unique brand for our golf course developments. She has designed golf courses that the entire family can enjoy. Her designs create challenges for top-notch golfers while being playable by others. She does not treat women golfers and their children who are learning as afterthoughts. Miss West is quickly becoming one of the world's most renowned and respected golf course designers."

"That is what you said about Lauren West's golf course designs when you signed the contract for her to design the Lake Tierra Golf Course."

"Mr. Hartley, I know you're a small-town Texas lawyer. If you understood anything about business, you'd realize I was puffing up promoting Lauren West and our golf courses to increase sales. The magazine interview was a sales pitch I created to get more clients for my developments. There's a little fraud in every sale, including my promoting Lauren West. If she had not been a former LPGA golfer, I would have likely picked another way of promoting our golf communities."

"Interesting," I say, carefully rifling through my papers, fearing I may have forgotten something. I catch jurors watching me with growing curiosity. "Because according to these emails you sent to Ms. West, you praised her work extensively. 'Innovative, inspired, a true game-changer.' In another email to your bank, you said, 'Lauren West's golf course designs will revolutionize the golf industry.' Are those your words, Mr. Benton?"

Benton shifts in his seat, thinking how to refute what he said in emails. He finally claims he was trying to encourage her and motivate her. He adds, "I believed that by complimenting her work, she would become more focused and generate more creative designs."

Trial lawyers are taught to never ask a question on cross-examination without knowing how the witness will answer. My next question will violate my rule.

"Mr. Benton, can you explain how your opinion of Miss West's golf course designs went from game-changing to amateurish?"

At first, Benton seems stumped by the question. He shifts in his seat. Finally, he says, "Those were different circumstances. When I emailed Miss West, I tried to encourage her, like a parent might praise a child, even though the child is making a mess with her painting. The testimony I'm giving now is my unfiltered opinion of her work. I'm not sugarcoating it now. I'm telling you the truth."

I hope the jury finds Benton's comparison of Lauren's golf course designs to a child's painting as offensive as I do.

I decide to ask another question, which I don't know how Benton will answer.

I ask him to tell the jury what specifically was amateurish about Lauren's golf course designs.

Benton sits stiffly in the witness chair. He pauses. Finally, he says, "I don't remember the specific flaws right now."

"You never said her designs were amateurish before today, isn't that true?"

"I doubt that it's true."

I grip the edge of the podium, leaning into it for support as a wave of fatigue hits me. My breath hitches, but I force myself to stay steady. I can't let Benton or the jury see just how much this is taking out of me. I continue asking questions, and Benton continues to make speeches during his answers, most of which have nothing to do with my questions. "Mr. Benton, did you fail to pay the Lake Tierra golf course general contractor the contract price you agreed to?"

Benton hesitates, and I show him the contract and documents reflecting payments. "I paid the contractor what I believed his work was worth."

"You decided the Lake Tierra golf course contractor's work was worth $250,000 less than the agreed contract price?"

"Yes," Benton says. "I had to fix some of their construction."

"What did you fix?"

Benton straightens up, a slight smirk on his face. "I had to address issues with the drainage system and make adjustments to the grading on several holes. Their work didn't meet my standards, so I had to bring in additional crews to get it right. It was a costly oversight on their part, and I wouldn't pay full price for subpar work."

I have Benton's accounting records. I can show his answer is untrue, but I decide to move on.

"And you also paid the Lake Tierra clubhouse contractor less than their contract amount, right?"

"Once again, I paid that contractor what their work on the clubhouse was worth. I once again had to make corrections."

"You have made it a habit of not paying your contractors and forcing them to sue you, haven't you?"

Benton rolls his eyes and gives me a dismissive glance. "No, that's not true. I don't let contractors get away with not doing what they are contractually obligated to do."

"Mr. Benton," I say. "Isn't it true that you ordered scorecards and brochures showing that Lauren West designed the Lake Tierra Golf Course?"

"No, that's not true."

I show Benton a purchase order with his signature on it. "Isn't that your signature on the purchase order for scorecards and brochures?"

"No, Miss West forged my signature on the purchase order,"

I show Benton another document with his signature. "You signed this document, didn't you?"

Benton looks at the document. “I don’t remember.”

I put the two documents on the screen for the jury and Benton to see. “Comparing the signature on the purchase order with the signature on this document, they are the same, aren’t they?”

“I can’t say. I’m not a handwriting expert.”

“You don’t recognize your signature?” I ask.

“As I said, Miss West became quite adept at forging my signature.”

“Do you know Steven Strong?”

“That name is not familiar to me.”

I show Benton a document and put it on the screen for the jury to see.

“Isn’t this the email you sent to Steven Strong telling him to stop printing brochures and scorecards showing Lauren as the Lake Tierra Golf Course designer?”

Robert Benton’s posture stiffens as if taken by surprise. “I don’t remember sending that email.”

"Do you remember not paying Steven Strong's company for printing the scorecards and brochures showing that Lauren West designed the Lake Tierra Golf Course?"

"I can't say. All I can say is I shouldn't have to pay a printer who mistakenly says Lauren West designed the Lake Tierra Golf Course."

Judge Hawkins interrupts me, his voice cutting through the tension in the room. "Mr. Hartley, we'll take a fifteen-minute recess. The court will reconvene at 10:45."

I nod, grateful for the brief pause, though I'm not finished with Benton yet. I watch as Benton steps down from the witness stand, his face flushed with anger. He avoids looking at me, his jaw clenched as he marches toward the exit with Morgan at his side. They exchange quick, hushed words, their heads close together. Carlotta Hampton follows them with her ear to her cell phone. It's clear I have Benton rattled, but I can't help wondering what they're planning next.

As they leave the courtroom, I catch a glimpse of Morgan's expression. He looks as cool as ever, undoubtedly plotting their next move. They don't stop to speak with the press this time, which tells me they're feeling the pressure, perhaps regrouping before making another public statement.

I turn to Lauren, who's been watching the exchange with intense focus. She looks up at me, her eyes searching for reassurance.

"Luke, do you think they'll try something during the break?" she asks, her voice tinged with worry.

I take a deep breath. "Morgan and Benton have nothing to try. Benton is not like the politician who can get by reading a teleprompter. All Morgan can do is share what he thinks I'll ask after the break and tell Benton how to answer my questions."

Lauren nods, though I can see the doubt still lingering in her eyes. "He's trying to twist everything, making it look like I had no right to design that course."

I place a hand on her shoulder, giving it a firm squeeze. "I've got this. Have faith. I'll take care of Mr. Benton."

She gives me a small, determined smile. "Okay. I'll be watching."

I smile back, but inside, I know this is far from over. Benton and Morgan are too seasoned to go down without a fight. As we head back to the courtroom, I mentally review what I have prepared for Benton in the next round.

For the next thirty minutes of my cross-examination, I meticulously review the Lake Tierra financial records. I get Benton to admit that the Hill Country Lake Tierra Development is his most profitable project.

I show Benton a profit-and-loss statement for the Lake Tierra Development. It shows a profit of over ten million dollars.

"If you hadn't terminated Miss West's contract, you would have owed her over one million dollars in profit, plus ten percent of any future earnings. Isn't that correct?"

"That's irrelevant to my decision to terminate her contract after she breached it. Our profits could have been twice as high if Miss West hadn't disparaged transgender athletes and exposed them to retaliation from right-wing extremists."

"Mr. Benton, can you explain why, after Lauren West filed her lawsuit, you suddenly paid the Benton Land Company a significant management fee, something you hadn't done with any of your other developments?"

Benton shifts in his seat, adopting a defensive tone. "Mr. Hartley, creating and then running a development like Lake Tierra is a complex and multifaceted operation. After Miss West filed her lawsuit, I reviewed the financials and discovered that Benton Land

Company had provided substantial management services without receiving proper compensation. Those services included overseeing construction, coordinating with contractors, handling marketing efforts, and ensuring the development was in line with our high standards. The fee was a legitimate expense, reflecting the value of those services. I hadn't charged a management fee in the past, but that didn't mean it wasn't warranted in this case. I decided to correct that oversight, making sure Benton Land Company received proper compensation for its role in the success of the Lake Tierra project."

"Isn't it true that you made this payment specifically to reduce the apparent profits of the Lake Tierra Development to avoid paying Miss West the bonus she earned?"

Benton stiffens slightly, his voice becoming more measured as he tries to maintain control. "Absolutely not, Mr. Hartley. I paid the management fees because the services Benton Land Company rendered demanded it. The timing may seem coincidental to you, but it was purely a business decision. You totally miss the point that the Benton Land Company was instrumental in the success of Lake Tierra development, and it deserved to be compensated accordingly. You are wrong to claim I terminated Miss West's contract to avoid paying her a bonus. Among other things, she hasn't earned a bonus."

As Benton delivers his answer, I keep my gaze on the jury. I know Benton's words are slick and well-rehearsed, but I'm more interested in how the jurors react. I see one juror, a middle-aged man in a plaid shirt, shift uncomfortably in his seat, his brow furrowing as if he's trying to piece something together. It's subtle, but I can see he's skeptical now.

"Mr. Benton, you've stated that you terminated Miss West's contract because of her stance on transgender athletes. Isn't it true that you've never taken a public stance on this issue before this lawsuit?"

Benton hesitates for a moment, his confident facade slipping slightly. "Well, Mr. Hartley, as a businessman, my focus has always been on running successful developments and serving my clients. I haven't felt the need to comment publicly on every social issue that arises. However, when Miss West's statements became a matter of public controversy, it affected the image and reputation of the Lake Tierra Development. I felt it was necessary to take a stance in this particular case to protect my business interests and the values of the community I serve."

I put a document on the screen and asks Benton to identify it. I get him to admit that in a public interview in 2022, he stated that he supported free speech and open dialogue in the workplace.

I see Benton shift in his seat, trying to appear more confident, but his eyes dart momentarily to the jury as if gauging their reaction to his words.

I ask, "But you terminated Miss West's contract, claiming she materially breached it when all she did was express her opinion on a public issue. Isn't that true?"

Benton shifts in his seat, jaw tightening as he prepares to respond. "What Miss West expressed wasn't just an opinion; it was hate speech that put the reputation of my development at risk. I had to act to protect my business and the people who invest in it."

I had expected the hate speech answer. I lean closer to the podium, my voice steady. "So, Mr. Benton, are you saying that, in your view, any opinion that contradicts your business interests qualifies as hate speech?"

He hesitates, clearly surprised by the question, his eyes flicking nervously toward the jury. I can see the uncertainty in his face, and I know I've struck a nerve. Benton shifts again, his voice faltering. "I wouldn't say that exactly. It's just that some opinions can cause actual harm, and in this case, it was harmful to the community we're building."

I can sense the momentum building, the jury's attention locked on Benton as I push forward. But as I move to ask my next question, a tightness grips my chest. I take a moment, trying to catch my breath without drawing attention to it, forcing myself to stay calm.

"Isn't it correct," I manage to say, my voice steady despite the strain, "that this dispute over transgender athletes only became an issue after you realized how much you owed Miss West under her contract?"

As I finish the question, I feel a sharp pang in my chest, but I can't let it show. Not now. Not when Benton is on the ropes. I keep my gaze on him, refusing to let the discomfort distract me, knowing that I have to stay in control, no matter what my body is trying to tell me.

Benton's face tightens, a flash of irritation crossing his features. He shifts in his seat, his bravado slipping just enough for me to notice. Then, with a defiant tilt of his chin, he leans forward, his voice taking on a dismissive edge.

"Mr. Hartley, you're twisting things to fit your narrative. This isn't about money. It's about principles. I've built a reputation for standing up for what I believe is right. Miss West's stance barring transgender athletes from competing in sports became a public relations nightmare. I had to act to protect the integrity of the Lake Tierra Development and my company. It's as simple as that."

He throws the words out there like a challenge, his tone sharp, almost daring me to push him further. But I can see the cracks forming beneath his bluster, the way his eyes flicker nervously to the jury, knowing that they might not be buying what he's selling.

I continue questioning Benton, driving home the point to the jury that his sudden support for transgender athletes conveniently surfaced only after he realized he owed Lauren over $1 million in bonuses.

I can tell my questions to irritate Benton. When I ask one more time about the timing of his support for transgender athletes, he testifies, "Mr. Hartley, I don't recall the exact timeline of events, but my concerns were always about the reputation of my development. Miss West's stance became a serious issue when it started affecting the image of Lake Tierra. Her public statements created a controversy I couldn't ignore, regardless of any financial discussions."

I nod slightly, not letting him off the hook. "So, to clarify, you didn't complain about Miss West's stance on transgender athletes until after she demanded her $1 million bonus. Isn't that correct?"

Benton's smile fades, replaced by a steely glare. "I didn't see the need to address the issue publicly until it became clear how damaging her statements were. The timing is irrelevant. My priority was to protect my business and the people who have invested in it."

Feeling the momentum shift, I press on. "You've never terminated a contract on moral grounds before terminating Miss West's contract. Isn't that true?"

Benton hesitates, his eyes narrowing as he searches for a way out. "I've always acted in the best interests of my company. Each situation is unique, and I decide based on what I believe is right."

I don't want to give him an inch. "So, to be clear, this is the first time you've ever terminated a contract on moral grounds. Yes or no?"

Morgan shoots up from his seat, his voice sharp. "Objection, Your Honor! Counsel is badgering the witness and asking repetitive questions."

Judge Hawkins, with an air of finality, looks directly at Morgan. "Overruled, Mr. Morgan. Mr. Benton. answer the question."

Benton shifts uncomfortably in his seat, clearly rattled. "I don't remember if this is the first time," he finally claims, his voice barely above a murmur.

I can sense the jury's attention locked onto Benton, their doubt growing with each evasive answer. I know I'm close to breaking through, and Benton knows it, too. His confidence is wavering, and the cracks in his defense are becoming impossible to ignore.

I take a deep breath, ready to deliver the final blow. "Mr. Benton, isn't it true that a private organization is funding your litigation and paying Mr. Morgan—"

Before I can finish, Morgan is on his feet and cuts me off. "Objection, Your Honor! Who is paying me is irrelevant to this case."

Judge Hawkins adjusts his glasses, eyeing Morgan with a measured gaze. "Mr. Hartley, please explain the relevance."

I turn to Judge Hawkins, choosing my words carefully. "Your Honor, understanding who is financing this lawsuit directly impacts the credibility and motives behind Mr. Benton's actions. If an outside organization with specific interests is backing this case, it indicates that Mr. Benton's claims might be driven not just by personal or business concerns but by that organization's broader agenda. Miss West has the right for the jury to consider this information when evaluating his testimony."

Judge Hawkins considers this for a moment, the courtroom falling into a tense silence. Finally, he nods.

"Objection overruled. Mr. Benton, please answer the question."

Morgan exhales sharply.

All eyes turn back to Benton. He shifts uncomfortably in the witness chair, adjusting his tie, and looks at Harvey Morgan as if asking for help.

He clears his throat. "I've received support from organizations that advocate for the rights of transgender individuals, including athletes in girls' and women's sports. There's nothing improper about that."

I press on, sensing his unease. "Can you name this organization providing support?"

Benton's eyes dart briefly to Morgan before returning to me. "I don't see how that's relevant. They're simply supporters who believe in my cause."

I maintain my gaze, unflinching. “So you refuse to name the organization paying Mr. Morgan and Miss Hampton for you?”

He straightens his back, attempting to regain some composure. “I prefer to respect their privacy. The important thing is that I’m defending my rights and the integrity of my business.”

I let a brief pause hang in the air, wanting the jury to absorb his reluctance to answer fully. I glance toward them and notice several jurors exchanging skeptical looks, their doubt evident.

Satisfied, I return my attention to Benton. “No further questions, Your Honor.”

As I walk back to my seat, I feel a mix of exhaustion and triumph. My chest tightens slightly, a reminder of the strain, but I push it aside. Lauren meets my gaze, offering a subtle nod of appreciation and support.

Judge Hawkins clears his throat, addressing the court. “We will adjourn for lunch before proceeding.”

I hear murmurs rise as people move about. I sink into my chair, slowly closing my eyes to steady myself. The hardest part may be over, but the battle is far from finished.

I understand from his witness list that Morgan intends to call potential Lake Tierra Development clients to testify that they reconsidered or withdrew their interest in purchasing property or investing in the development after hearing Lauren's comments. Then, he's calling a public relations professional who will claim that Lauren's comments were a significant threat to the Lake Tierra Development's reputation. Still, from the look on Robert Benton's face when he left the witness stand, I don't know what he and Morgan will do next. In the meantime, the courtroom buzzes around me. I can't shake the feeling that something big is about to unfold.

Chapter 34

Lauren

I gather my papers and glance at Luke, who meets my eyes with a reassuring nod. For the first time in days, I'm optimistic. Luke took care of Robert Benton better than I had expected.

We walk out of the courtroom together, weaving through the bustling hallway where whispers and hurried footsteps fill the air. People are talking, their voices low but charged with energy, as if the weight of Luke's cross-examination has set something in motion. I can feel the eyes of those around us, curiosity mixed with unease, as if they know a storm is brewing.

When we step outside into the afternoon heat, the sun feels almost too bright and too harsh after the dark intensity of the courtroom. Conversations seem to pause as we emerge, and a few heads turn our way, their expressions a mix of anticipation and uncertainty. I adjust my blazer, trying to shake off the anxiety that clings to me like a second skin, and my eyes scan the crowd gathered on the courthouse steps. I can feel the tension as if everyone is waiting for the next move, the next twist in this unfolding courtroom drama.

Luke's voice is steady as he comments on the media circus outside, but I notice a subtle shift in his posture. He follows my gaze, his eyes narrowing as he watches Benton and Morgan bask in the attention as arrogant as ever.

"Of course, they couldn't resist," Luke mutters, irritation lacing his tone. His jaw tightens, and I can see the exhaustion etched in the lines of his face. The heat is oppressive, bearing down on us as we stand there, and I catch a slight hitch in Luke's breath.

He shifts his weight almost imperceptibly, but I can see it. I also see his shoulders tensing as he tries to maintain his composure. His hand reaches for his side, just below his ribs, and he takes a deeper breath, but it's not quite enough. His chest rises and falls a bit too quickly, his breath coming in short, shallow bursts.

"Luke?" I say softly, concern creeping into my voice.

He nods, dismissing it, but I can tell he's struggling. His hand grips the railing beside us as if anchoring himself, and for a moment, I think he's going to brush it off and keep moving. But then he pauses, his breath catching again, and I can see the strain in his eyes.

"Just give me a second," he murmurs, his voice tight. "Damn it," he says.

I step closer, instinctively reaching out to steady him. "You should sit down for a minute," I suggest, glancing around for somewhere we can escape the relentless sun.

Luke hesitates, his pride warring with the obvious need to catch his breath. Finally, he nods, conceding to the exhaustion. We move to a nearby bench, and I can feel the heat radiating off the pavement as I guide him to sit. He leans forward, elbows on his knees, taking slow, deliberate breaths as he tries to regain control.

For a moment, we're both silent, the noise of the reporters and the crowd fading into the background. All I can focus on is the rise and fall of Luke's chest, each breath a reminder of the toll this trial—and everything leading up to it—has taken on him.

My smile tightens. "Let them try. Anyone who was in that courtroom knows you put Benton on the ropes. You might have even knocked him to the canvas."

"Exactly," Luke replies, placing a hand on my shoulder, grounding me. "We have all the momentum. The jury saw right through Benton's act. I'm dying to know how he and Morgan are spinning his testimony."

I catch Luke's eye, and he gives me a reassuring nod. "No matter who they call next, I'm ready."

I smile, trying to let his confidence reassure me as we continue down the steps. But I worry about his breathing.

We head to Rosie's Diner, our usual lunch spot. The familiar routine of this place has become a small comfort in the middle of this storm. By now, I'm a regular, and Rosie and her staff know me by name. They know what I like to order, and something is soothing about not having to make another decision in a world where so much feels uncertain.

As soon as we step inside, the comforting aroma of home-cooked meals surrounds us, and the tension in my shoulders eases for a moment. Rosie spots us and waves us over to our usual booth by the window, a small gesture that brings a smile to my face. The familiarity is soothing, even if my order isn't always the same.

Rosie doesn't bother asking what I want. "How about the tuna salad today? It's fresh, and I can pair it with a side of mixed greens," she suggests, her pen poised.

"That sounds perfect," I reply, feeling grateful that she always knows what will hit the spot.

"And for you, Luke, the grilled chicken breast with steamed vegetables and a whole wheat roll?"

"Perfect," Luke replies, his voice steady. It's the kind of meal that keeps him going through these long afternoons in court. Rosie nods and heads back to the kitchen, leaving us alone with our thoughts.

I try to push the morning's events out of my mind, but they keep replaying in my head. I glance out the window, watching people go about their day as if everything is normal. It's surreal how life goes on around me while I'm in the midst of this battle.

Luke seems to sense that I need a distraction. "Do you remember the first time we came here?" he asks, leaning back in the booth.

I can't help but smile at the memory. "How could I forget? You insisted that this place had the best coffee in town. You were right."

He grins, a rare sight that makes me feel a little lighter. "I'm always right," he teases, and I laugh softly. It's a small relief, a reminder that there's still room for moments like this, even now.

As we wait for our meals, we avoid discussing the trial. Instead, we chat about past projects, and places we'd like to visit once this is all over and even share a few silly stories. Luke tells me about his early days as a lawyer and I share my biggest flops on the golf course. For a little while, it's enough to help me forget about the pressure of the trial.

When Rosie returns with our meals, I feel more at ease. The food is as good as always, and I can tell that Luke is doing his best to keep me calm, to keep me focused. I appreciate it more than I can say. As we finish our lunch, I catch Rosie's eye, and she gives me a thumbs-up, a silent message of support that warms my heart.

But as we leave the diner, stepping back into the sunlight, I'm still tense. Carlotta's tense phone call, the way Benton and Morgan seemed so smug outside the courthouse. I know how Morgan and Benton operate. It destroys their opponent at all costs. Whatever they are planning creates a sense of dread I can't ignore.

We walk back toward the courthouse in silence, the familiar routine of lunch at Rosie's already fading as we approach the steps. I glance at Luke, seeing the same determination in his eyes that he's had since the beginning of this fight. "Whatever happens next," he says, his voice sounding confident, "we've got this won."

That's the first time Luke said that, and I want to believe him, but I know Morgan and Benton aren't done with me. As we enter the courthouse, I see Harvey Morgan. He's waving for Luke to come with him.

Luke walks away with Morgan, their heads bent together in conversation, and my mind immediately jumps to the worst scenarios. I know I was careful on the stand, that I answered every question truthfully, but Morgan is clever and ruthless. I can easily picture him twisting my words, convincing the jury that I'm dishonest.

Standing there, alone amidst the courthouse crowd, I try to steady my breathing. Luke said we're going to win, but the uncertainty gnaws at me. I hate this feeling of being out of control, of not knowing what they're discussing.

Time seems to stretch as I wait for Luke to return, my thoughts spiraling. I glance down the hallway, searching for some sign that everything is still on track, but there's just an endless stream of people oblivious to the turmoil I'm feeling.

This trial has been a long battle, and though we're nearing the end, I sense something disastrous is about to unfold. I pace the hallway. The courthouse, usually bustling with activity, now seems suffocatingly still. The voices of the people around me blur into a low hum, and all I can focus on is the tension coiling tighter in my chest.

Luke said at lunch, “We’ve got this won.” I want to believe him, but the nagging voice in the back of my mind won’t let me rest. I know Robert Benton. He has never admitted defeat. I also know Harvey Morgan. He claims he has never lost a case.

I glance at the clock on the wall. My fingers drum nervously against my side, and I catch myself chewing on my lower lip, a habit I thought I’d long outgrown. I can’t help it.

Finally, I see Luke approaching, his face a mask of calm determination, but I’ve learned to read him well enough to notice the subtle tension in his jaw, the slight furrow in his brow. He stops in front of me, and for a moment, I can’t tell if the news is good or bad. My heart hammers in my chest, and I swallow hard, bracing myself.

“What did Morgan want?” I ask, trying to keep the anxiety out of my voice.

“He wanted to discuss a settlement,” Luke replies, his tone calm but with an underlying tension that tells me this is serious.

“Settlement? Benton’s never come close to offering anything reasonable. What’s his offer this time?”

Luke nods. “Morgan asked what you would accept, and as we agreed, I told him you’d settle for one million dollars plus my attorney's fees. I also told him you're willing to let Benton claim co-designer credit for the Lake Tierra Golf Course."

I pause, taking in his words. Benton owed me one million dollars when we filed suit. He owes me more now, but I'd definitely take one million. I've already decided I'm okay with Benton taking some credit; I believe people will know who truly designed the course. Still, hearing it confirmed like this brings a mix of emotions, victory laced with a bit of resentment.

"And what did Morgan say?" I ask, my voice steadying.

"He wasn't happy. He said you'd regret not taking the earlier offer, that Benton won't back down, and that we're in for a long fight. But he's bluffing, Luke says firmly. They know they're losing."

"Maybe," I reply. "But I know Morgan. He takes risks."

"But it's not up to Morgan or Benton. It's up to whatever organization that's funding the lawsuit. They can tell Morgan to settle and he has no choice."

"Do you think the organization funding Benton will settle?"

Luke takes a moment before answering. "If whoever controls the money was sitting in the courtroom or watched Benton testify on Court TV, that person will persuade the organization to settle on our terms."

We walk back toward the courtroom, expecting Morgan to call his next witness. As we enter the courtroom, I immediately notice something is off. Benton is not sitting with Morgan. He's not in the courtroom.

While I'm looking for Benton, Morgan approaches Luke and calls him aside. They talk quietly for a few moments, and I watch them, my anxiety creeping back in. When Luke returns to me, his expression is serious.

Luke says, "Benton or I should more properly say the organization that is funding the litigation has agreed to the settlement. He'll pay the one million dollars and my attorney's fees, but there will be no future bonuses. You may work for other developers right away."

Ten minutes later, we're in the courtroom. Judge Hawkins tells the jurors that he needs them to stand by while he takes care of some other matters and then he excuses them to go back to the jury room. We retire to the witness room and sit anxiously, waiting to hear that Morgan's client has wired the funds to my account. Five minutes later, there's a knock on the door, and Morgan advises Luke that his client had wired the funds to my account. I call my bank and verify the funds they've received. We sign the settlement documents Luke has prepared and the three of us go to Judge Hawkins' chambers to advise him.

I feel a strange mix of relief and disbelief. We've won, but it's not the victory I expected. Still, it's enough. I take a deep breath, knowing I'm free to leave the courtroom behind and go back to work.

After Judge Hawkins excuses the jury, we pack up our files. Luke's movements are slow and deliberate, as if he doesn't want to leave. He reaches down and puts his hand on top of mine. I look at him and let out a deep breath. The lines etched into his face speak volumes of the fatigue he bore, a testament to the long months we had both endured. His hair is tousled, no doubt from the countless times he'd run his hands through it in frustrated contemplation. We exchange a look, silently acknowledging the relief we both feel ending our fight with Benton and Morgan.

"It's over," I say. Luke grasps my hand. I feel the warmth of his touch. It's like we've waged war together and somehow survived. Luke gives me one more nod, and we turn and leave the courtroom, looking back one last time. As I step out, I hear the swinging door close behind me. Hopefully, this will be my last time exiting a courtroom.

We navigate through a sea of bodies as we leave. I see Benton has suddenly reappeared and is speaking to the press again. He tells the reporters that he must keep the terms of our settlement agreement secret. Still, he's proud of standing tall against MAGA discrimination and in favor of transgender athletes who want the chance to compete in high school, college, and professional sports in their identified gender.

When the reporters see us, they come over in a group. One reporter asks, "Miss West, do you have any comment for us?"

"Yes," I say. I feel my heart racing as I continue. "I'm glad it's over, so I'll have the chance to do more productive things."

"What about your position on trans athletes?"

"More accurately," I say. "It's my support of girls and women athletes. It hasn't changed. But I've learned since I first answered a question during an interview that the issue is far more complicated than I originally thought. I feel it's important to discuss it constructively."

"That sounds like a change in your original position."

"No, I haven't changed my views. I support fairness, safety, and privacy in girls' and women's sports. Since my original interview, I've learned lots of new terms, and hateful people have threatened and harassed me and frightened my mother. That's why I say the issue should be one to discuss and not put people on either side at risk."

"Can you elaborate on that?"

"When I gave the first interview, no one had ever called me Karen. I had never heard of the term doxxing until protestors showed up at my house, blocking me from entering and terrifying my mother. I wasn't aware people were posting deepfake photos and videos until I discovered there were lewd photos and videos of me on a porn website. Someone had posted fake videos of me saying hateful things about transgender people. I had never heard the word swatting, and I didn't know people were making fake emergency calls until the police showed up at my front door. They showed up several times and once again terrified my mother. Finally, in all my years, no one had ever thrown a rock through the window where I was staying. I wonder when and why civil debate has become so rare in our country. When did it become okay to demonize and bully those who think differently? I'd much rather engage in thoughtful discussions on complex issues."

Luke holds my hand and whispers, "Your father would be proud of you."

I smile, thinking of my father.

"Lauren," Luke begins, his voice dropping to a tender register laced with fatigue from our ordeal. "Do you remember when you quoted what Atticus told Scout about not knowing a person until you climb in his skin and walk around in it?"

"Sure, I wanted to get to know you."

"After a tough trial, a client once told me, 'You never really know a man until you pack salt with him.' He said he suspected it may have originated in the Russian Gulag salt mines. We packed salt together over the last several months, fighting against Morgan and Benton. In some ways, the weight of the world is off my shoulders. In other ways, I don't want to lose my connection with you."

In the silence that follows, our roles as lawyer and client fade away, leaving us as two individuals who have seen each other's weaknesses and strengths. There is a strong bond between us, reminding me of the bond soldiers coming out of a battle together. I reach out and hug Luke, partly because I don't want him to see I am crying.

With a hint of a smile, I gather my thoughts and ask, "So, are you planning to dive into another case like this anytime soon?"

Luke chuckles softly, the sound rich with the fatigue I sense from trying a case while still suffering the side effects of COVID. "Let's just say I'm looking forward to time with my girls... at least for a little while."

"I agree," I say, thinking about his daughters eagerly waiting for their father at home. "Will you be heading for home?" I ask.

I try to grasp what I'm feeling now. I feel joy and relief that the ordeal is over, and a twinge of apprehension thinking about the future. I'm eager to have more quality time with him, but I am at a loss for what to do next. For my sanity, I need another mountain to climb. But for now, I don't know what mountain to climb.

"Yes," Luke replies. "Call your mother. We'll pick her up, go to my house, and celebrate tonight."

What will I do tomorrow?

Epilogue

Lauren

Following a night of festivities, I woke up the next day with an unexpected heaviness in my chest. The joy and relief of winning the case faded, leaving behind an inexplicable sadness. I couldn't understand why I felt so down after such a significant victory. I called Luke, searching for answers. He told me trial lawyers and their clients feel this way after a lengthy and emotional court battle. We had invested so much time, effort, and emotional energy fighting Benton and Morgan that, now that it was over, a void replaced the intense focus and adrenaline that had fueled us for so long.

Luke was right, but for me, there was something more. After we settled the lawsuit, I found myself, for the first time in my life, without a stretch goal to drive me. There were no golf tournaments to win, no award-winning golf courses to design, and no pitched battle against Benton and Morgan to keep me occupied. I suddenly had all the time in the world to do what I wanted, but I had no idea what that was.

The sense of purposelessness gnawed at me, and it wasn't just about the case. I realized that the bond I had formed with Luke, built on shared battles and countless hours spent together, was fraying. We had spent months side by side, meeting for coffee each morning and eating dinner with our mothers and his daughters every week, all centered on defeating Benton. Now that the fight was over, so were the reasons to spend time together. I found myself back in Dallas with my mother while Luke was in Corona with his girls, the distance between us growing in more ways than one.

I was frozen, unsure what to do next.. My availability spread like wildfire through the golf course development community, and the calls started coming in. Developers eagerly sought me to design their courses, but I realized that the idea of constantly being on the road, away from home, no longer appealed to me. The fulfillment I once found in creating golf courses felt hollow. I spent days in a funk, pondering what I truly wanted.

As the days turned into weeks, the feeling of purposelessness deepened. Each morning, I felt more lost, the weight of uncertainty pressing down on me. I felt adrift, no longer anchored by the fight against Benton and Morgan. I didn't know who I was or what I wanted without the daily battle.

In search of clarity, I visited my sports psychologist. Years ago, she had given me the Myers-Briggs test, and I retook it. The result was the same: ENFP, which stands for Extraverted, Intuitive, Feeling, Perceiving. She explained that people with this personality type are often enthusiastic, charismatic, charming, energetic, and independent. I saw how these traits had driven me to succeed as a golfer and a golf course designer. She also pointed out the weaknesses typical of ENFPs—needing approval, being indecisive, struggling to follow the rules, and quickly getting bored. It was like she was describing me to a tee.

At the end of our session, she suggested that teaching and coaching might be avenues worth exploring. The idea struck a chord, but it also filled me with questions. Could I really find fulfillment in something so different from what I'd always known? Could I redefine who I was after all this time?

As I left her office, I realized that my journey wasn't over. The court battle might be behind me, but the fight to find my purpose was only starting. And as I stood on the edge of this new chapter, I knew it was time to take the next step, whatever that might be.

One afternoon, my cell phone rang as I sat alone in my home office. To my surprise, a group of homeowners called from a conference room at the Lake Tierra Golf Course clubhouse. They asked if I would consider becoming the golf pro at Lake Tierra. The idea of using my skills and experience to teach young girls to play golf was something I had never considered. My career had always kept me too busy for teaching. But now, with a void in my life and a yearning for purpose, the idea began to take root. I thought back to the time I had spent with Abby before the trial and how much I had enjoyed it.

I told the homeowners I needed to discuss the idea with my mother. I doubted she would be willing to leave her church friends in Dallas. To my surprise, she embraced the idea with enthusiasm. I also talked with Luke, unsure how he would feel about me returning to Corona. He said he would be happy for me to return, especially because Abby wanted me to continue teaching her to play golf. With their encouragement, I agreed to meet with the homeowners the following week.

When my mother and I drove through the gates of the Lake Tierra development, memories flooded back. I wanted to get into a golf cart and view the beauty of the golf course I had created. The homeowners greeted us with warm smiles and genuine enthusiasm. They spoke highly of my design of the Lake Tierra Golf Course and appreciated my passion for the sport. They were eager to revitalize the golf program and believed I was the perfect fit to lead their efforts.

As I listened to their vision for Lake Tierra's golf program, which included expanding opportunities for both adults and juniors, organizing local tournaments, and establishing outreach programs for children, I felt a spark ignite within me. It was as if fate had brought me back to the site of my most significant golf course design, offering me a new sense of purpose.

After returning to Dallas, I put my townhouse on the market. It sold the first weekend. Four weeks later, after the closing, my mother and I moved into a new home in Corona with a clear goal: to help develop the next generation of top girls and women golfers, not only in the Hill Country but beyond.

Settling into my new role, I reached out to local schools and organizations, offering free golf lessons to young girls. It wasn't long before a group of enthusiastic girls showed up at the golf course, eager to learn. Their energy and determination reminded me of how I had felt at their age, falling in love with golf.

Week after week, we gathered on the driving range, and I taught the girls everything I knew about golf. But my focus wasn't just on perfecting their swing or mastering a chip shot. I aimed to instill confidence, resilience, and discipline—skills that would serve them well beyond the golf course. As word spread, girls from all over Texas attended my summer clinics at Lake Tierra, and I quickly built a reputation for developing college scholarship golfers.

My father had always driven me hard, pushing me relentlessly to become the top girls' and women's golfer in the world. While his approach got results, I knew it wasn't something I wanted to replicate when I started teaching. Instead of pushing the girls to the brink, I focused on nurturing their passion for the game and building their confidence. I recognized that each girl was unique, so I tailored my coaching to fit their individual strengths and challenges.

Beyond golf, I integrated life lessons into my coaching—handling pressure, maintaining focus, and developing mental toughness. My goal was to help them grow into well-rounded individuals, not just outstanding golfers. And that approach has made a real difference. The girls aren't just improving their swings; they're becoming strong, independent young women ready to excel in college and beyond. That's why so many of them are earning scholarships. The girls I teach and coach make me love what I'm doing now.

In this newfound chapter of my life, surrounded by passionate young minds eager to learn and grow, I discovered that sometimes the greatest healing comes from helping others find their own way.

Under the warm sun of Corona's skies, we embarked on an adventure that would forever change us all, one swing at a time.

One afternoon, as I waited for my client, a young golfer approached the practice green nearby. I recognized her as Madison Lee, a teenager with an impeccable swing. Madison had spoken passionately about inclusion in sports during a recent town hall. I watched the video later, and my curiosity piqued by her eloquence.

"Miss West?" Madison said hesitantly. "I wanted to thank you for standing up for fairness in sports."

I nodded. "Thanks, Madison. But fairness isn't always black and white, is it?"

Madison tilted her head. "What do you mean?"

I gestured to the course, the rolling hills I had designed to challenge even the best players. "Golf teaches us precision, patience, and perspective. It also teaches us how different challenges test us in different ways. I know I've spoken out against allowing transgender athletes to compete in women's sports because I believe in protecting the integrity of competition. But I've also come to understand that it's not just about fairness. It's about inclusion, identity, and people wanting to belong."

Madison's eyes widened. "So, do you think you were wrong?"

I thought for a moment. "No, I don't think I was wrong. But I do think I was too quick to judge. There's pain on all sides of this debate, and I've learned that listening is just as important as speaking up. We need to find solutions that don't tear people apart."

Madison smiled. "That's a good way to think about it."

I watched her walk away, her swing as graceful as ever. For the first time, I felt that understanding the issue wasn't about taking sides. It was about finding a way forward together.

In December 2024, the LPGA updated its gender policy, instituting new eligibility criteria for its competitions. Effective from the 2025 season, the policy stipulates that players must have been assigned female at birth or have completed their transition before the onset of male puberty to be eligible to compete.

The Dallas reporter called me and asked for me to comment about the change. I told her I didn't want to get back in the news so I didn't comment.

I continued to work with Abby, who was passionate about learning and a joy to be around. My mother and I resumed our weekly dinners with Luke, his mother, and his girls. Our two mothers made no secret of their hopes that Luke and I might become more than friends. Abby and Megan constantly teased us, convinced that we were already a couple.

Whether we will ever officially be a couple, I'm not sure. Luke's mother-in-law remains steadfast in her opposition, which is a stumbling block. But as I spent more time with Luke and his girls, I wondered if maybe, just maybe, there was a future for us beyond our lawyer-client battle against Robert Benton. The thought both excited and scared me, like a teenager experiencing her first crush. I was the girl who skipped her high school prom to play in a golf tournament and whose father made sure there was no room for a serious relationship during my college and professional golf years. Now, at this stage of my life, I'm probably one of the few who would feel nervous about stepping into something so serious. Yet, that same nervousness carried with it a new excitement about the possibility of what might come next.

www.ingramcontent.com/pod-product-compliance
Lightning Source LLC
LaVergne TN
LVHW050940210926
848482LV00013B/686
9798295880902